Faith MATTERS

365 DAILY DEVOTIONS

with

LEITH ANDERSON

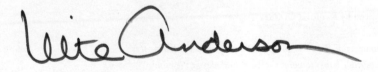

summerside
PRESS™

Summerside Press™
Minneapolis 55438
www.summersidepress.com
Faith Matters
© 2011 by Leith Anderson

ISBN 978-1-60936-134-1

Cover and interior design by Müllerhaus Publishing Group |
www.mullerhaus.net

Edited by Ramona Cramer Tucker

*Summerside Press™ is an inspirational publisher offering fresh,
irresistible books to uplift the heart and engage the mind.*

Printed in China

Introduction

Faith really does matter!

I am often impressed by the frequency of a statement made on television reports and interviews of people who have faced some of life's greatest challenges. After battles with illness, financial setbacks, relational breakups, and personal traumas, the newscaster says, "Her faith got her through" or, "His faith sustained him." This describes ordinary people in extraordinary situations who believe in God and his goodness when too much has gone wrong. Their faith matters.

Not that faith is only for the worst times of life. Faith in God is for the best times of life and the ordinary days of life. "Faith is being sure of what we hope for and certain of what we do not see," according to the New Testament author of Hebrews 11:1. "And without faith it is impossible to please God, because anyone who comes to him must believe that he exists and that he rewards those who earnestly seek him" (Hebrews 11:6).

My own faith in God was born in childhood and has been honed in adulthood. It is a faith rooted in a commitment to Jesus Christ as my Savior and Lord. But the laboratory of my faith has included thousands of others I have known and observed. I could not be more impressed with the boys and girls and men and women who have soared to the heights of success and have walked through the valleys of death—all with amazing faith in God.

You are invited to walk this journey of faith each day of the year with *Faith Matters*. The Bible quotes, devotional readings, and concluding prayers range over a wide variety of experiences and topics from funny to serious and ancient to modern—because that's the way we live faith, in the broad experiences of life. Take just a few minutes every day to hear what the Bible says, read a few thought-triggering paragraphs, and pray to the God we believe in and know rewards those who earnestly seek him.

May your faith grow stronger every day!

❧

LEITH ANDERSON

Eden Prairie, Minnesota

JANUARY

Looking Ahead

———◈———

"The God of heaven will give us success."
Nehemiah, in Nehemiah 2:20

Robert Kennedy once said that some people look at the way things are and ask why; others look at the way things might be and ask, why not?

Nehemiah was that kind of man. When he scanned the city of Jerusalem, in ruins for generations, he saw it with walls and gates rebuilt, temple worship restored, and its discouraged people uplifted. He was a man of vision whose life was consumed with "what God has put into my heart to do for Jerusalem."

People of vision don't look at yesterday; they look at tomorrow. They look ahead. They see things others cannot see.

If you want to do something great, the place to begin is by asking God for the vision. Don't settle for some second-best human substitute. Dream big dreams, and open your heart and mind to the vision that God wants to give you.

———◈———

God of heaven, give me your vision for this New Year.
Guide me every step of every day. Give success to your
dreams in my life. In Jesus' name, amen.

Bloom Where You Are Planted!

The desert and the parched land will be glad;
the wilderness will rejoice and blossom.
Like the crocus, it will burst into bloom;
it will rejoice greatly and shout for joy.

Isaiah 35:1-2

Remember that little plaque, BLOOM WHERE YOU ARE PLANTED? A very pleasant idea, right? But the concept also raises a nagging question: What does God want from me where I'm planted? Or, another way of putting it: What is the purpose of my life?

Many people have no idea why they were born. Others think what matters is being successful, having a good time, making lots of money, becoming famous. But they miss out on what matters most.

Your life will be transformed when you begin to see that your purpose is to show others the love of God in whatever place you are planted. Then you will grow the fruit God has called you to produce. Your attitude will be different. You'll face disappointment with courage and accept success without pride. You truly will bloom where you are planted!

Here I am, Lord. This is your place for me right now.
Please show me your purpose and help me love others.
May I bloom for you where I am. Amen.

Attitude Check

<hr />

Whatever you do, work at it with all your heart, as working
for the Lord, not men, since you know that you will receive
an inheritance from the Lord as a reward.

Colossians 3:23-24

Long ago in England a passerby walked up to three construction workers
and asked each what he was doing.

The first responded, "I'm earning money."

The second one said, "I'm laying bricks."

The third workman said, "I'm building a cathedral."

All three men were working at the same job—one saw it as money earned,
another saw it as a task to be accomplished, another saw it as fulfillment of
a vision. The difference? Attitude!

How you feel about your work has a lot to do with your overall contentment.
You could have a super job, yet complain all the time. Or a terrible job, but
still be content. Working to please God and not men can bring dignity and
integrity to both the best and the worst jobs. Try thinking of God as your
boss and see the difference it can make in your work!

<hr />

*God, you are my Boss. I work for you. My desire is to serve you well and do
for you the very best job I can do. Pleasing you is my top priority. Amen.*

Person of the Year

———————◦◦◦◦◦———————

We pray this so that the name of our Lord Jesus may
be glorified in you, and you in him, according to the grace
of our God and the Lord Jesus Christ.

2 Thessalonians 1:12

The Ford Thunderbird is a special car—distinct from all the rest. The first
Thunderbird sports car, manufactured on October 22, 1954, cost $2,700.
Today it's a valuable collector's item. In six decades it's the only car that has
won the CAR OF THE YEAR designation four times.

How special is this car? When Katie Couric signed a $65 million contract
with NBC to host the *Today Show* for four years, to celebrate she traded in
her old Honda on a 2002 Thunderbird. She could have bought any car she
wanted, and she chose a Thunderbird.

But all T-Birds combined are not even close to being as special as one
Christian. Every car is labeled FORD, CHRYSLER, MERCEDES, OR BMW. You
wear a label too. Never forget how special you are if you wear the name of
Jesus Christ. God gave his Son for you. You are more valuable than any car.
You're God's person of *every* year!

———◦◦◦———

Lord Jesus Christ, I am called a "Christian" because I am named for you.
Thank you for your love and goodness. My worth and meaning in life come
from you. My desire is to honor your name by the way I live this year. Amen.

A Masterful Tune

"But as for you, be strong and do not give up,
for your work will be rewarded."
Azariah, in 2 Chronicles 15:7

The mother of a young piano student once bought two tickets for the brilliant Paderewski's concert, thinking it might inspire her son to practice.

They arrived early to get front seats in the hall. While the mother visited with friends, the little boy slipped away and started exploring. He wandered backstage, saw the beautiful piano, and sat down to play his last week's lesson piece (not very well, I might add). In his concentration he was oblivious to the hush of the crowd, the opening of the curtain, and the rising lights. The great Paderewski walked onto the stage, came up behind the child, and began to play along, turning the childish effort into something musically magnificent. When the boy realized what was happening, he began to pull his hands back, but the maestro whispered in his ear, "Keep on playing, keep on playing."

And that's what God does for you. He comes up behind you, puts his arms around you, and turns your battles into victories and your tunes into masterpieces. He whispers, "Keep on fighting; keep on playing."

---

*Dear God, you know I don't have world-class talents.
I'm just me, trying my best. Please put your hands over
my hands to make your beautiful music. Amen.*

First Things First

"Seek first his kingdom and his righteousness,
and all these things will be given to you as well."
Jesus, in Matthew 6:33

A lecturer once asked his audience to guess how many rocks would fit into a wide-mouth gallon jar. After everyone had guessed, he fit as many rocks into the jar as he could. "Is the jar full?" he asked. All agreed it was. He dumped some gravel into the jar, shook it until it settled in between the rocks, and asked again, "Is the jar full?" The audience started to catch on. Next he poured some sand into the jar between the rocks and gravel. Then he poured in a quart of water. "What's the point of all of this?"

"There are always gaps, and if you work at it, you can fit more into your life," someone said.

"No," he replied. "The point is, if you hadn't put the large rocks in first, you never would have gotten them in."

If you fill up the jar of your life and then try to fit God in last, there will be no room. But if you put God first, there will be room for everything else you need.

Be first in my life, God! There are so many things to do and so much "stuff" that fills my days that I sometimes leave you until the last. I don't want to squeeze you in at the end. I want you always to be Number One. Amen.

An Amazing Change

———— ✦❧❧✦ ————

"If anyone is in Christ, he is a new creation;
the old has gone, the new has come!"
Paul, in 2 Corinthians 5:17

Change is at the very center of Christianity. God created a perfect world that was changed by sin, but he didn't allow that change to be permanent. He intervened by sending his Son, who changed his place of residence from heaven to earth, becoming a human being and taking the name of Jesus. During his thirty-three years on our earth, Jesus continued to instigate change. He changed blind people to sighted, disabled people to walkers, hungry people to full, ignorant people to informed, and sinners to saints. Jesus himself changed from life to death when he was crucified and from death back to life when he was raised from the dead at Easter.

Jesus' great offer is to change you—to make you like him. The process begins the moment you accept Jesus Christ as your Savior and continues until he takes you to heaven. It's a most amazing and wonderful change!

∿

God of change, thank you for changing me! I accept Jesus as my Savior and say good-bye to the old and hello to my new life with Jesus. I know you aren't finished changing me yet and welcome the transformation to come. Amen.

A Simple Plan

———— ✦⟨◈⟩✦ ————

Commit to the Lord whatever you do, and your plans will succeed.
Proverbs 16:3

The little book of Haggai starts out with a financial crisis. God wanted the Hebrew people to rebuild the wall of Jerusalem, but he found them to be poor managers of their finances. He said, "You earn wages, only to put them in a purse with holes in it." Hey, I can relate to that!

But then God says, "Give careful thought to your ways." In other words, take inventory and make a plan to do what God wants. Figure out what you have (your assets), what you owe (your liabilities), and how your money is spent (your expenditures). Then figure out what money you have coming in (your income). Make a simple financial plan that reflects your philosophy and your priorities.

Many people have done this with amazing results! Going through this process has wonderfully affected their finances, their family, their happiness, and their whole lives. Why not try it for yourself?

⟨◈⟩

*Thank you, Lord, for all your blessings. When I compare myself
to others in history and most people today, I am truly rich. Yet
I am not the money manager you want me to be. I need a better
plan and your help in following the plan you want for my life.
I ask you to be my financial adviser and commit to be the best
possible steward of your blessings to me. In Jesus' name, amen.*

The Power of Words

———— ❧❧ ————

May the words of my mouth and the meditation of my heart
be pleasing in your sight,
O Lord, my Rock and my Redeemer.
Psalm 19:14

Martin Luther King, Jr., inspired people across the nation with his famous words, "I have a dream." John F. Kennedy said, "Ask not what your country can do for you. Ask what you can do for your country." Both men captured the imagination of a generation of Americans with their powerful words.

But a person need not be a celebrity to exercise the power of words. There is life-changing power in an ordinary person saying "no" to drugs, or "yes" to a marriage proposal, or in simply saying "I love you" to a lonely child.

Children taunt one another with the words, "Sticks and stones may break my bones, but words can never hurt me." But that isn't true. Words shape history. Words make or break careers. Words can make a marriage succeed or fail. So make your words count for good in someone's life!

∽◦∾

*O Lord, my Rock and Redeemer, may your Spirit guide my
thoughts and give right words to my mouth. I want what I say
to build up, not tear down, to help, not hurt, to inspire, not
discourage, and to please you while blessing others. Amen.*

The Solution

Jesus Christ was chosen before the creation of the world,
but was revealed in these last times for your sake.

1 Peter 1:20

Did you know that God chose Jesus to be our Savior before he created the world?

It would be easy to surmise that it happened this way: God created the world, then humans chose sin, and sin introduced a million evils that have permeated everything and totally wrecked God's perfect creation. Caught by surprise, God had to come up with "Plan B." Sending his Son to die on the cross and pay for human sin and mistakes was an expensive rescue but, oh well, God didn't know what else to do.

But that's not the way it was at all. Before God created the world, he knew what humans would do. He knew we would all choose sin and mess up our world. God anticipated every situation and provided Jesus as a solution.

Truth is, God knew you before you were born. You can totally trust him to solve your deepest problems.

You are the all-knowing God, smarter than any genius. You have problems figured out before they start. Before the first human sinned, you planned for your Son, Jesus, to come as our Savior. You know more about me than I know about myself and have my problems solved before they begin. I trust you, God and Father of my Lord Jesus Christ. Amen.

Choose Hope

❧

"For I know the plans I have for you," declares the Lord,
"plans to prosper you and not to harm you, plans to give
you hope and a future."
Jeremiah, in Jeremiah 29:11

Michelangelo spent another long day lying on his back painting the ceiling of the Sistine Chapel at the Vatican in Rome. His painting portrayed God creating the world. It was lonely work. Michelangelo's body ached as the last sunlight disappeared. He climbed down the ladder off the scaffolding and ate dinner alone. Before going to sleep, he wrote a sonnet. The last line said, "I am no painter." He was so discouraged that he felt incompetent as an artist.

But when the sun rose the next morning, he returned to the Sistine Chapel and resumed painting one of the greatest masterpieces of art. How did he do it? He simply chose to go on. He chose to hope.

If you believe in God, you have an enormous advantage. You can choose hope because you know God is on your side. You can always expect a better tomorrow.

❧

*Dear God, I choose you. And because I choose you, I choose hope.
And because I choose hope, I will keep going even when I am tired
and discouraged. You will strengthen me, encourage me, and give
me hope and a future. I trust you. In Jesus' name, amen.*

Which Way?

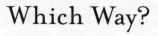

The wisdom that comes from heaven is first of all pure;
then peace-loving, considerate, submissive, full of mercy
and good fruit, impartial and sincere.

James 3:17

Yogi Berra, that great American baseball player and folk-philosopher, once said, "When you come to a fork in the road, take it." Of course, which way you take makes all the difference as to whether you end up in Canada or Mexico, or in Portland, Oregon, or Portland, Maine.

The same situation occurs in the spiritual realm. We're traveling on a road called Wisdom. Suddenly we come to a fork, and we have to decide which way to go. The sign for one says DEVIL'S WISDOM, and the other is marked GOD'S WISDOM.

Each of us has to choose which fork we will take, and the choice we make is the difference between heaven and hell. Choosing God's wisdom, or God's way to live, is not just an add-on to the rest of life. It is a total way of life—the way of eternal life. It is radically different than earthly wisdom, with radically different results!

To you, the all-wise God, I look for wisdom in my life. Help me always to choose your way and protect me from ever choosing the devil's way. May I recognize the difference between what is right and what is wrong and always go your right way. I follow you in faith, trusting you completely. Amen.

The Small Stuff

———— ❧❧ ————

"Consider the ravens. They do not sow or reap...yet God feeds
them. How much more valuable you are than birds!"
Jesus, in Luke 12:24

Have you ever heard the old gospel song lyrics, "His eye is on the sparrow,
and I know he watches me"? They're a wonderful reminder that we can
always trust God to take care of us.

Sometimes it's easier to trust God in the most extreme circumstances, such
as when we're diagnosed with cancer or when we're totally broke. Perhaps
that's because, right there in the midst of our troubles, we're finally able to
fully trust God.

When lesser troubles come, though, we're less likely to turn to God. Instead,
we trust in our own money, time, and expertise to solve them. We're in
control, we feel, so why do we need God?

But if you truly want to experience peace, learn to trust God for the small
stuff...because most of life is composed of the small stuff.

———— ❧ ————

*You take care of the birds, God, but you always take better care of
me. You have stayed by my side through the worst storms of life. You
have stuck with me when I turned my back against you. I know you
can be fully trusted for absolutely any situation, yet I get all worked
up and worried about today's problems that will be forgotten by next
week. So, today I am going to trust you for the small stuff. Amen.*

Stranded?

His divine power has given us everything we need
for life and godliness through our knowledge of him
who called us by his own glory and goodness.

2 Peter 1:3

One year during the Super Bowl, FedEx ran a commercial parody on the movie *Castaway* with Tom Hanks. The movie is about a FedEx employee who's stranded on a desert island with a FedEx package he never opens. When he finally is rescued, he delivers the package, never knowing what is in it.

But in the Super Bowl ad, the rescued survivor delivers the FedEx package and can't resist saying to the recipient, "If I may ask, what is in the package?" The woman opens the package and shows him the contents. "Oh, nothing, really. Just a satellite telephone, a GPS, a compass, a water purifier, and some seeds."

Everything he needed to survive was in that box, but he had never opened it!

Are you feeling stranded in your life? Remember that, in Jesus Christ, you have everything you need. Grace and peace are yours in abundance.

Help me, Lord, to recognize your gifts and to use them well for Christian living. When I feel weak, give me your strength; when I am poor, give me your wealth; when I am anxious, give me your peace. Better yet, help me claim and use these blessings that are already mine. Amen.

Through All Generations

The Lord is good and his love endures forever;
his faithfulness continues through all generations.

Psalm 100:5

Some scholars consider theologian Jonathan Edwards to be the most brilliant philosopher America has ever produced. His writings and sermons were a catalyst in the American Great Awakening, a revival that brought large numbers of people to Jesus Christ, as well as effecting enormous social change.

This devout man of God faithfully prayed for the salvation of his children and grandchildren and future generations yet unborn. Sociologists studied the faith and careers of Jonathan and Sarah Edwards' descendants over a period of one hundred years. Not only were they believers, generation after generation, but they became some of the most effective leaders of this nation—judges, pastors, governors, senators, congressmen, and a vice president of the United States. The Edwards' family is a stunning example of God's enduring love and faithfulness.

What wonderful encouragement to pray faithfully for your own family members—even for those yet unborn! God's faithfulness continues through all generations.

This is my prayer, Lord: that all of my family will know Jesus and live godly lives.
Beyond my generation, I pray for my grandchildren and great-grandchildren,
for my nephews and nieces and their children—not that they will all be rich and
famous but that they will all be faithful and righteous for Jesus. Amen.

Just Like John

---◦❧❧◦---

"And you, my child, will be called a prophet of the Most High;
for you will go on before the Lord to prepare the way for him."

Zechariah, in Luke 1:76

Before Jesus was born, God blessed his uncle Zechariah and aunt Elizabeth with a miracle baby. Picture the elderly Zechariah, standing over the crib of newborn son John, singing praises to God. Every devout Jew of Zechariah's generation remembered the words from the last page of the Old Testament—that God would send an Elijah-type prophet who would prepare for the Messiah's coming. God had told Zechariah that *his* son would grow up to be that prophet!

God had a unique, special plan for John, but he still uses people like John today to prepare others to believe in Jesus. When we make friends with those who don't know Jesus, when we are loving and kind and invite them to church, when we pray for their needs, we are marvelously preparing them for Jesus Christ. We are just like John.

---◦❧◦---

*Use me, Lord. Make me an influence for good in the lives of
everyone who knows me. Bless and transform my family and friends
through me. Like John, I want to be a path to Jesus. Amen.*

The Secret to Contentment

I have learned to be content whatever the circumstances.

Philippians 4:11

Life without money is impossible for all but the very few. The president of the United States doesn't need cash when he travels, but even a first grader has to pay for field trips and milk at lunchtime. Good or bad, rich or poor, we all deal with money. The question is, what kind of relationship with money do we have? Do we love it or hate it? Do we control it, or does it control us?

The Bible says to seek contentment in what we have, instead of being continually driven to acquire more and more. But contentment doesn't come naturally. If we want it, we have to practice it. Why not decide to drive your present car or wear your winter coat another year? When an item breaks, consider doing without before looking for a replacement. See if, like the apostle Paul, you can "learn to be content."

Teach me, Holy Spirit, to be content. It's a lesson I need to learn. Too often I want more of everything, even though I already have so much. Too often I am driven by greed instead of need. Thank you for all I have and help me to settle down and be satisfied. Amen.

One More Shot

———◆❦❦◆———

But you, O Lord, are a compassionate and gracious God,
slow to anger, abounding in love and faithfulness.
Turn to me and have mercy on me;
grant your strength to your servant.

Psalm 86:15–16

Jesus often used parables, or stories, to teach concepts. One time he told about a man who had planted a fig tree in his vineyard. When it hadn't produced any fruit in three years, he told his gardener to cut it down. The gardener begged the owner to give the tree one more year—a second chance to do what it was supposed to do.

Jesus is just like that gardener. He intervenes on our behalf to give us another chance. If we have wasted years, living without purpose and direction, and have borne no fruit for God, Jesus says, "Give it one more shot. Allow one more year. Let her try again. Give him another chance."

This is the second chance we've longed for. Accept it as a gift from Jesus. Don't waste another day just taking up space. Be and do what God wants you to be and do.

———❧❦———

God of the Second Chance, please forgive me and let me try again.
Give me courage, wisdom, and strength to do better next time.
Help me to get it right. For Jesus' sake, amen.

Stressed Out?

—⟨co⟩—

Elijah was afraid and ran for his life...and prayed that
he might die. "I have had enough, Lord," he said.
1 Kings 19:3-4

The prophet Elijah knew well the toll stress takes on your body. After all,
he took on all the pagan prophets. He called down fire from heaven in one
of the greatest demonstrations of divine power in the Old Testament. He
took on the kingdom and army of King Ahab and won. These were amazing
miracles.

But they produced an enormous amount of stress. Elijah was spiritually,
emotionally, and physically spent and, as a result, very vulnerable. When
wicked Queen Jezebel threatened Elijah, he fell apart. Because she had
ordered the death of many other prophets, she intimidated him as no one else
had. He fled into the wilderness, where he became depressed and suicidal.
Exhausted, he fell asleep, and an angel brought him food and water.

What Elijah needed at that point wasn't a miracle—he needed a good night's
rest and a decent meal. Proper diet, exercise, and rest are responsible
therapies for stress.

—⟨∾⟩—

*Lord, I feel like running away, or quitting, or just giving up. Tell me what
to do. If I need a miracle, then give me a miracle. If it's sleep or food I need,
show me the bed and table. Please give me what I need to go on. Amen.*

A Twist on History

The prayer of a righteous man is powerful and effective.
James 5:16

It was the British poet Alfred, Lord Tennyson who wrote: "More things are wrought by prayer than this world dreams of."

When I read Tennyson's words, I think, *If we only knew!* I believe that history from heaven's perspective reads quite differently from school history books. If asked to list the greatest people of power in our history, we would list names like Washington, Jefferson, Lincoln, Roosevelt, Eisenhower, and Reagan. But someday we may visit the Library of the Universe in heaven and discover a twist on history. The names we thought were famous have only an obscure footnote. The names that made the difference, the greatest names, will be those we never knew: poor widows, enthusiastic teenagers, faithful Sunday school teachers, obscure missionaries...otherwise ordinary people who faithfully and effectively prayed in such a way that they shaped human history for good.

God of history, I pray to you as you asked me to pray.
My requests are for our world, nation, community, church,
and family. I believe that my prayers can change everything
because they go directly to you through Jesus Christ. Amen.

A Distinctive Style

———— ✦⟨ফ্র⟩✦ ————

Men spoke from God as they were carried along by the Holy Spirit.
2 Peter 1:21

Did you know more than forty different authors wrote the Bible over fifteen hundred years? These authors were young and old, spoke Hebrew and Greek, and had good moods and bad moods and unique personalities. They included: David, a poet; Moses, a lawgiver; Luke, a physician; Paul, a theologian; and Peter, a fisherman. Each had a distinctive style that came through in his writings. All were recruited by God and were given material and divine supervision. They had to stay within the assignment but had the freedom to be themselves.

Compare it to a professor who selects a few graduate students with whom to share her research data. She assigns them papers to write, allows them to work on their own, but edits their writing for accuracy. Every paper contains her information but is different and distinctive due to the personality and style of the student writing it. Are these the professor's papers or the students' papers? Both.

So it is with the Bible. It is a divine/human book. The origin is God (giving content and ensuring accuracy), and the origin is human (reflecting the personality of the writer). There is no other book like it!

———— ⟨ফ্র⟩ ————

*Thank you, God, for the Bible—your amazing book that
speaks your truth to my heart and life. My desire is to read,
listen, believe, and obey your holy Scriptures. Amen.*

"Rocky" the Disciple

These are the names of the twelve apostles:
first, Simon (who is called Peter)....
Matthew 10:2

Simon Peter was the kind of guy who never looked scared. He jumped out of a boat to walk on water; he declared Jesus the Messiah when others were silent; he lopped off the ear of a guard when Jesus was arrested. Even his nickname, *Peter*, means "Rocky." He was the Sylvester Stallone prizefighter of the disciples.

It was Peter's friendship and love for Jesus that made him courageous the eve of Jesus' crucifixion. What started out as a nice Passover dinner ended up in one disaster after another—soldiers, arrest, assault, threats. All were scared. Most of Jesus' followers went into hiding. But Peter loved Jesus enough to stay nearby. Unfortunately, before the night was over, brave Peter succumbed to fear. He failed Jesus. But the story doesn't end there. He repented and went on to become one of the great heroes of the Christian faith. He learned an important life lesson: that Jesus is greater than our fears.

Jesus, what is your nickname for me? I'd rather be a fighter than a coward. I'd prefer you call me Faithful or Loving or Courageous or Loyal rather than some lesser name. Call me what you want me to be and help me to live up to that name. Amen.

It's What You Do

Love is patient, love is kind. It does not envy, it does not boast,
it is not proud. It is not rude, it is not self-seeking, it is not
easily angered, it keeps no record of wrongs. Love does not delight
in evil but rejoices with the truth. It always protects, always trusts,
always hopes, always perseveres.

1 Corinthians 13:4–7

Jesus told us to love our neighbors as ourselves, but how do we *do* that?
Love isn't mostly about what we *feel*; it's mostly about our *actions*. But with six
billion people in the world and so many needs, what can one person with
limited resources do?

Begin with the needs of people you know. What can you do to love them in
Jesus' name? Make a list of your neighbors. Divide the list into seven parts
so you can pray for one-seventh of your neighbors every day. Ask God to
show you their needs. Then give some of your time. Everyone has 168 hours
in the week. Two hours a week spent loving and serving a neighbor is about
1 percent of your hours. Tutor. Build. Pray. Teach. Coach. Shovel. Visit.
Clean. Babysit. Time is the truest currency of love.

*Loving Lord God, I want to be like you. Just as you patiently
love me in all that you do, I want to love the people in my life
in the way I treat them. Here are their names. Amen.*

A Continual Promise

———————⟨❧⟩———————

He who began a good work in you will carry
it on to completion until the day of Christ Jesus.
Philippians 1:6

You've probably seen the sign that says, PLEASE BE PATIENT, GOD ISN'T FINISHED
WITH ME YET. That slogan is based on the promise made by God in Philippians
1:6. God reshapes and retools every person who believes in Jesus Christ. He
repairs and replaces parts when necessary. He fixes us up as good as new or
better. Whenever something is wrong, God goes to work making it right. He
refines and adjusts our attitudes and actions and never stops until he makes
us perfect.

Imagine what it would be like if you were stuck the way you are forever—
if you could never improve! Imagine if God never corrected us when we are
wrong and never lifted us when we are down. God continually promises to
work for good in our lives and to continue to do it until he takes us to heaven
someday to forever be with him.

———⟨❧⟩———

*You do good work, Lord! And I am very grateful for all you've done so far in
my life. But I know you're not finished with me yet. So I pray that today you'll
fix me, change me, improve me to make me the way you want me to be. Amen.*

Rebuilt and Restored

❧

The God of all grace, who called you to his eternal glory
in Christ, after you have suffered a little while, will himself
restore you and make you strong, firm and steadfast.
1 Peter 5:10

A man owned a 1958 Chevrolet Impala convertible when he was a teenager. He loved that car. But eventually he sold it, and the car was resold and resold. When he reached his forties, he wanted that Chevy back, so he hired a private detective to trace all the owners through motor vehicle registrations and interviews. At last he tracked that car across thousands of miles in multiple states and found it in a junkyard—wrecked and rusted out. After traveling across country to buy the wreck, the man invested thousands of hours and tens of thousands of dollars rebuilding and restoring his once beautiful convertible. Eventually, it was as good as new. For him, it was twice loved and twice owned.

God first owned us as our Creator. Then some of us wandered away from him and ended up in the junkyard. But God doesn't easily give up. He lovingly tracks us down and rebuilds and restores us through Jesus Christ.

❧

*I'm kind of run-down and rusty, Lord. Make me your
restoration project. Fix me up. Remove the rust. Put me
back the way you designed me to be. Amen.*

The Golden Rule

Be careful to do what is right in the eyes of everybody. If it is possible, as far as it depends on you, live at peace with everyone.

Romans 12:17–18

You're probably familiar with the Golden Rule: "Do to others what you would have them do to you." As I try to live this way, I'm amazed at the power of Jesus' teaching. When people criticize me, I try not to criticize them. When somebody writes an unkind letter, I try to respond with love. When a waiter treats me poorly, I try to leave a generous tip.

Does this always work? No. But the goal isn't to change the other person; it's to please God. Our generosity shouldn't be based on the other person's behavior but on how we would like to be treated and how God has treated us.

But what about the people who are impossible to get along with? As Christians, we are to do what is right, no matter what the other person does. So if someone wants to fight, make every effort to live in peace. Be kind, loving, and forgiving—like Jesus.

God, there are some mean and grouchy people in my life. Some who claim to be Christians are among the grouchiest. Give me wisdom and courage to treat them the way Jesus would and love them no matter what they say or do. In Jesus' name, amen.

100 Percent Loyal

❦

The mouth of the righteous man utters wisdom,
and his tongue speaks what is just.
The law of his God is in his heart;
his feet do not slip.
Psalm 37:30-31

Every employer who has had a 100 percent loyal employee can tell you what that sort of person is like. He may not be the smartest person who has ever worked for the company, but he's totally dependable. She may not be the most talented person on the staff, but she'll do anything; no assignment is too menial. He's willing to stay late if he needs to; she's willing to take a pay cut if the company's budget is slipping behind.

The righteous person in Psalm 37:30-31 has that kind of loyalty to Jesus Christ. He doesn't push his own agenda or complain. She is willing to go wherever and do whatever God says, absolutely without question. Interestingly, here's what is *not* mentioned about this righteous person: no spelling out of all the good works accomplished, or praying long hours, or having great faith. The righteous person simply loves God and lives for him. How about you?

❧

God, I pledge my allegiance to you—to always love you, serve you, and be faithful to you in every circumstance. I promise through Jesus. Amen.

What Really Counts

"For whoever wants to save his life will lose it,
but whoever loses his life for me will save it."
Jesus, in Luke 9:24

Some books have exceptional impact on our lives. I suppose it's as much the moment as the message. For me, the moment was in my later teens when I read Jim Elliot's biography, *Shadow of the Almighty*.

Jim Elliot was a young man determined to do whatever God wanted. The vision God gave him was to reach the Auca Indians of Ecuador with the gospel of Jesus Christ. After six years of prayer and much preparation, Jim and four other men landed a small plane near an Auca village where they had been dropping gifts. They hung hammocks high above the jungle floor and waited. On a Friday, five American men and isolated natives met for the first time. Two days later, on January 8, 1956, the Aucas killed Jim and his companions. It was a high price, five lives, yet through their deaths the Aucas came to know Jesus as Savior.

The way to do something significant with your life, to make it really count, is to do something significant for God.

*You know I'm not looking to die, Jesus. But I want you to
know that I love you more than life itself. I give everything
I am and have to you, including my life. Amen.*

A Call to Love

—◈—

*"Lord, when did we see you hungry or thirsty or a stranger
and needing clothes...and did not help you?" Jesus will reply,
"I tell you the truth, whatever you did not do for one of the
least of these, you did not do for me."*

Matthew 25:44–45

The most famous verse in the Bible is John 3:16: "For God so loved the
world that he gave his one and only Son, that whoever believes in him shall
not perish but have eternal life."

When we hear those words we think of ourselves, of how much God loves
us. That's true, but that's not all. God loves others just as much. He loves
Europeans, Africans, Latin Americans, and Asians. He loves poor people
and rich people, the beautiful and the unattractive. He loves the able-
bodied and the disabled, the CEO, the native born, the immigrant, the
crack addict, the Eagle Scout, the gay and the straight. And God wants us
to love whom he loves. In fact, he *calls us* to love whom he loves. It's not an
option. Jesus went so far as to say that the way we treat others is the way we
treat God. That certainly puts things in perspective, doesn't it?

—◈—

*Thank you for loving me enough to send your Son. Fill me so full of your love
that I love others as you do. And may my love come from my heart and flow
through my actions toward everyone—especially those hardest to love. Amen.*

The Power Connection

---❦---

Hear my prayer, O God;
listen to the words of my mouth.
Psalm 54:2

I'm old enough to remember the first time computers were installed in my office. Shortly afterwards, when I was working alone on a Saturday, I pushed the print button on a document I'd finished and walked down the hallway to the laser printer, expecting to find the sheets cranking out. Nothing. I checked for paper in the tray, returned to my office, and tried again. No results. I read the manual to make sure I was doing the commands in the proper sequence. I worked at it for hours but never got that document to print. Several days later, I realized the cable from my computer wasn't connected to the printer. It went up into the ceiling somewhere and stopped.

Sometimes our prayers are like that. We work long and hard to get them exactly right, but there is no power. It's as if the prayer goes up out of sight and never connects. It's the connection to God that will make our prayers effective.

❧

*Can you hear me now, O God? Can you hear me? Listen and
I will speak. Answer the prayer of my heart. I believe and know
we are connected—that you will hear and answer because I am
praying in the name of Jesus my Savior and Lord. Amen.*

A Fabulous Book

———◦❦◦———

All Scripture is God-breathed and is useful for teaching, rebuking, correcting and training in righteousness, so that the man of God may be thoroughly equipped for every good work.
2 Timothy 3:16–17

The Bible is so much more than just good literature. It is rich and deep and full of wisdom. It's good for:

- *Teaching.* It's the textbook for knowing God and understanding life.

- *Rebuking.* It confronts errors in our beliefs and thinking, acting as a plumb line to show us where we are out of whack.

- *Correcting.* It shows us what's wrong with our lives and helps us correct what's wrong—with God's help.

- *Training.* It shows us what is right—what we ought to do. Why spend life avoiding bad stuff? Be trained to do good stuff!

- *Good works.* It equips us to do good in a world that has a huge shortage of good works.

In short, the Bible will equip us to do good in *every possible situation.* Now that's a fabulous book!

———◦❦◦———

When I read the Bible, help me understand and do what you say. Teach me. Rebuke me. Correct me. Train me. Equip me to do every good work you want me to do. Lord, thank you for your Word. Amen.

FEBRUARY

Reshaped

We know that in all things God works for the good of those who love him, who have been called according to his purpose.

Romans 8:28

Have you ever watched a potter at his wheel, his hands working the clay as it spins? A touch here, a squeeze there, and a beautiful bowl or vase appears, as if by magic. But sometimes, when the creation looks almost finished to my inexperienced eyes, the potter will squash the clay back down into a formless clump and start all over again. Why? Because it wasn't quite right; it wasn't quite perfect.

And that's what God does with us. We are like clay in the potter's hand, and he desires our perfection. Taking the half-formed creation that is us, he remolds it until we are formed in the image of his Son, Jesus Christ. I'm not pretending it isn't painful to be smashed down and reshaped on that potter's wheel. However, spinning around while the master potter works on you is quite different from aimlessly spinning out of control. In all things, God is working for your good.

You are the Potter; I am the clay. I love your touch, and I am grateful you are so close. While I don't like setbacks, redesigns, and start-overs, I do trust you. You love me and know what you are doing with me. Thank you. Amen.

The Most Valuable Paper in the World

Let us hold unswervingly to the hope we profess,
for he who promised is faithful.

Hebrews 10:23

Remove a dollar bill from your wallet. It's really only a piece of paper with ink on it, isn't it? The intrinsic value is practically nothing. Every bill has a picture of a dead guy and signatures of government officials most of us have never heard of. Yet we value the money, and many people will do almost anything to get a larger pile of it. We save it. We believe in it. Though it has no intrinsic value, it's the promise behind the paper and ink that makes it valuable, because we believe the United States of America will make the paper's promises come true.

The Bible is also merely paper and ink. It doesn't have any intrinsic value. But it contains many promises: that God will meet our needs, answer our prayers, heal our bodies, comfort our grief, forgive our sins, and get us to heaven. With the guarantee of God himself behind those promises, that makes the Bible the most valuable paper in the world!

Faithful God, your Word is good and true. You keep your promises. I know I can always count on you. When I read the Bible I know that you stand behind it completely. How wonderful you are and how grateful I am for the dependable Bible in a world with too many broken promises. Amen.

Love Him Back!

———— ❧ ————

To all who received him, to those who believed in his name,
he gave the right to become the children of God.

John 1:12

One of the most familiar verses in the Bible is, "For God so loved the world that he gave his one and only Son, that whoever believes in him shall not perish, but have eternal life" (John 3:16). What it says is astonishing: God loves us! He loved us enough to give his Son. He loves us every day, in every situation, and more than we could ever love ourselves.

But we need to accept God's love and love God back. We have to say "yes" to this love. And when we do, we become his daughters and his sons. How can we accept this love? Through Jesus Christ! Jesus told us, "Love the Lord your God with all your heart and with all your soul and with all your mind" (Matthew 22:37). The most important relationship we'll ever have is with God. So accept his love—and then love him back!

———— ❧ ————

You love me. How wonderful and amazing that you, God, love me
so much. There are no adequate words to thank you or describe
how grateful I am. I just want to say over and over that I love you,
God. I love you. I love you. I love you. I love you. Amen.

Apron Blessings

"Freely you have received, freely give."
Jesus, in Matthew 10:8

A woman once invited her neighbor from the next farm to go to church with her. The neighbor said, "I'd be glad to come, and I'll wear my best apron." The first woman knew no one else wore aprons to church, so she phoned other women in the church and asked them to wear aprons the next Sunday so as not to embarrass her guest. Months later the neighbor found out why everyone had worn aprons that Sunday. She was so touched by their sensitivity that it influenced her to become a Christian, like those who had cared so much for her. For the women in that church, sharing their faith was far more important than what they wore.

God has given us salvation, money, jobs, health, and a thousand other gifts. While he is glad to give us those things, he wants us to freely share those blessings with others.

My generous God, I am blessed. The list of your gifts is longer than I can remember. Yet I am often selfish and proud, wanting things my way and wanting more gifts from you. Forgive my pride and help me think of others ahead of myself. Make me a blessing as I adapt to meet the needs of others for Jesus. Amen.

Active Evidence

———— ✦ ————

But someone will say, "You have faith; I have deeds."
Show me your faith without deeds,
and I will show you my faith by what I do.
James 2:18

Imagine you're asked to stand before a judge and prove you are a Christian. At the trial your friends, coworkers, and family members are called as witnesses. Questions are asked, and testimony is given. Your checkbook is examined, tapes of your conversations are played, and evidence is offered on everything from church attendance to treatment of people who have hurt you. Such evidence doesn't make you guilty or not guilty. It merely proves or disproves your plea as defendant. What counts is the truthfulness of the plea.

The same goes for being a Christian. Good works and Christian behavior do not make you a Christian. They are evidence of your plea of faith. As you act on your beliefs and live out your life day to day as a Christian, your actions are the evidence of the truth of your commitment to God before the juries of earth and heaven.

———— ✦ ————

Dear Jesus, may my actions prove my faith. I believe in you with all my heart and want to live for you with all my life. When others check me out, may they see you in my deeds. May they see you in me. Amen.

On God's Team

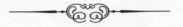

"Your will be done on earth as it is in heaven."
Jesus, in Matthew 6:10

One of the greatest differences between earth and heaven is that in heaven everything is done according to one will—God's will. Earth is currently operating with over six billion wills because each of us has our own. That's why there are ethnic conflicts, racial strife, and fights within families. But in heaven, God's will rules. His will is everyone's will.

The best comparison I can think of is those unusual moments in team sports when every member works perfectly together. It's the synergism of five basketball players smoothly moving the ball down the court for basket after basket. It's the rhythm of a rowing crew skimming over the water. It's the indescribable coordination of a World Cup soccer team. It's hard to describe and tough to beat.

Maybe that's a little of what heaven is like. It's everyone on God's team together, pulling in the same direction.

Our Father in heaven, hallowed be your name. Your kingdom come, your will be done on earth as it is in heaven. Make me an example of your ways and your will. May I move in perfect harmony with what you want. My prayer is that I will make all choices and carry them out so that others will see a preview of heaven in my life. Amen.

An Invitation

---❦---

"It is God who works in you to will and
to act according to his good purpose."
Paul, in Philippians 2:13

Most people interpret life by one of three categories: secular, evil, or God. Secularists believe there is a reasonable explanation for everything. They don't think of God as being involved. Their lives center on themselves. Those who interpret life in terms of evil don't necessarily worship or follow Satan, but they see the hand of evil in everything that happens. They always assume the worst.

Then there are those who interpret all of life in terms of God. They see God in everything. They have a never-ending sense of his presence and power, even in the smallest and most ordinary events, and do everything for the glory of God. Their whole lives center on God himself.

What's your perspective? I invite you to look for God in every detail of life. See him in your relationships. Expect him in your home. Honor him in all you do. The most ordinary events become extraordinary and supernatural because of God's touch.

---❧---

*I'm always looking for you, Great God. I expect to meet you
when I wake up in the morning and say "good night" to you when
I go to sleep at night. I search for you in the miracles and the
miseries of my life. I know you are there, working to accomplish
your good purpose in everything I experience. Amen.*

Protected from What Might Have Been

—◦⟨◦⟩◦—

Deliver me, O my God, from the hand of the wicked,
from the grasp of evil and cruel men.
Psalm 71:4

Do you ever stop to thank God that you have lived so long? Have you praised him for preserving you from all the possible things that could have gone wrong?

When one of our sons moved across country, I worried. He was driving through winter weather, pulling a trailer over the Rockies, and I feared everything from loose lug nuts to drive-by shooters. When he safely arrived, I thanked God for preserving him.

Later, while on an airplane, I noticed the man in the window seat cross himself as the wheels touched the ground. I smiled to myself. *That's not a bad idea. This guy is grateful to God for getting him back on earth again.* What I had seen as routine, he had turned to praise.

Sometimes it's good to be reminded not just to praise God for what went right, but also to praise him for all the things that don't go wrong!

—◦⟨◦⟩◦—

God my Protector, you have protected and preserved me from ten thousand dangers I never knew. I am safe when others are under attack. I am alive when others my own age have already died. I am surrounded by your presence. As you have preserved me in the past, I will trust you to preserve me now and tomorrow. Praise to you, Lord. Amen.

Angels on Earth

❦

For he will command his angels concerning you
to guard you in all your ways;
they will lift you up in their hands.
Psalm 91:11-12

When someone does something really special for you, you might say, "You're an angel!" It's a high compliment because angels are among the most wonderful, magnificent creatures in all of God's creation.

The popularity of angels has soared in recent years. Stories of encounters with angels frequently appear in magazines, books, and on national TV. The Bible also makes many references to both good and bad angels and the roles they play. When God sends good angels to guide and protect you, you should be grateful, but you shouldn't focus on the angel.

If a mail carrier brings you a love letter from your fiancé, you don't kiss the mail carrier, do you? He is merely the messenger. When flowers are delivered to you, it isn't the deliveryman to whom you are grateful, it is the sender. Angels are messengers from God, but our focus should be on the God who sent them.

❧

King of kings and Lord of lords, you are the Boss of heaven and earth. All the angels of heaven work for you. They are supernatural, super-powerful, and super-wonderful. Thank you for sending these heavenly creatures to be your messengers to us on earth. But it is you I love and praise and worship, not your messengers. You are my King, my Lord, and my God. Amen.

Motive, Means, and Opportunity

Make the most of every opportunity.
Colossians 4:5

You're on jury duty, and soon you have to decide, "Did he do it, or didn't he?" The prosecutor looks you in the eye. "I ask you to consider three critical factors in your verdict: *Motive.* Did the defendant have good reason to do what he is accused of doing? *Means.* Did the defendant have a way to do what he is accused of doing? *Opportunity.* Did he have a time and a place where he could do what he is accused of doing? If all three are present, then the charges must be true."

Those three factors—motive, means, and opportunity—are also important in your spiritual life. The Bible says to love God with all your heart—and your neighbor too. That's *motivation.* The Bible also says that you can do all things through Christ. That's *means.* And the world is full of *opportunities* to show God's love to others.

Are you motivated? Do you have some means? Will you grab an opportunity to show God's love to others?

Count me in. I love you, God, and want to live out my love. Love is my motive. Christ is my means. Life is full of opportunities. I delight to live out love for you with all my heart, mind, soul, and body. Amen.

A Fresh Start

─────❦─────

Peter, an apostle of Jesus Christ.... Praise be to the God
and Father of our Lord Jesus Christ! In his great mercy
he has given us new birth into a living hope through
the resurrection of Jesus Christ from the dead, and into
an inheritance that can never perish, spoil or fade.

1 Peter 1:1, 3–4

The Bible contains many stories about Jesus' twelve followers who heard his teachings, observed his miracles, and memorized his sayings. One of these men was Peter. Originally named Simon, this fisherman was introduced to Jesus by his brother, Andrew. Soon Peter became one of Jesus' closest friends.

Peter loved all the action surrounding Jesus—the crowds, the miraculous healings, the confrontations with politicians. But Peter was a "fair weather friend." He skipped out when Jesus really needed him. His denial of Jesus remained a painful memory and regret for the rest of Peter's life, but he did something we all should do when we miserably fail: learn a lesson from our mistakes.

Peter made a fresh start and remained steadfastly faithful to Jesus for the rest of his life. So can you. Simply tell Jesus you are sorry for your mistakes and you want to start over.

─────❧─────

Thank you for the story of Peter, who failed you and was restored. That's my story too. I say I love you and am loyal, then deny you out loud. I am so sorry. Please forgive me and renew me through the great mercy of Jesus. Amen.

Your Heart's Desires

Delight yourself in the Lord,
and he will give you the desires of your heart.

Psalm 37:4

When I first heard this verse I understood the words to say, "If you like God, he'll give you everything you want." It sounded like a good deal to me.

I'll never forget the day I understood these words in a totally different way. I was a graduate student teaching a summer class at church when a college sophomore home for the summer said, "Here's what I understand it to mean. If we make God the delight of our lives, he will cause our hearts to desire what he wants them to desire."

Now, why didn't I think of that? She got it right! What if the desires of our hearts were totally changed so we desired what God wants us to desire and then God gave us the fulfillment of those desires? Life would be completely different!

If you make God your heart's desire—loving him, pursuing him, pleasing him—then he will give you the desires of your heart.

Beloved God, you are a delight! You are so good, so great, so holy, so loving, so kind, and so totally marvelous. I thrill to think about you. And, I know you have the very best plans and dreams for me. May you give your desires to me so that I can make them the desires of my heart. Amen.

The Lemon Clause

———— ✦❦✦ ————

God demonstrates his love for us in this:
While we were still sinners, Christ died for us.
Romans 5:8

Everyone wants to be loved—to be needed and important in someone else's life. Problem is, most love is based on desirability: looks, talents, and how much money we have. Wouldn't it be great to just be loved for yourself? To have someone know the "real you" and still love you?

When my wife and I shopped for a used minivan, the salesman tried to show us one for a very low price. He said it had been repurchased by the Chrysler Corporation under the "Lemon Law." I wouldn't have wanted that car at any price. I've had enough cars that ended up being lemons without starting out with one that was officially a lemon!

The amazing thing about God's love, though, is that he loves us "as is." He buys us even though he knows we are lemons. Not only that, he's willing to pay top price—the suffering and death of his own Son.

———— ❧ ————

Lord God, you know my name. I am a sinner. I am a "lemon"—filled with mistakes, stupidity, and deliberately evil choices. You know all that and love me anyway. I am amazed but deeply grateful. You love me as is and gave your Son, Jesus, to pay the price for my life and the debt for my sin. Wow! Amen.

Four Words for Love

And now these three remain: faith, hope and love.
But the greatest of these is love.
1 Corinthians 13:13

In English we have only one word for *love*, even though it can mean different things. In Greek, the language in which the New Testament was written, there were four words for love.

Storge. Natural affection, especially between a mother and a child.

Philia. The affection between friends and those we really like.

Eros. Strong attraction, especially sexual love.

Agape. An extreme love that unselfishly gives for the benefit of another person.

All four kinds of love are gifts from God. The first three come the easiest because they are based on the attraction to the ones we love and the benefits we can get back. Agape love is based on the person doing the loving, not the person being loved. It is completely to benefit another rather than to get benefit for ourselves. Only God's love is agape—great to get but supernatural to give.

"God is love"—that's one of my favorite truths about you in the Bible, Lord. I love to be loved by you. No one loves better than you love. Thank you for the many ways you love me and for the many ways you give me to love you and others. I want to be a lover just like you. Amen.

The Real Thing

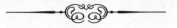

Love must be sincere.
Romans 12:9

Relationships between two people often come to a crossroads when one person behaves in a way the other person sees as inappropriate. Our reaction is, "What was she thinking?" or, "How can he *do* that?" *These* are the times when we need love.

Love is thinking and acting in a positive and caring manner toward other persons regardless of their attitude or behavior. In the Greek language the word *sincere* literally means "without wax." The Greeks often patched cracks and defects in marble statues with wax. The repairs were invisible when the statue was cool; but in the heat, the wax melted and the defects reappeared. Sincere love is the real thing. It looks the same when relationships heat up!

It's easy to make everything be about *us*. But the Bible says to honor others with sincere love whether they are nice or not.

Yes, God, there are some hard-to-love people in my life. You know who they are, and you know what they say and do. Loving them is not easy. Loving them would be impossible if it weren't for you. Carve into my life the marble of unflawed love for these less-than-lovable folk I'm thinking about. Make my love for them as sincere as yours. Amen.

The Final Authority

It is the Lord Christ you are serving.
Colossians 3:24

Do you ever feel isolated? Like you're the only one with difficulties in your life? Truth is, we all have issues. For some, they are job-related, maybe an unfair or unkind boss. For somebody else, it's a marriage that's troublesome at best.

What's the most liberating way to deal with these issues? Realize that God has the final authority. It's not the boss who has the final say over your job success; it is God. It is not the teacher to whom your child has been assigned who will determine her academic outcome this year; it is God. It is not the physician's diagnosis that determines your health; it is the Great Physician.

God is one thousand times more important than anyone or anything else in your life, and he has a plan for you. You can trust him with absolutely anything. He won't disappoint you.

Lord Christ, you are in charge. While it looks like the final say comes from teachers, employers, judges, and doctors, I know better. You are the final authority. It's up to you. You truly are the Lord. Amen.

Upsize It

"'Which of these three do you think was a neighbor
to the man who fell into the hands of robbers?'
The expert in the law replied, 'The one who had mercy on him.'
Jesus told him, 'Go and do likewise.'"
Luke 10:36-37

We all know what upsizing is from McDonalds and Burger King. When you order a combo, the server asks you if you want to upsize it for an extra 49 cents. For the extra money, you get a Biggie Coke™ and a Super Size fries with your sandwich.

Jesus was good at upsizing his stories too. We all know we should love those who are like us, but Jesus took it a step further. When a lawyer asked him to define who his "neighbor" was, Jesus told a story about a Jewish man who was beaten and robbed. Two other Jewish men saw the injured man and crossed the street to avoid him. Then a Samaritan came by and took care of the man. Though Jews and Samaritans traditionally disliked one another and avoided contact, this man took care of someone who wasn't like him.

Who is your neighbor? Anyone who has a need.

---

*God of love, mercy, and grace...make me a modern Samaritan.
Where there is injury, help me to heal. Where there is hatred, let
me show love. Where there is poverty, let me be generous. For
Jesus' sake, I will go and do like the Samaritan. Amen.*

A Habit for Life

"If anyone would come after me, he must deny himself
and take up his cross daily and follow me."
Jesus, in Luke 9:23

Magazines and books are full of phrases like "be true to yourself." But Jesus makes it clear that Christianity is not about putting yourself first; it is about self-denial. It's about voluntarily giving up something you want and could have. It's about putting others first and not insisting upon your own way. It's about letting go of anger when you've been wronged.

I have a challenge for you—and for me. Think of something that's important to you and then think of ways that denying yourself of that could help others in the name of Jesus Christ. It may be watching less TV or getting up earlier to pray for the needs of others. It may be choosing to live more simply so you have more money to share with others. The point is to do it once, then twice, and gradually every day until it becomes a habit for life.

*This doesn't come naturally to me. It only comes supernaturally.
I like to be comfortable and keep what I've got. It isn't that I don't
want to help others but that I don't want to hurt myself. Then I think
about you, Jesus, and how you left heaven and died on the cross for
me. Now that I am your follower I want to take the supernatural
way of Jesus, deny myself, and take up my cross every day. Amen.*

The Right Thing

---◆◈◆---

"If we confess our sins, he is faithful and just and will forgive
us our sins and purify us from all unrighteousness."
John, in 1 John 1:9

Think, for a moment, what a miraculous statement 1 John 1:9 is! It's saying
that if we go to God and sincerely confess our sins, God promises to forgive
those sins and totally purify our souls from any stain of those sins. How
amazing and wonderful—to receive forgiveness from God!

Confessing sins to God isn't the only kind of confessing we need to do.
God also tells us to go to anyone we've sinned against, confess, and ask for
forgiveness. When you do, that person might look you in the eye and say,
"I'll never forgive you." But it's still the right thing to do.

The Christian life is all about doing the right thing—not always the easy
thing. And the benefits of doing the right thing, both in the short-term
and the long-term, are *always* worthwhile.

◈

*Father, forgive me. I have sinned. Let me be specific—you know my
sins, but I need to name them to you. Thank you for your guarantee
to forgive these sins I have now confessed. Go with me as I seek
the forgiveness of those against whom I have sinned. Amen.*

Number One...

"The Son of Man came to seek and to save what was lost."
Jesus, in Luke 19:10

CEO Charles Schwab once offered a challenge to management consultant Ivy Lee: "Show me a way to get more things done. If it works, I'll pay anything within reason."

Lee told him to write down what he had to get done the next day, and then number the items in order of importance. "Work on number one first thing tomorrow, and stay with it until it is completed. Then work on number two until it is completed. If you can't complete everything on your list, don't worry. At least you will have taken care of the important things before getting distracted by items of lesser consequence. The secret is to do this daily. Establish priorities, record your plan of action, and stick to it."

A few weeks later Schwab sent Lee a check for $25,000, saying it was the most profitable lesson of his entire business career.

That's because the success of life is tied to making and keeping priorities. No one was better at priorities than Jesus. His number-one priority was, and still is, to reconnect people to God.

Jesus, I want to prioritize like you. You came to earth with the clear purpose of seeking and saving those who are lost from God. You always know what is most important. In my busy life I want to get the top opportunities and responsibilities on my list and put them in the right order. With your help I'll always make you Number One at the top of my priorities. Amen.

An Ambassador of Good Will

—⚬❦⚬—

"He who is least among you all—he is the greatest."
Jesus, in Luke 9:48

I watched a TV interview of prize fighter Muhammad Ali, with clips of his early career—all the way back to when his name was Cassius Clay. In those clips this young, trim, in-your-face athlete quoted often what became his most famous line: "I am the greatest." Although he was the three-time world heavyweight boxing champion, Ali turned a lot of people off with his superior attitude.

What a sharp contrast to the older man I saw interviewed. Because of Parkinson's disease, he had trouble walking and could no longer box. His speech was slow and difficult to understand. He no longer claimed to be the greatest. Yet streets and parks have been named after him, he became known as an "ambassador of good will," and his face is one of the most recognized around the world. It certainly seems as if Muhammad Ali became far greater in his weakness than he ever was in his strength. His story is a modern-day example of the principle Jesus taught.

—⚬❧⚬—

You are my King, and I am your ambassador. You are the greatest, and I am your servant. My desire and goal is to represent you well wherever I go and whatever I do. As a Christian, I am always a representative of Jesus. Amen.

What Makes Heaven

"Do not let your hearts be troubled. Trust in God; trust also
in me. In my Father's house are many rooms; if it were not so,
I would have told you. I am going there to prepare a place for
you. And if I go and prepare a place for you, I will come back
and take you to be with me that you also may be where I am.
You know the way to the place where I am going."

Jesus, in John 14:1-4

When my wife and I traveled to Australia, we discovered that Australians sometimes resent having Americans refer to their country as being "down under." Down under what? In fact, almost every Australian souvenir shop sells maps of the world that show Australia on the top, with Europe and North America on the bottom. In other words, up and down depends on where you are and where you are talking about. It's about relationship.

The same may be said about heaven. What makes heaven is not up or down, but relationship. To put it simply: heaven is the home of God. Heaven is where Christians on earth are headed. Heaven is where Jesus came from. And if heaven is where you want to end up, you have to have a relationship with Jesus!

---

*I'm coming, Jesus. Get everything ready. I'm coming to heaven to be
with you at the address you're getting ready right now. Amen.*

At Any Cost

———— ⌘ ————

"Foxes have holes and birds of the air have nests,
but the Son of Man has no place to lay his head."
Jesus, in Luke 9:58

My first serious camping experience was on the coast of Maine as a teenager. A friend of my father's took me and a friend of mine camping. It was cold and wet and he told us to be careful not to touch the tent because it would leak. That night, as the wind howled and the rain poured, I decided to test his advice; I touched the canvas over my face. Sure enough, it leaked on my head the rest of the night.

I didn't try camping again until college. Camping across Europe was fun, but not as much fun as staying in a nice hotel with a color TV and a private bathroom. I guess I'm just not wired to camp.

But in Luke 9:58 Jesus isn't telling us to be campers or homeless, he is calling us to consider him more important than family, home, job, safety, or comfort. We are to follow him *at any cost*.

———— ⌘ ————

It sounds like you were homeless, Jesus. I know you moved around a lot and didn't have a permanent address during the last years of your life. It's not that you want me to be homeless but that you want me to be devoted to you. So, whatever you ask, wherever you want, count on me to follow. Amen.

Too Cluttered?

"Do not take a purse or bag or sandals;
and do not greet anyone on the road."
Jesus, in Luke 10:4

One of the pieces of advice Jesus gave his followers was, "Don't get cluttered with possessions." He wasn't forbidding people to wear shoes or to have purses or saying we shouldn't have any possessions. But he was saying, "Don't let the things you have define who you are."

Some time ago I read an article in *Money* magazine about lottery winners who were sorry they had won. They wished they could go back to when they had less, when life was simpler, even though it may have been more of a struggle. They were drowning in clutter.

Following that piece of advice, Jesus said that when you go out, *"do not greet anyone on the road."* In other words, stay focused. Don't become distracted from what is really important in life. Do you let things define who you are? Don't get too cluttered. Stay focused.

We have a lot of stuff. The truth is, God, that some of us have so much stuff that we rent storage homes for our possessions and go visit them a few times every year. Personally, I have more than most people in the world, and I still want more. Bless me with a life lived for who I am and not what I have. Amen.

Simple Faith

—⟨ও৩⟩—

"I praise you, Father, Lord of heaven and earth,
because you have hidden these things from the wise
and learned and revealed them to little children."
Jesus, in Matthew 11:25

This is a very Jesus-type statement, made while talking with his disciples and sharing various bits of wisdom. Jesus was insisting that people who position themselves as the smartest, best educated, and most sophisticated often don't understand God's greatest spiritual truths. They're too smart for their own good.

Some people are convinced their plan or formula will beat the stock market, only to discover that the return on their money is half what they would have received with the S&P 500. Or someone develops an elaborate diet and drug therapy to treat a condition, only to discover their client would be better off simply taking aspirin. Others get graduate degrees in philosophy but ignore the basic truths of God in the Bible.

But children? They have simple faith. Their approach to God is uncomplicated. If we stay simple, like children, we won't miss the basics of God's spiritual truths.

—⟨৩⟩—

God of all truth, you give wisdom and knowledge. Education and insight are among your many good gifts. But please protect me from ever thinking that I am smarter than you are or that my ways are better than your ways. You are my Father, and I always want to believe in you as your child. Amen.

Holding On to Hope

————❦————

We also rejoice in our sufferings, because we know that suffering
produces perseverance; perseverance, character; and character, hope.
And hope does not disappoint us, because God has poured out his
love into our hearts by the Holy Spirit, whom he has given us.

Romans 5:3–5

Admiral James Stockdale was the highest-ranking United States military
officer in the notorious "Hanoi Hilton" prisoner-of-war camp in North
Vietnam. From 1965 until 1973, he never knew when, or if, he would be set
free. He was cruelly tortured over twenty times, walked the rest of his life
with a limp, and never fully recovered from the brutal treatment.

How did he endure? How did he keep up hope for eight years? "I never lost
faith in the end of the story," Jim Stockdale said. "I never doubted not only
that I would get out, but also that I would…turn the experience into the
defining event of my life, which, in retrospect, I would not trade."

For Stockdale, surviving his experience was all about not losing hope. As a
Christian, you can always hold on to hope, for God will do what he promised!

————❦————

*Some days I don't have much hope. Problems are too many. Pain is too much.
Tomorrow looks like more of the same. If it weren't for you, my loving God,
I don't think I could go on. But you give me hope that the future will be better,
that the difficulties will pass, and your promises will all come through. Amen.*

Spectacular Things

———◦⬦◦———

Elijah was a man just like us. He prayed earnestly.
James 5:17

When we read the prophet Elijah's biography, we discover quite a list of accomplishments. He prayed for a drought, and it didn't rain for three-and-a-half years. Then he prayed for rain, and the rains came! When a widow's only child died, Elijah prayed, and her son came back to life. When Elijah prayed for fire from heaven, an altar piled with wet wood was zapped into flames. As if all that weren't enough to convince us he was no ordinary man, his biography ends in a most extraordinary way. Elijah never experienced physical death! God took him directly to heaven.

Yet Elijah was an ordinary person, just like us. He could get terribly discouraged. He didn't always know what to do, and he struggled with some of his relationships. The message of Scripture is clear: God does spectacular things when ordinary men and women pray earnestly.

∽◦∾

I'm one of those ordinary people. Not famous. Not all that important. Most people have never heard of me. But I'm talking to you, God. How great is that! Ordinary me praying to spectacular you. And you listen. And you answer. How amazing to pray and be heard in Jesus' name. Amen.

Alone Time

Humble yourselves, therefore, under God's mighty hand,
that he may lift you up in due time.
1 Peter 5:6

Between the first forty years of his life, when he was in the court of the pharaoh of Egypt, and the last forty years of his life, when he was leading the people of Israel, Moses spent forty years in the wilderness—pretty much alone, being trained, prepared, and shaped by God.

Jesus spent forty days and forty nights in the wilderness, a time during which he was alone with God—and when he was also tempted by Satan.

Three formative years in the desert shaped Paul's life, preparing him for the significant and great pioneer ministry he would have as an apostle to the Gentile world.

All of us could benefit much from time alone with God. So read the Bible to learn more about God. Talk to him in prayer. Tell him how great he is. Focus on God himself. It will revolutionize your relationship with him!

This is my time for you, my God. Whether these are brief moments
of meditation and prayer or days and years out in the desert,
it's you and me together. Protect and keep and bless me through
this time as you blessed Moses and Jesus and Paul. Amen.

MARCH

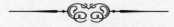

Center Stage

Come, let us bow down in worship,
let us kneel before the Lord our Maker;
for he is our God
and we are the people of his pasture,
the flock under his care.
Psalm 95:6–7

Teddy Roosevelt once said, "Even if the preacher can't preach for sour apples, and the choir is more than a half note off-key, you can always get something out of worship if you will put yourself into it." And that's true. The more we put in, the more we get out.

The famous Danish philosopher, Søren Kierkegaard, compared worship to a play. The few who stand up in front—the musicians, the pastors—are the prompters. The people in the congregation are the actors. The church building is the stage. And the audience is an audience of one, and that's God.

What a revolutionary perspective! You don't go to church to be an audience, but to be a participant. You don't come to see friends or the pastor, but to speak to God. God is the invited guest. At church we worship him by acknowledging his worth—centering on him and not on ourselves.

Our Creator and Lord, we love you and worship you. I am not alone. I join with others to praise you and to hear from you. Together we are many, but you are one. You are the one true God worthy of all honor and glory. Amen.

God's Idea

---※⟨⟨⟨⟩⟩⟩※---

Above all, you must understand that no prophecy of Scripture came
about by the prophet's own interpretation. For prophecy never had
its origin in the will of man, but men spoke from God
as they were carried along by the Holy Spirit.

2 Peter 1:20–21

The Bible is a unique book. It claims to be divine, and it is called the *Word
of God.* When the Bible speaks, it speaks for God himself. It stands alone in
terms of its authority and power in our lives because it was God's idea, not
somebody else's. He outlined and planned the contents. It's his book. God
revealed information in the Bible that we wouldn't have otherwise known,
and he "inspired" it. That means he gave his breath and life to the Bible
when it was written.

Look at it this way. If you are going to have a pacemaker placed in your
chest, you want to make sure that it's a trustworthy, accurate device from
a respected manufacturer and that it's properly installed. After all, it's a
matter of life and death.

Believing in the Bible's truths is also a matter of life and death. God's Word
is trustworthy and accurate because it comes from God. There's no better
source.

---⟨⟨⟩⟩---

*Speak to me through your written Word. God, sharpen my mind and soften my
heart to hear all you have to say. Remind me that the Bible is unique because it is
from you. When I hear the words of the Bible, I hear the words of God. Amen.*

Three Strikes and You're Out?

———⋅⋙☙⋘⋅———

"Before the rooster crows, you will disown me three times."
Jesus to Peter, in Matthew 26:34

I'm sure you're familiar with the baseball rule, "Three strikes and you're out." When Jesus was put on trial, his close friend Peter stepped up to the plate.

The first pitch came from a servant, who lobbed a passing comment Peter's way: "You were with Jesus of Galilee." Peter's reaction was, "I don't know what you're talking about." Strike one.

The second pitch was a curve ball—spoken to someone else but the words unexpectedly came right at Peter: "This fellow was with Jesus of Nazareth." Peter could have admitted it—or said nothing at all. Instead, he panicked and blurted, "I don't know the man." Strike two.

The third pitch was major league. A whole group of people said, "Surely you are one of them, for your accent gives you away." This time Peter had to swing hard to defend himself. "He swore to them, 'I don't know the man!'" Strike three. Worse, his profanity was proof he was lying.

Later, Peter felt awful about denying he knew Jesus. But you know what? Jesus still loved him and forgave him. He'll do the same for you.

———☙⋙———

Never ever do I want to deny you, Jesus. I don't want to do
what Peter did. I don't want to strike out. With your help
I will keep my eye on you and be faithful always. Amen.

Just Say Thanks!

———— ✦ ————

*Always giving thanks to God the Father for everything,
in the name of our Lord Jesus Christ.*
Ephesians 5:20

Two of the most important words in the English language are "thank you."
How we like to hear them. They let us know we are appreciated and that
what we do is significant. How easily hurt we can become if we do something
for someone and never hear a word of thanks.

If you have children, you're undoubtedly in the practice of regularly
reminding them to say "thank you" until it becomes a habit. Did you know
that God likes to hear "thank you" from his children too? Too often we are
quick to *ask* God for things and very haphazard about thanking him. How he
delights when, without being asked, we say, "Thank you."

Do you regularly thank God not only for your food but for all he's done for
you? Tell him. Thank him for his multitude of blessings. God loves to hear
"thank you"!

———— ✦ ————

*Lord God above, thank you for everything. Thank you for abundant grace
I do not deserve; thank you for life, food, shelter, family, friends, and so
much more. But, most of all, I thank you for Jesus my Savior. I thank you for
everything in the name of my Lord Jesus Christ. Amen.*

Pray Like Nehemiah

———◆◆———

"Oh, Lord, let your ear be attentive
to the prayer of this your servant."
Nehemiah, in Nehemiah 1:11

After the kingdom of Israel was led away captive to Babylon, only a small remnant remained in Jerusalem. A man named Nehemiah rose to the influential position of cupbearer to Artaxerxes, the king of Persia. When Nehemiah's brother visited Jerusalem and reported back how the holy city was in shambles, the walls had been torn down, and the Jewish people there were in dire straits, Nehemiah was greatly distressed. He fasted and prayed for four months.

Then, aware of his position of influence as cupbearer to the king, Nehemiah prayed, "Give your servant success today by granting him mercy in the presence of this man." He didn't ask for release from captivity or for the walls of Jerusalem to be rebuilt. All he asked was that God would turn the heart of Artaxerxes to do what was right and good.

How different from the prayers I've prayed in times of trouble. I'm prone to tell God exactly what I want him to do. But how much better to pray like Nehemiah—to just give God the problem and trust him to do what is right and good.

———◆———

O Lord, let your ear be attentive to me, your servant. I pray not with answers that I ask you to approve. Instead, I pray with questions I ask you to answer. Here are my problems...I trust you to show me what to do. Amen.

The Greatest Political Promise

"Why do you stand here looking into the sky? This same Jesus,
who has been taken from you into heaven, will come back
in the same way you have seen him go into heaven."

Angels, in Acts 1:11

Almost two thousand years ago a politician made an amazing promise...
in fact, a real shocker.

The politician? Jesus. It may seem inappropriate to refer to him that way,
but think about it: his life was riddled with politics from the beginning.
When he was born, the Magi came looking for a king. King Herod ordered
all Hebrew baby boys killed, because he didn't want to risk this up-and-
coming politician threatening his throne. On Palm Sunday the crowds went
wild, hoping Jesus would be crowned king and throw off the cruel Roman
yoke. On the cross the sign posted over his head read KING OF THE JEWS.

It was when Jesus left earth to return to heaven that he made the greatest political
promise in history. Actually, his press agents made the announcement. Two
angels appeared and told his followers that someday Jesus would come back.

Since that day Christians have been waiting for the fulfillment of that
promise. Whenever dictators rule or governments become corrupt,
Christians repeat, "You just wait. Jesus is coming back!"

*Jesus, we often look around at problems instead of up to you in anticipation of
your return. Thank you for your promise to come back. Now would be a very good
time! Until you arrive I pledge you my full devotion. You are my King. Amen.*

Where It All Started

The disciples were called Christians first at Antioch.
Acts 11:26

Have you ever wondered where the name *Christian* originated? It obviously has to do with Christ, you say, but when and how did Christ's followers come to be known as *Christians*?

It all goes back to the city of Antioch. Antioch was located in present-day Turkey, about fifteen miles from the eastern shore of the Mediterranean. The city had a reputation for hanging nicknames on people. When the Roman emperor Julian came to visit, the people started calling him "The Goat" because of his beard. To his dismay, the nickname stuck!

Since the followers of Jesus were always talking about the Christ, they were nicknamed *Christians*. The *ian* ending literally meant "belonging to the party of" or "a follower of." At first, *Christian* was a derogatory nickname, but the name stuck, and soon they even began calling each other Christians. They wanted to be known as belonging to the party of Christ or as followers of Jesus Christ.

And it all started in Antioch.

Dear Jesus Christ, I am honored to bear your name. For me to be called a Christian is a total privilege. My desire is to carry your name well. May others always see you in me. Amen.

Forgiveness Times 77

———◆◆◆———

*"Forgive us our sins, for we also forgive
everyone who sins against us."*
From the Lord's Prayer, in Luke 11:4

How many times should you forgive someone?

First-century Jewish rabbis taught that you ought to forgive three times. With this as the background, Peter, one of Jesus' disciples, asked him one day, "Lord, how many times shall I forgive my brother when he sins against me?" Figuring Jesus would agree with the rabbis, Peter tried to look even more magnanimous by saying, "Up to seven times?" He probably figured he'd double what the rabbis said and then throw in one more for good measure.

Peter had a gift for saying outlandish things, but Jesus liked to turn Peter's blatherings into teaching opportunities. This time Jesus shocked everyone by answering, "I tell you, not seven times, but seventy-seven times."

The root meaning of *forgiveness* is to "let go," to surrender all claims. The idea is to release ongoing resentment, bitterness, or any desire for revenge. Jesus was saying that, as his followers, we are to forgive limitless times.

———◆◆———

*Heavenly Father, I never get tired of being forgiven, but I do
get tired of forgiving others. Give me a greater appreciation
for your forgiveness of my sins so that I may become more
generous in forgiving those who sin against me. Amen.*

Do You Remember When?

"So I will always remind you of these things, even though
you know them and are firmly established in the truth
you now have. I think it is right to refresh your memory
as long as I live in the tent of this body."

Peter, in 2 Peter 1:12−13

Memories can change over time. As each generation dies, history is forgotten. The worst of memories can be suppressed, and even the best of memories fade with time. Nursing homes are filled with residents who can remember conversations that took place fifty years ago but cannot tell you what they had for breakfast. Their long-term memories are intact, but their short-term memories are fragile. An elderly friend wrote recently, bemoaning the fact he was running out of people to whom he could say, "Do you remember when…?"

The older the apostle Peter became the more he realized the transforming power of recalling the words Jesus spoke. Going through the exercise of remembering the good things Jesus and the prophets taught will give you the strength to face the bad things in your own life. Remembering is good for today—and for tomorrow.

You are the God who remembers everything. I am a human who easily forgets. Refresh and strengthen my memories, Lord. I must not forget your truths, your blessings, and your faithfulness. Amen.

Secret Sins

---✦❧❦❧✦---

Search me, O God, and know my heart;
test me and know my anxious thoughts.
See if there is any offensive way in me,
and lead me in the way everlasting.

Psalm 139:23-24

When you take a flight, you know your luggage will be screened. If you have any knives, handguns, hand grenades, or rocket launchers, you take them out of your luggage before you go. If you don't, the scanner will reveal them, and the security people will confiscate your secret weapons.

But the light of Jesus Christ is more powerful than any airport security equipment. So shouldn't the reality of being exposed to his brilliance be enough to motivate us to dump our secret sins?

Author Lee Strobel told about a baptism service where people were invited to write their secret sins on a piece of paper, then come forward to pin the paper to a large wooden cross before being baptized. One woman was so afraid someone would read her paper that she almost didn't go up front. Then God whispered to her, "I love you. It's okay. You've been forgiven."

If you have a secret sin, let the light of Jesus expose it. Confess it to God so you too can experience forgiveness and the freedom of a better tomorrow.

～⚬～

God, I ask you to scan every part of my life for every sin.
Show me what I've done wrong so I can confess, receive your
forgiveness, and start all over again. In Jesus' name, amen.

Uncle Herbert's Opportunity

Be very careful, then, how you live—not as unwise but as wise,
making the most of every opportunity, because the days are evil.
Therefore do not be foolish, but understand what the Lord's will is.

Ephesians 5:15–17

Born and raised in England, my uncle Herbert and his wife emigrated to the United States where, in addition to being a tool and die maker, he also invested in the stock market. He was never wealthy, but by the time he died he had a portfolio worth tens of thousands of dollars.

When I was about twenty and Uncle Herbert was an old man, he told me a compelling story. Many years earlier a salesman had come to his door selling stock for a few cents a share. Uncle Herbert had declined the offer because he had never heard of the Coca-Cola Bottling Company. He was still shaking his head over that missed opportunity.

Don't miss out on the opportunity to invest your life in God's work. God has great dreams for you, and he promises eternal returns. May none of us end up like Uncle Herbert, who came to the end of his life regretting he'd missed out on a great investment opportunity.

*I pray for wisdom to run from danger and to make the
most of every God-given opportunity. God, too many times
I can't tell the difference. I can get myself into a mess.
Protect me from foolishness and make me wise. Amen.*

A New Dream from Old Pieces

And Naomi was left without her two sons and her husband.
Ruth 1:5

Naomi, a godly woman who lived over three thousand years ago in Bethlehem, had a simple dream: to be a wife and mother. During a famine, her husband moved them to Moab, a different country. It wasn't where Naomi wanted to be, but while they were there her dream of motherhood came true. She loved her two boys. But then her husband died and part of her dream died with him. Now her dreams focused on her sons—that they would marry godly Jewish women and give her grandchildren. But her sons married Moabite girls—unbelievers. Then Naomi was blasted with the deaths of both sons. Her former dreams were forever gone.

But the story doesn't end there. Naomi's daughter-in-law Ruth loved Naomi and her God. Ruth accompanied Naomi back to Bethlehem and remarried, giving birth to a son. That grandson, Obed, grew up, and his grandson was named David. David became king of Israel, and one of his descendants was Jesus. God took the leftover parts of Naomi's broken dream and made them into Jesus Christ, the Savior of the world.

---

*Thank you, God, for protecting me from the worst of my dreams—
it's a good thing they didn't come true. Comfort me, Lord, in the loss
of the best of dreams that were not meant to be. Pick up the pieces
and shape them into something even better. Amen.*

Chosen for God's Team

—⟨ତ⟩—

"You are a chosen people...a holy nation,
a people belonging to God."
1 Peter 2:9

I have never been a very good athlete. I remember well the youthful pain of picking teams during grade-school gym classes. I always hoped I wouldn't be chosen last. A few times I was chosen as one of the first—not because I was good, but because the person choosing was a friend who did it out of loyalty. It felt great! I felt important and included, and it made me want to do my very best.

If you are a follower of Jesus, God has chosen *you* for his team—not because you are good, but because he likes you. You are chosen as part of a "holy nation." *Holy* means "different." You don't look like, think like, or behave like any other team.

In the Olympic games every athlete wears the name and flag of the nation he or she represents. If you are a Christian, you are on God's team in the Olympics of life. You wear his name and flag. What an indescribable honor!

—⟨ତ⟩—

*You are my Captain, God, and I am absolutely thrilled that you chose me
for your eternal team. You make me feel so important and
wanted. I promise I will give you my very best. Amen.*

A Servant's Heart

Be rich in good deeds, and…be generous and willing to share.
1 Timothy 6:18

One cold wintry day a beggar asked Martin of Tours, a Christian Roman soldier, for some money. But Martin had none. Instead, he took off his coat and split it with his knife. He gave half to the cold, shivering beggar and put the other half back on.

That night he had a dream in which he saw heaven and the angels and Jesus. In his dream Jesus was wearing half of a Roman soldier's coat. When one of the angels asked, "Master, why are you wearing that battered old coat? Who gave it to you?" Jesus answered, "My servant Martin."

On Judgment Day may we, with Martin, hear him say to us, "I needed clothes and you clothed me, I was sick and you looked after me. Come, you who are blessed by my Father; take your inheritance, the kingdom prepared for you since the creation of the world" (Matthew 25:36, 34).

May I see you, Jesus, in those who are hungry, hurting, and poor. And when opportunity comes to share the blessings you have showered upon me, give me a tender and generous heart. Make me the agent of your love and generosity. Amen.

Getting Rid of Demons

For I am convinced that neither death nor life,
neither angels nor demons, neither the present nor
the future, nor any powers, neither height nor depth,
nor anything else in all creation, will be able to separate
us from the love of God that is in Christ Jesus our Lord.

Romans 8:38-39

The Bible contains amazing stories about Jesus casting out demons, but sometimes it's hard to relate to them, isn't it? After all, our lives today are so different. But evil is still evil, and all of us struggle. Let me ask you: who or what has a lock on your life and just won't let go?

Whatever it is, let Jesus Christ take it on. With his authority and power as the Son of God, let him chase those demons away and set you free. You say, "Well, that would be great! How do I do it?"

It takes more than just believing, for even demons believe in God. You must commit your whole life completely to Jesus Christ so that he, and he alone, has full power and authority over every part of you. If you do, you'll be astonished at the difference Jesus can make. Why not try it? You have nothing to lose but your demons!

All-powerful God, kick the demons out of me. Whatever they are, they get between you and me, and I want to get rid of them. May Jesus Christ have full authority and control of me from the inside out. Amen.

First Class—or Coach?

———————— ❧❧ ————————

"If anyone wants to be first, he must be the very last,
and the servant of all."
Jesus, in Mark 9:35

Have you ever received an upgrade to fly first class? First class is nice. You get to board early, the seats are wide, the bathroom is first class only, and the flight attendants hang up your coat for you. But flying first class is more than the additional space and other perks. There's a certain sense of privilege—even superiority—you feel when the coach travelers have to walk past you, wishing they were in first class.

The opposite feeling comes when you fly coach. One time as I walked past those first class seats I thought, *I belong up here. They all act like they are so much better.* Then I went to the back of the plane, where the seating is cramped, there's a line for the bathroom, and you have to wear your jacket or roll it up and jam it between suitcases in the overhead rack.

I took my seat, feeling sorry for myself. Then I was reminded of the time Jesus' disciples argued about which one of them was the greatest. Suddenly it didn't matter where I sat.

————— ❧ —————

Jesus, you deserve first class every time. Yet you volunteer to let others get the best seats, and you settle for the end of the line. You are stunningly humble and generous. I want to sit with you! Amen.

Come On In!

---❦---

Enter into his gates with thanksgiving
and his courts with praise.
Psalm 100:4

It's always a privilege to be invited to someone's home, for it is a very private, personal place. Psalm 100 invites us to God's place and to his presence. When the ancient Jews sang these words of invitation, to them it meant the Temple in Jerusalem. As God's chosen people, they had access to his place of residence on earth, but there were limits. Ordinary Jews were allowed only in the outer courts of the Temple. The Holiest Place, where God's presence was greatest, could only be entered by the high priest once a year on Yom Kippur, the Day of Atonement.

But Jesus changed all that. The moment he died, the thick curtain separating the Holiest Place ripped in half from the top to the bottom. It's as if God shouted to the whole human race, "Come on in!" There are no longer any distinctions or limitations. All are now invited into the presence of God now and into the place of God forever.

---❧---

Dear God, I am praying in response to your invitation to me. My answer is yes. I am ecstatic to be invited into your holy presence. I am unworthy but thrilled. I come in the name of Jesus, who gave me your invitation. Amen.

God Is Good

Give thanks to the Lord, for he is good;
his love endures forever.
Psalm 107:1

What you believe about the goodness of God has a huge impact on your everyday life. If you believe God is not good, you begin to fear him. Many live in constant fear that God will zap them with bad things—punish them with sickness, make their businesses fail, or otherwise bring calamity. And expecting the worst becomes a self-fulfilling prophecy.

On the other hand, if you believe God is good, you decide that God knows best. You trust him to bring good into your life and don't expect the worst. Instead of looking for a demon behind every bush, you expect God to show his goodness through every circumstance, even the difficult ones.

True gratefulness is hard to counterfeit. Those who truly believe in the goodness of God are grateful, and those who don't believe in the goodness of God are not. If you believe God is good, it will transform your life!

*In our troubled world there are people who say you are not
a good God. I believe you are. You are my starting point for
everything. I look for your goodness every day in everything. Thank
you for who you are and for being so good to me. Amen.*

True Compassion

———◈———

Have mercy on me, O God,
according to your unfailing love;
according to your great compassion
blot out my transgressions.
Psalm 51:1

In *Les Miserables,* by Victor Hugo, a Frenchman is cruelly sentenced to prison for five years for stealing a loaf of bread. Repeated escapes keep him in the prison for nineteen years. Upon his release, he finds refuge in the home of a Catholic bishop. Bitter and angry, the ex-convict doesn't believe God is good or that there is any goodness to be found in himself. He returns the bishop's kindness by stealing his silverware. When the Frenchman is caught, it's a sure sentence back to prison and probably to death.

But the kindly old bishop has compassion for the man and tells the police, "No, it was a gift." For further proof, he gives the ex-convict a pair of valuable silver candlesticks as well.

That bishop was kind, merciful, and good, just like God. His example of Christian character had a far-reaching effect on the ex-convict because he experienced firsthand the goodness of God through a Christian. And that goodness transformed his life and changed his view of God.

∽

Compassionate God, you have shown mercy and generosity to me more times than I can remember. Bless me to show compassion to others as you have shown compassion to me. Release me from the fear of "being taken advantage of" so that I can be merciful regardless of the outcome. Amen.

Random Kindness

———— ❧❦❧ ————

The Lord's servant must...be kind to everyone.

2 Timothy 2:24

I like those billboards that say, COMMIT A RANDOM ACT OF KINDNESS. It's actually a very Christian concept. It's so easy to get caught up in the cyclone of selfishness that causes us to put ourselves and our own priorities ahead of everyone else. But God says that the measure of a person is not money, clothes, title, or power. It is in the good we do for others.

It's things like welcoming a new neighbor when everyone else is too busy. It's caring for someone else's child. It's helping the seniors down the street. It's sending a note of encouragement and sharing resources to meet the needs of others. God doesn't measure us by wealth or position, but by all the random acts of kindness that we do for others and the attitude we have when we do them.

————— ❧ —————

Open my eyes to opportunities for kindness. Let me see the little things I can do or say today to help and encourage others. When I go to bed tonight, may I remember all of the ways that God showed me kindness and that I showed kindness to others today. Amen.

How Much Does Your Prayer Weigh?

---◈---

"Do not keep on babbling like pagans, for they think they will be heard because of their many words."
Jesus, in Matthew 6:7

Charles Spurgeon, a late nineteenth-century English preacher, once said, "Prayer is measured by weight, not by length." That's what Jesus was talking about when he cautioned his followers to not think long prayers are more effective.

To his listeners, this was liberating. The Jews of first-century Jerusalem were overloaded with prayer requirements. They had to recite the Eighteen Petition Prayer word for word three times a day, pray two prayers of confession, table grace for every meal, and various prayers of praise throughout the day. Prayer had become a burden, not a communication with God.

Many people still believe God is more likely to listen to ten thousand words than to one thousand. They exhaust themselves with hours and hours of prayer to prove their sincerity. But Jesus disagreed with the idea that the longer you pray, the better God listens.

I'm reminded of the words of the great reformer, Martin Luther. He said prayers should be "brief, frequent, and intense."

---◈---

God, I love you 100 percent! Bless me, I pray. In Jesus' name, amen.

Who's the Boss?

"No servant can serve two masters. Either he'll hate the one and love the other, or he will be devoted to the one and despise the other. You cannot serve both God and Money."

Jesus, in Luke 16:13

Take a look at the words *God* and *Money* in Jesus' words. Note that both are capitalized. They are presented as competing deities. Only one can be the top one, the boss in your life. If it's Money, it's not God; if it's God, it's not Money.

If someone were to ask your best friends what is most important in *your* life—God or Money—my guess is that those who know you best wouldn't take long to answer. It's obvious who the boss is. We can't fool our friends.

Jesus is saying that the best way to manage money is to let God be the boss. "Don't ever let Money become your god. Don't treat the really important decisions in life as primarily financial decisions." If you make God the boss of your life, it's the best financial decision you will ever make!

Money is so important in my world. It's easy to let money rule my life and treat it like a god. Lord, forgive me. You are the only God. You are first. I want to live for you and not for possessions that will eventually fade away. Amen.

Listen...

---◆❦◆---

"Be still before the Lord and wait patiently for him."
Psalm 37:7

Each morning I read the Bible and pray. Usually I write out a weekly prayer list, and at the top I write the word *listen*. I do that because I know I'm prone to be in a hurry. I eat my food too fast, fill my schedule too full, and when I'm praying, I tend to do all the talking. It's too easy for me to say, "God, this is what I've got going today. These are my worries, and this is what I'd like you to fix. Thanks. I've got to go."

I have to remind myself to listen to God, to focus on him, to meditate on what I've read from the Bible, and to be silent long enough to allow the Spirit of God to communicate with my spirit. It's hard for me to just sit there, be quiet, and seek to listen. But it's important—for me, and for you too.

❧

Here I am, Lord. Now I will be silent...and listen to you. Amen.

Secret Loyalties

"O Lord...keep this desire in the hearts of your people forever,
and keep their hearts loyal to you."
David, in 1 Chronicles 29:18

During Jesus' life on earth he invested himself in a group of twelve close
followers—men hand-picked by him. Judas, the treasurer of the group, had
great potential. But he never quite fit in. He never fully believed. He was
loyal to Jesus during the best of times, but when things didn't go well, he
sold Jesus out to his enemies for thirty silver coins.

Judas revealed the secret place where Jesus went with his followers in the
Garden of Gethsemane outside Jerusalem. He made arrangements to
identify Jesus to the police with a kiss. At the prearranged time, Judas ran to
Jesus and said, "Greetings, Rabbi," and kissed him. Jesus replied, "Friend,
do what you came for." Then the men stepped forward, seized Jesus, and
arrested him (Matthew 26:48-50).

What a loser Judas was. He could have gone down in history for his loyalty
to Jesus. Instead, he is forever remembered for his kiss of betrayal. What
about you? Where do your loyalties lie—in the best of times and in the worst
of times?

*Would I ever betray you, Lord? I pray not! May my kiss affirm
my loyalty and never betray you with treason. When life is easy,
I will be true to you. When life is hard, I will not forsake you.
When temptations are many, I will be faithful. Amen.*

Choosing the Shadows

❦

"Whoever wants to be first must be your slave."
Matthew 20:27

Typically we think of the greatest person as the man up front, the woman in the spotlight, or the leader with the most recognition. But that's not Jesus' way. The people he chooses for greatness are those who are humble, who would prefer to stay in the shadows.

Moses stuttered and didn't want to be up front. But God took him out of the shadows and made him the greatest lawgiver in history. Saul was a young Jew who hid when the prophet Samuel came to anoint him king of Israel. Saul didn't want the spotlight, but God chose him to be king. John the Baptist became the most popular man in Israel but then insisted on stepping back into the shadows so he could point people to Jesus.

If you want to be great, give the spotlight to Jesus. Trust God to give you the recognition you need.

❧

It's all about you, God. It's not about me. I do not seek fame,
fortune, or power. I seek you alone. If you want to make me a
celebrity or you want to keep me in the shadows of obscurity,
it's up to you. I totally trust whatever you choose. Amen.

Investing in Forever

———❦———

Do nothing out of selfish ambition or vain conceit, but in humility
consider others better than yourselves. Each of you should look not
only to your own interests, but also to the interests of others.

Philippians 2:3-4

A twenty-eight-year-old sat by me at a banquet. When he greeted a
prominent businessman at the head table, I asked, "How do you know him?"
My new acquaintance said his father had died when he was sixteen. The
businessman read about it in the newspaper and phoned him. "I realize you
don't know me," the man said, "but I know this is a hard time in your life,
and I wonder if I could take you out for breakfast." For the past twelve years,
that businessman has taken him out for breakfast every Tuesday morning!

While I don't know that businessman's assets, I assume he is well off. But
obviously that isn't what his life is about. Here's somebody who cared enough
to invest in the life of a fatherless teenager...and continues to do so.

How many people will be in heaven because you invested in them on earth?
Let's live with eternity in view. Let's put God first and invest in forever.

———❦———

*Since you are the God who knows everyone, you know whom
I could help. Bring that person into my life or show me who is
already nearby and waiting for my help. I welcome the opportunity
to pour myself into the life of another for Jesus' sake. Amen.*

Remembering as if I'd Been There

---⟨◈◈⟩---

I will remember the deeds of the Lord;
yes, I will remember your miracles of long ago.
I will meditate on all your works
and consider all your mighty deeds.
Psalm 77:11–12

One of my special childhood memories is of a lake cabin my parents owned. I can still hear the screen door slamming and see our family dog, Tucker, running across the lawn, chasing the ball. I remember swimming in the lake with my brothers and fishing off the dock. Here's the irony: my parents sold the cabin before I was born, and I've never been there. But I've seen the home movies and heard them talk about it so often that I remember it as if I'd been there.

That's how God wanted the celebration of Passover to be for every Jew of every generation. He wanted them to remember the angel of death passing over every house in Egypt that was marked with lamb's blood on its doorframe, sparing the Hebrews from losing their firstborn sons. God told them to celebrate Passover every year thereafter in vivid ritual form so each child would remember this dramatic reminder of God's power and love as if he or she had been there.

∽◠◡∾

Your faithfulness in past generations must not be forgotten, Lord.
When I learn and remember all you have done in the past, my faith
is strengthened for today. You are the same God who delivered the
people of ancient Israel and who will deliver modern me. Amen.

Celebrating Jesus!

———— ✦❦✦ ————

They took palm branches and went out to meet him, shouting,
"Hosanna!"
"Blessed is he who comes in the name of the Lord!"
"Blessed is the King of Israel!"
John 12:13

The day we know as Palm Sunday was a great day in Jerusalem. The city was crowded with visitors from all over the world who had gathered for the coming Jewish Passover. On this particular day, stories circulated about the miracles Jesus had done, most recently the raising of Lazarus from the dead. The crowds were wild to get a glimpse of him. As he rode into the city on a donkey, thousands paved the road with palm branches and shouted, *"Hosanna, blessed is the King of Israel."*

For the religious leaders, it was an awful day. They were disgusted and frightened by the popularity of Jesus. To them, it was like a standing ovation for the enemy.

But for those who believed in Jesus, it was a wonderful day. They waved palms, shouted praises, and danced with excitement. Did they understand everything that was going on? Not really. But that didn't stop them from celebrating Jesus!

———— ❧ ————

Jesus, I wish I could have been there. My voice would have shouted your praise. My hands would have waved palm branches. My heart would have been full of excitement. Instead, I praise you now with my voice, I lift my hands in worship, and my heart is pounding for you. Amen.

A Faith for Every Season

Remember your leaders, who spoke the word of God to you.
Consider the outcome of their way of life and imitate their faith.

Hebrews 13:7

After the celebration of Palm Sunday, things started to go downhill. On Thursday Jesus was betrayed by Judas and then arrested. He was on a fast track to the cross, and just about everyone was abandoning him at a record pace.

John recorded what happened. After Jesus was arrested, John and Peter followed as the soldiers took Jesus to see the high priest. Since John knew Caiaphas, the high priest, personally, he was able to go into the courtyard with Jesus while Peter had to wait outside. It was as though John had security clearance. But this, of course, put him in great danger, for historically when a leader or a conqueror is overthrown, those closest to that leader are either forced out of office or executed. But John's faith did not waver. His was a faith for every season. Faith in celebration. Faith in danger. And faith in duty. How about yours?

Jesus, I want to faithfully follow you just like your friend John—even if that means going into dangerous places. Good days. Bad days. Safe places. Scary places. Wherever you go, I will follow and totally trust you. Amen.

A Special Assignment

When Jesus saw his mother there, and the disciple whom he loved standing nearby, he said to his mother, "Dear woman, here is your son," and to the disciple, "Here is your mother." From that time on, this disciple took her into his home.

John 19:26-27

This was the climax of history: Jesus dying in our place, to pay for our sin. Yet Jesus had a personal, practical need too. As the eldest son of a Jewish widow, he was responsible to find someone to care for her after he was gone. In his darkest hour of need, Jesus turned to the one person he could depend upon—John, the only one of the twelve disciples who showed up at the cross to stand with Mary, the mother of Jesus.

In the years following Jesus' death and resurrection, all his disciples went out as missionaries to spread the message of Jesus across the empire...except John. He stayed behind to care for Mary until she died, because that's what Jesus wanted him to do.

Faith in Jesus calls some of us to special assignments. They may not be glamorous, and they may not be easy, but our duty is to do whatever Jesus calls upon us to do.

If you want me to stay close to home like John, I'll stay, Jesus. If you ask me to leave home for a different assignment, I'm willing to go. Whatever you need and want, just ask, and my answer will be yes. Amen.

What Love!

---❦❦---

This is how we know what love is: Jesus Christ
laid down his life for us.
1 John 3:16

We all love to be loved. The trouble is we don't deserve it. We're sinful. But God decided, before we were born, that he loved us no matter what.

In 1987 Northwest Airlines flight number 225 crashed shortly after takeoff from the Detroit airport. Only one of the 156 passengers survived—four year-old Cecelia Chican from Tempe, Arizona. Rescue workers originally assumed she was a passenger in one of the cars on the highway where the plane crashed, but when they checked the flight manifest, they confirmed she had been on the plane.

How did she survive? When the plane was going down, Cecilia's mother had knelt in front of her, put her arms around the four-year-old, and held her tightly as the plane crashed. She loved her daughter who couldn't save herself, loved her enough to die so Cecilia could live.

That's what Jesus did for us on Good Friday. We couldn't save ourselves from sin, so he stretched out his arms on the cross and died so we could live. What a demonstration of love!

---❧---

Jesus, you love me more than words can describe. You demonstrated
your love in the biggest possible way when you died to save me.
All I can say is "Thank you! I love you so much!" Amen.

APRIL

Risk Takers

Joseph of Arimathea asked Pilate for the body of Jesus. Now Joseph was a disciple of Jesus, but secretly because he feared the Jews. With Pilate's permission, he came and took the body away. He was accompanied by Nicodemus, the man who earlier had visited Jesus at night.

John 19:38-39

After the crucifixion, two secret followers of Jesus claimed his body. One was Joseph from Arimathea, and the other was Nicodemus, a well-known leader in Jerusalem. By stepping forward, they endangered themselves, for everyone associated with Jesus was at risk.

In that culture women prepared bodies for burial, so these men—wealthy, prominent—were especially unlikely candidates for the job. Also, according to Jewish religious teaching, anyone who touched a dead body was temporarily disqualified from participation in worship, which meant these men would be excluded from the holy festival of Passover. But they did it anyway, out of respect for Jesus. It was a time of profound sadness—their teacher, leader, Messiah was dead. They were burying their hope.

But three days later Jesus came back to life. It was the greatest miracle God has ever done—proving that Jesus is the Son of God, as he said he was!

Lord Jesus, I'm not much of a risk taker. My name wouldn't appear on a list with Joseph and Nicodemus. But when it comes to you, I pray for boldness. Give me courage to serve you anytime and anywhere, even if it's a risky thing to do. Amen.

Evidence for Doubters

Then Jesus said to Thomas, "Put your finger here. See my hands.
Reach out your hand—put it into my side. Stop doubting. Believe."
Thomas said to him, "My Lord and my God!"
John 20:27-28

When the eyewitness reports of Jesus' resurrection started flooding in, one of Jesus' followers had difficulty believing they were really true. Thomas was not with the other disciples when Jesus appeared to them after his resurrection. Although his closest friends told him Jesus was alive again, Thomas insisted on tangible evidence. "Unless I see the nail marks in his hands, and put my finger where the nails were and put my hand into his side, I will not believe it."

A week later, when the disciples, including Thomas, were together in a house, Jesus came and greeted them, "Peace be with you." And then he spoke to Thomas about his doubts.

It was just like Jesus to open himself to inspection, for he always meets doubters more than halfway. Just as Thomas needed to touch Jesus' hand and side in order to believe, Jesus wants us to touch him with our faith, believing he died for us and rose from the dead.

---

*I have my doubts, just like Thomas. Jesus, I pray for
bigger faith and smaller doubts. Please teach me and show
me so that I will better believe in you. Amen.*

To Touch Jesus

—◦⟨⟨⟩⟩◦—

"I have seen the Lord!"
Mary Magdalene, in John 20:18

Several times I have met U.S. presidents, and I remember the occasions well: where I was, what I wore, and what was said. But the most memorable moment was when we shook hands and looked into each other's eyes. It's one thing to see a world leader from a distance or on television, but quite a different matter to actually touch that person.

Imagine what it must have been like to touch Jesus. When Mary Magdalene went to his tomb on Easter morning, she was devastated. She assumed Jesus was dead and would stay dead. When his body was missing, it never occurred to her that he had come back to life again. As she encountered him, her vision was blurred with tears. She assumed he was the gardener: "Sir, if you've carried him away, tell me where you've put him and I'll get him." But then Jesus said her name. She immediately recognized him and threw her arms around him. Mary touched Jesus, and her life was forever changed.

≈

Let me come close to you, Lord Jesus. As much as I would love to touch
you as Mary touched you, that is not what I ask. My prayer is to know
you, to sense your presence, and to be as near to you as I can be until that
day in heaven when I will see you face to face...and touch you. Amen.

Royal Genes

King of kings and Lord of lords.
Revelation 19:16

Jesus had many critics and powerful enemies. They made false accusations, lied about him, and eventually had him arrested on false charges and crucified. But they never denied his royal heritage. Even his enemies knew he was qualified to be the Messiah.

What they failed to realize was how royal he *really* was. Jesus was a descendant of King David, so, humanly speaking, he had royal genes. But he was much, much more. He was the King of kings, the absolute sovereign who had the right and the power to order anyone to do anything. No army or court could ever force him to do anything he didn't choose to do.

That's what makes the account of Easter week so stunning. In one week the crowds went from worshipping him to falsely accusing him, beating him, crowning him with thorns, and nailing him to a cross with the sign THIS IS JESUS, THE KING OF THE JEWS. They killed their king!

If you were in that crowd, what would *you* have chosen to do with Jesus?

King Jesus, they didn't all crucify you. It was just some. Count me among those who would never try to hurt you. I hate what they did to you. But, I also know that my sins helped nail you to that awful cross. You were crucified in my place. You suffered and died for me. I thank and praise you forever. Amen.

Love So Amazing

❧◆❧

He was despised and rejected by men,
a man of sorrows, and familiar with suffering....
Surely he took up our infirmities
and carried our sorrows,
yet we considered him stricken by God,
smitten by him, and afflicted.
But he was pierced for our transgressions,
he was crushed for our iniquities.
Isaiah 53:3–5

Nearly eight hundred years before Jesus was crucified, the prophet Isaiah graphically described the event in Isaiah 53. There is no one on whom I could ever wish or inflict such pain as that suffered by Jesus. Had I witnessed the crucifixion, I'm sure I would have wanted to look the other way. It was too painful to watch. And the horror of horrors is that *my* sin was the cause for what he suffered.

How could any of us not be grateful? not be transformed? It is no wonder that many who witnessed Jesus' crucifixion were willing to give up everything to serve him and to spread his story. Experiencing the enormity of Jesus' sacrifice caused them to completely redirect their lives. I'm reminded of the words of the old hymn, "Love so amazing, so divine, demands my soul, my life, my all."

❧◆❧

Jesus, your crucifixion takes my breath away. What they did to you is too awful to describe. It's too painful for me to keep looking. And, that you died for me...what amazing love. Your love and sacrifice demand my everything in response. Amen.

Ready to Believe?

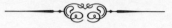

John saw and believed.
John 20:8

Jesus had told his followers he'd come back to life; but frankly, it was too much to believe. When Mary Magdalene told Peter and John that the stone was rolled away from the entrance of Jesus' tomb, and there was no body, they took off at a run. John went inside the tomb. Technically, he didn't see much of anything—only folded-up grave clothes. But he didn't need to see, hear, or touch Jesus, or even fully understand what was happening. Why? Because John was ready to believe. He *knew* Jesus was alive!

I doubt John was surprised by the resurrection. He must have thought, *Well, of course Jesus came back to life.* I can just picture him outside that empty tomb, throwing back his head and laughing with pure joy. Are you ready to believe? Join the celebration, run to the resurrection, share the laughter, and believe in Jesus, the risen Lord!

My Risen Lord Jesus, I believe. I know you died and then rose from the dead. Death could not hold you. Of course not! You are Jesus—the Son of God! Amen.

The Welcoming Committee

For the Lord himself will come down from heaven, with a loud command, with the voice of the archangel and with the trumpet call of God.... And so we will be with the Lord forever.

1 Thessalonians 4:16–17

When Jesus ascended to heaven forty days after his resurrection, his followers stared in amazement. The Bible says, "Suddenly two men dressed in white stood beside them" (Acts 1:10). These men announced great news: Jesus is coming back someday!

Just as Jesus' first coming to earth as a baby was predicted thousands of years in advance, so was the prediction of his second coming. The first time Jesus came to earth as a poor peasant; the next time he will come as a conquering king. When Jesus returns, he will right the injustices caused by sin in the world. He will judge evil and bring all the loose ends of history together in complete fulfillment of God's plan.

We may not know as many details about his return as we'd like, but I like the way one Bible student approached the return of Jesus: "I'm not on the Time and Place Committee. I'm on the Welcoming Committee!" Are you?

Come on back, Jesus! You've been gone a long time, and we need you here again. Along with millions of others, I'm ready to shout my "Welcome!" as soon as you come. Amen.

The Most-Watched Film in History

For what I received I passed on to you as of first importance:
that Christ died for our sins according to the Scriptures, that he
was buried, that he was raised on the third day according to the
Scriptures, and that he appeared to Peter, and then to the Twelve.
After that, he appeared to more than five hundred.

1 Corinthians 15:3–6

The *Jesus* film—a dramatization of the life of Jesus seen by millions of people around the world—may be the most watched film in history. Some scenes are powerfully graphic, and many who watch the film are hearing the story for the first time.

When the *Jesus* film was shown on Good Friday in Chittagong, Bangladesh, people in the audience began to gasp and weep over Jesus' agony and death. Then one boy jumped up from the crowd and shouted, "Don't be afraid! He gets up again! I saw it before!"

And he was right. Because Jesus didn't stay dead—he got up again!—we're on the resurrection side of Jesus' death. That means you don't need to fear your own death, either. If you believe in Jesus' death and resurrection, *you* will get up again! You'll share in Jesus' resurrection.

Easter is not a new story for me. I know how it ends—Jesus comes alive again! Even though I know what happened, I'm still excited and amazed. Because of Jesus, I don't need to be afraid to die. Amen.

No More *If*

If we have been united with him like this in his death, we will
certainly also be united with him in his resurrection.

Romans 6:5

Did you know that, because of Easter, you can live forever? Read the Romans
6:5 words of St. Paul again. They apply to everyone who believes in Jesus.
Isn't that fabulous? If you believe in Jesus and what happened when he died,
then you live forever. It's the best deal anyone could ever get!

But note that very important word *if*: "If we have been united with him...."
Why not make today the day you clear up that *if*? Do you personally believe
Jesus died on the cross to save you from the consequences of your sins? If so,
take the next step. Commit the rest of your life to Jesus as Savior and Lord.
Tell God you believe in Jesus, accept him as Savior, and that you will choose
to trust him for the rest of your life.

Once this faith is in place, there is no more *if*. It's a settled deal: "we will
certainly also be united with him in his resurrection."

*Jesus, I go on record with you today. I believe in you as my
Savior from sin and commit to you as the Lord of my life.
Through faith I am forever united to you. Amen.*

The Choice

John, the man who saw it, has given testimony,
and his testimony is true. He knows that he tells the truth,
and he testifies so that you also may believe.
John 19:35

Just before the execution of a captured spy, a Persian general gave the condemned man a choice he typically offered condemned prisoners: firing squad or big black door. The captured spy thought for a long time, then chose the firing squad. It wasn't long until the shots rang out, and the spy was dead.

"They almost always choose the firing squad," the general told an aide, "because people prefer the known to the unknown."

The aide asked the inevitable question: "What's behind the big black door?"

"Freedom," the general explained. "But I've only known a few men brave enough to choose it."

Many of the eyewitnesses of the events leading up to Easter made poor choices. Judas chose betrayal. Peter chose denial. The religious leaders and the Roman politicians chose to execute Jesus. Thomas chose doubt. But John? He bravely chose faith. Some might have considered that the "black door"—the unknown—but John saw it as freedom.

Which of the eyewitnesses do you most want to be like?

---

*Lord, I choose freedom. I'm with John, who so fully believed
in Jesus and so boldly invited others to believe as well. How
wonderful to live with faith and freedom! Amen.*

Work Matters

May the favor of the Lord our God rest upon us;
establish the work of our hands for us—
yes, establish the work of our hands.

Psalm 90:17

The job you do is important to God. How do I know that? Because so many individuals in the Bible are identified by the jobs they did: Cain the farmer, Joseph the slave who later became prime minister, Aaron the priest, Esther the queen, Ezra the scribe, Jesus the carpenter, Matthew the tax collector, Luke the physician, and Lydia the textile merchant.

Whatever your job, consider it your current assignment on God's team. Work hard and well, knowing that how you work matters to God. If you've attained a high-level position, don't become selfishly proud of your job. If you are serving in a lowly position, don't be ashamed. Carry out your duties honorably, and trust him for the final outcome.

You may be rich or poor, famous or unknown, powerful or powerless, the boss or a minimum wage worker. Whatever position you hold, count your job to be of the highest importance—because God does!

---

*Creator God, you are such a hard worker, and your work
is so good. You created the universe, and your Son, Jesus,
worked in a carpenter shop. I dedicate my job and my work
to you. Show me favor in all I do…for you. Amen.*

The Empty Egg

*As they entered the tomb, they saw a young man dressed
in a white robe sitting on the right side, and they were
alarmed "Don't be alarmed," he said. "You are looking
for Jesus the Nazarene, who was crucified. He has risen!
He is not here. See the place where they laid him."*
Mark 16:5-6

In a Sunday school class of ten eight-year-olds, Philip did not fit in very well because he had both mental and physical disabilities. One Easter the teacher instructed the children to go outside and fill their plastic, egg-shaped pantyhose containers with symbols of new life. The children *ooh-ed* and *aah-ed* as each egg was opened. Flowers, leaves, and even a butterfly became Easter object lessons. But one container was empty. "That's stupid," the class jeered, "there's nothing there."

Philip whispered to the teacher, "It's mine."

The others said, "You don't ever do anything right, Philip."

Philip answered, "I did so do it right. It's empty, because the tomb is empty."

That day a miracle took place. The children grasped the truth of Easter for the first time—and they accepted Philip as one of their own.

That summer Philip died suddenly from an infection. At his funeral nine eight-year-olds walked to the front carrying nine empty, egg-shaped pantyhose containers. They got it! The tomb is empty. He has risen!

*Wonderful. Miraculous. Priceless. The tomb is empty. Jesus,
you defeated death for us all. You have risen! Hallelujah!*

Guardian Angels

For he will command his angels concerning
you to guard you in all your ways.

Psalm 91:11

Stories circulate from all over the world of Christians who have received supernatural protection.

A hostile mob attacked missionaries in a remote compound, intending to kill them. But at the last moment the attackers suddenly fled. The next two days the same attackers came...but again the mob dispersed. A year later, one of the missionaries met the leader of the attacking tribe. He told the missionary the tribe hadn't killed them because of the hundreds of soldiers guarding the missionary compound.

A man riding on a train on an overnight journey awakened as the train came to a screeching halt in the middle of nowhere. A farmer had frantically flagged down the train, causing it to stop only a few yards from a washed-out bridge. The farmer said a stranger had awakened him in the middle of the night and told him to go to that spot and do everything possible to stop the train.

What might guardian angels commanded by God have protected you from?

God, there's a lot you do for me that I don't know.
You supernaturally protect me with unseen resources. I am glad,
and I am grateful. Protect me, I pray, from every evil. Amen.

The Polisher

———◦◦◦◦———

"For my thoughts are not your thoughts,
neither are your ways my ways,"
declares the Lord.

Isaiah 55:8

I had a job operating a commercial floor polisher during college. The assignment seemed simple enough. All I had to do was turn the machine on and polish the floor. Well, the first day I turned it on, it polished me right into the wall! It was obvious I needed a stronger grip, so I dragged the thing back into the middle of the room and squeezed as hard as I could. *Wham!* I hit the wall on the other side even faster.

A guy who'd done it before flipped the switch with one finger and gently guided the polisher back and forth across the floor. "Don't fight it," he said. "The harder you try, the less control you will have. Just tilt it in the direction you want it to go, and the power of the polisher will do everything for you."

I tried it his way—and it worked!

Sometimes that's how we pray—trying so hard that we hit the wall. Instead, we simply need to trust the power of the Polisher.

∿

*My Father, I admit that I try to pray harder to convince
you to do what I want. Remind me that the power of
prayer comes from you and not from me. Amen.*

Unlikely People

❦

"Saul is my chosen instrument to carry my name before the
Gentiles and their kings and before the people of Israel."
The Lord, in Acts 9:15

First-century Saul hated Christians. He persecuted them. He arrested and
murdered them. He was the Osama bin Laden of his generation. Not in
anyone's wildest imagination would Saul become a follower of Jesus or a
leader of the Christian church.

Then, one day, as Saul walked the highway to Damascus, Jesus appeared in
a bright light and spoke to him. Saul fell to the ground and immediately
believed in Jesus. His life was transformed. But most of the Christians didn't
believe him. They thought it was a trick, a way to infiltrate their ranks so he
could murder more of them. Fortunately, a few believed God could perform
this great a miracle and welcomed Saul. As a result, the murderer became a
missionary. He took the gospel from Asia to Europe and wrote much of the
New Testament.

God changes people with a past, and he uses unlikely people in magnificent
ways. He will use you too if you give your life to him.

∼◌∽

*Change me, God, to be all you want me to be and do all you want me to do.
And grow my faith that you can change anybody—even those I've given up on.
You can and do transform the worst of sinners into the best of saints. Amen.*

Fight to Win!

❖

"Go and make disciples of all nations, baptizing them in the name of the Father and of the Son and of the Holy Spirit, and teaching them to obey everything that I have commanded you. And surely I am with you always, to the very end of the age."

Matthew 28:19-20

When Jesus was wrapping up his ministry on earth, he gathered his little group of followers and challenged them to change the world. Jesus was like a coach, talking to his team at halftime in the locker room. "Okay, now, listen up. This next half determines everything. If we win, we go to the playoffs. If we lose, we're done for the season. It's up to *you*. Go back out there and fight to win!"

So who is the *you* he's talking about? It's the whole body of believers—you, me, and other Christians around the world. Jesus trusts us to pray, give, and go *together*—in order to tell others about him. He knows there will be errors and mistakes, but he trusts us, the church, with his name, his gospel, his Bible, and his plans. So let's go back out there and fight to win!

❖

Coach Jesus, I hear you! I'm ready to go, to fight, and to win the victory for you. Starting now, wherever I go, you can count on me to recruit more disciples for you. Amen.

His Sheep

—❦—

We are his people, the sheep of his pasture.
Psalm 100:3

When God described his relationship with us, he could have used master/slave terms. After all, it is technically and legally true that God created us, and as "his people" he can do anything he wants with us. We cannot overpower or overrule him.

But God's emphasis is not on controlling us as slaves but on caring for us as sheep. Shepherds love their sheep. Shepherds care for their sheep. The safest and best place any sheep can be is in the shepherd's pasture. For it's in the pasture where food is plentiful, where dangers are few, and where the shepherd is always close by.

The New Testament says that Jesus is the Good Shepherd who lays down his life for his sheep (John 10:11). Think of it! We are his sheep, and Jesus the Shepherd loves us enough that he actually died for us. It's a truth that can transform your life.

∼❦∼

Good Shepherd, you are so caring and kind. You love me, protect me, feed me, and stay close to me. You are the very best. Knowing you and seeing all you do makes me love you and want to serve you more and more. Your shepherding is transforming my life for good. Amen.

The Good Stuff

By the grace of God I am what I am,
and his grace to me was not without effect.

1 Corinthians 15:10

When St. Paul was describing how his life had changed from being a persecutor of Christians to being a follower of Christ, he was not being proud or arrogant. He was saying, "If you look at everything about me, and you see good stuff in me, it's there because of God."

So what's the good stuff about you? Are you kind, loving, a wise counselor? Are you an effective parent, a good marriage partner, a gifted artist? If there is good stuff in your life, it is because God put it there. You are who you are because of God.

Sometimes I surprise myself. I say and do really loving things. I love people who are not very lovable. I demonstrate wisdom I didn't know I had. When that happens, I realize that it's all because of God. He gives grace to everyone who believes. That means me—and you too.

I love the good stuff in my life. I don't mean the gifts I have received but the gifts I give. When I am godly, righteous, kind, generous, and loving, it is all because of your grace in me. You are truly good to me, Lord, and it really shows. Amen.

Feeling Hassled?

———◦⊱❦⊰◦———

They sold Joseph as a slave into Egypt. But God was with him and rescued him from all his troubles. He gave Joseph wisdom and enabled him to gain the goodwill of Pharaoh king of Egypt; so he made him ruler over Egypt and all his palace.

Acts 7:9-10

If you think you have job hassles, let me tell you about Joseph. Joseph was a man of integrity and truth, but his jealous brothers sold him into slavery. He was taken off to Egypt where he worked as hard as he could for an extended period of time. His thanks was that his master's wife tried to seduce him. Joseph resisted her advances, but she falsely accused him, and he was sent to prison. During his long years there, Joseph went through hassle after hassle but continued to work diligently and remained faithful to God.

What Joseph didn't know was that God had a masterful plan all along. He was preparing Joseph to become the ruler of Egypt, to preserve his chosen people.

You see, it's not the hassles that are important but how you handle them! May you handle your job hassles with patience, integrity, and contentment, always remaining faithful to God—just like Joseph.

———⊱❦⊰———

Come with me to work, Lord God. When I am stressed, relax me. When I fall behind, help me to catch up. When I am down, encourage me. Give me all I need to work well for you. Amen.

Pledging Allegiance

Our citizenship is in heaven.
Philippians 3:20

My mother lived in the United States for years as an "alien." In fact, when I was a boy, I delivered her alien registration to the post office every January. Switching her citizenship was not a spur-of-the-moment decision. It was a deliberate, careful choice. It required not only pledging allegiance to the U.S. but renouncing her citizenship and allegiance to the country of her birth. It was nothing to be done lightly.

The same is true of becoming a Christian. It is a conscious switch of allegiance from the way you were born to God himself. It happens on a specific day by a deliberate choice. It not only requires pledging your allegiance to God as your King but renouncing citizenship in any other kingdom not ruled by God.

Has God's kingdom come to you? Are you a citizen of his reign? If not, you have an invitation from the King himself.

---

*My God and my King, I renounce all other loyalties and swear
my allegiance to you alone. I choose to be your subject and
obey your commands. I gladly announce to others that I am a
citizen of your kingdom. All through Jesus Christ. Amen.*

The Power of Compounding

*These have come so that your faith—of greater worth than gold...
may be proved genuine and may result in praise, glory and honor
when Jesus Christ is revealed.*

1 Peter 1:7

If you put money into an interest-bearing account of 7 percent, your money will double in ten years. If you get 10 percent interest, your money will double in seven years. It's the power of compounding. When you believe in God, he compounds your faith. And faith is the most valuable of assets, worth more than gold. It just keeps going and growing.

But sometimes you need to audit your account—to check to make sure your asset is there and performing properly. The way to test faith is to see if it works when life is tough. Do you still trust God when you are disappointed, in pain, and facing circumstances you would never choose? When you face problems by trusting God, you discover that your faith works! And then you get a great audit report showing how much your faith has increased. It's the power of compounding!

*God of every situation, give me strength to face difficult times.
When the storms of broken relationships, physical pain, financial
setbacks, and personal problems howl through my life, may
my faith be strong to survive and to thrive. May the traumas
make my faith larger and stronger. In Jesus' name, amen.*

Faith Works

———— ❧ ————

Serve wholeheartedly, as if you were serving the Lord,
not men, because you know that the Lord will reward everyone
for whatever good he does.

Ephesians 6:7–8

In his book *Taking Your Faith to Work,* Al Glenn tells of a speaker who went to a college fraternity. He asked the president of the fraternity, "What are you living for?" The young man replied, "I'm studying to be a pharmacist." The speaker said, "I understand that's what you're going to do for a livelihood, but what are you living for?" The young man paused in his embarrassment and finally blurted, "I'm sorry, sir, but I haven't thought that through yet." It turned out that almost all of the thirty fraternity men present knew how they planned to earn their livelihood, but only two knew their purpose for living.

Do you know your purpose for living? As far as the Bible is concerned, you are not called to be a carpenter, a teacher, or a business person. You are called to serve God. Regardless of your vocation, it is God for whom you work!

———— ❧ ————

*My purpose in life is to live and work for you, my God. Your current
assignment is my place of employment, so I want to do a good
job for you there. I get a paycheck, for which I am very grateful,
but my greatest reward comes from pleasing you. Amen.*

Tempted

———✦⟨⟨◦⟩⟩✦———

"It is written: 'Man does not live on bread alone,
but on every word that comes from the mouth of God.'"
Jesus, in Matthew 4:4

Jesus was once in a desert wilderness for forty days without food. That's almost a thousand hours! And most of us say we're starving if we go more than six hours without a meal.

A healthy thirty-year-old American male consumes about 4000 calories per day. But even if Jesus needed only 2,500 calories per day to maintain his body weight, not eating for forty days meant losing forty pounds. If he started out weighing 160 pounds, his weight would have dropped to 120 or less. He was *starving*.

Therefore, when Satan showed up to tempt him to turn the stones into bread, Jesus was weary and weak. He must have considered doing it—he was hungry! But Jesus didn't want to be controlled by Satan. He wouldn't let someone evil make him do even a good thing—like eating bread.

What can you learn from Jesus? Don't let physical needs take control over your spiritual needs...and don't take orders from anyone but God.

∽◦∾

Deliver me from the evil one, my Savior. When I am weak and weary, when I am thinking about giving in to temptation, give me your strength to resist evil and do what is right. Amen.

Catching On

---❧❧---

Cast your cares on the Lord
and he will sustain you;
he will never let the righteous fall.

Psalm 55:22

A trapeze artist was once asked, "What's it like the first time you swing from a high trapeze to be caught in the air by your partner on the other trapeze?"

He answered, "There are two things you need to know. First, you have to trust the other person completely. Second, you have to let go before you can catch on. That may sound simple, but that's one of the most difficult parts of all. You can swing back and forth on this trapeze, but the only way you can get to the other side and to the other person is by letting go of the first side."

There are a million different areas of life where you can trust God and some are pretty high...and scary. But God will always be there to catch you, and you'll be safe in his arms. You simply have to trust him and let go—so that he can catch on.

---❧---

My faithful God, I know you are always dependable. You are always there for me. You would never let go or let me fall. Right now there are some things I'm holding too tight and need to let go. I'm coming to you. I know you will not let me down. Amen.

Just Try It!

—◦◦❦◦◦—

Taste and see that the Lord is good.
Psalm 34:8

I was an embarrassingly picky eater as a boy. My two basic rules: don't eat anything green, and don't eat anything new. When my family went to Joe's Pizzeria, I promptly informed my parents, "I don't eat pizza." They asked why, and I said, "Because I don't like pizza." They said, "How do you know if you've never tried it?" I told them that I just knew. I quickly turned a happy family outing into a disaster.

Several visits later, I did something wild and courageous. I ate a bite of pizza and discovered it to be quite good. In fact, I ate a whole piece! Pizza became a lifelong favorite food in spite of my initial stubbornness.

Once you get a taste of reading the Bible, praying, and you grow to know God better, you'll discover the joy of being a fully committed follower of Jesus. But you won't know until you try it!

—◦◦❦◦◦—

I have hunger that no ordinary food can satisfy. I hunger and thirst for you, Lord. Your words fill me, prayers satisfy me, and your presence nourishes me. Discourage me from spiritual junk food, and let me feed on your truth and righteousness. Amen.

Don't Forget Jesus

———◆⬥◆———

"This is my body, which is for you; do this in remembrance
of me." In the same way, after supper he took the cup,
saying, "This cup is the new covenant in my blood;
do this, whenever you drink it, in remembrance of me."

The Lord Jesus, in 1 Corinthians 11:24-25

The year before Charleen and I married, we lived several states apart. I kept pictures of her everywhere—in my wallet, on my desk, and on the bedroom dresser. I looked at them all the time. After we married, I no longer surrounded myself with her pictures. I had her! Why did I need a picture?

The same goes for communion. You see, while Jesus is gone from our physical view, we need a picture, a reminder. That's why we celebrate communion, so we'll be reminded of him while he's in heaven and we're on earth. Most major commitments in life require a signature—a marriage license, a mortgage, or a car loan—tangible proof of commitment. Communion provides a tangible reminder of our faith. When we eat the bread and drink from the cup, it's a physical expression of our spiritual belief.

Communion is to be observed until we're together with Jesus someday. And then there will no longer be a need for reminders.

———◆———

*Come, Lord Jesus, and let me experience you in the bread
and cup. Let me see your face in communion. Amen.*

Garbage In, Garbage Out

———————

Whatever is true, whatever is noble, whatever is right, whatever is pure, whatever is lovely, whatever is admirable—if anything is excellent or praiseworthy—think about such things.

Philippians 4:8

You're probably familiar with the expression "garbage in, garbage out." Every day we are bombarded with words and images that compete for our attention. Some people continually dwell on negative thoughts that eventually destroy them from the inside out. Others are habitually positive, thinking good thoughts that in turn produce a good life. Both extremes illustrate you are what you think.

"Yeah, yeah," you say. "But I don't have any control over what I think. I just think what I think. Thoughts float into my head."

But you're wrong. According to God, you do have control over what you think. When an idea or image floats into your mind, you choose whether to dwell on it or let it go by. If you use the Bible as a filter, you'll let good thinking in and keep bad thinking out.

If you are what you think, it's important to make sure you think good thoughts!

———————

Father, forgive me for all the garbage I think about. My brain needs a good cleaning by your Holy Spirit. I commit to think better. I will make a conscious effort to unthink the bad and rethink the good. Be the Lord of my thoughts. Amen.

Forgiven and Forgiving

"For if you forgive men when they sin against you, your heavenly
Father will also forgive you. But if you do not forgive men their
sins, your Father will not forgive your sins."
Jesus, in Matthew 6:14–15

James Edward Oglethorpe, the founder and first governor of Georgia, once
proudly told a young British missionary, "I never forgive anyone." The young
missionary, named John Wesley, replied, "Then, sir, I hope you never sin."

Wesley was referring to the Lord's Prayer where Jesus teaches us to pray,
"Forgive us our sins as we forgive those who sin against us." St. Augustine
called that line the "terrible petition," because anyone who says that prayer
and fails to forgive is actually petitioning God not to forgive him.

There is no virtue more central to Christian life than forgiveness. There is no
practice more necessary for the well-being of God's people than forgiveness.
Jesus modeled forgiveness when he forgave even those who crucified him.

Is there someone who has sinned against you that you have not forgiven? If
so, who is it? Will you decide right now to forgive that person and then act
on that decision?

---

*No one has been sinned against as much as you have, God. Yet you
forgive the worst of sins through Jesus. You are amazing! Please forgive
me of my sins. But help me also to forgive those who have sinned against
me. Even if they don't ask, help me to forgive, for your sake. Amen.*

The Family Story

———◦✦◦———

"These are the Scriptures that testify about me."
Jesus, in John 5:39

My family journeyed with my mother to her birthplace in White Haven, on the English Coast of the Irish Sea. After visiting the house where she was born, we traveled to Workington, where she lived with her mother, sisters, and grandparents after her father died. We saw their house, her grandfather's butcher shop, and the schools she attended.

But the most memorable moment was coming across her father's broken tombstone in the cemetery. My mother had few memories of her father, who had died when she was about five years old. She had never visited his grave before. The emotion caught her by surprise and gripped us all with unexpected feelings. This was our history—part of who we were, and are, as a family.

To understand more about Jesus, study the Bible, for it contains the whole story of Jesus and the family from which he descended.

———◦✦◦———

Father...I love to call you "My Father" because I am part of the family of God. Jesus is not only my Savior and Lord but also my "older brother." You have brought all of my history into your divine family and have brought me into your forever family. Thank you, my Father and my God. Amen.

Expect the Supernatural!

---❦---

Now to him who is able to establish you by my gospel and the proclamation of Jesus Christ, according to the revelation of the mystery hidden for long ages past, but now revealed and made known through the prophetic writings by the command of the eternal God, so that all nations might believe and obey him—to the only wise God be glory forever through Jesus Christ! Amen.

Romans 16:25-27

When you visit another country and culture, your expectations differ from your expectations at home. In China, you expect to eat with chopsticks rather than knives and forks. In Australia, you expect to drive on the left rather than the right side of the road. If you go to the equator in the winter, you expect the weather to be hot rather than cold.

Your expectations also shape your experience. For example, if you go to Australia expecting to drive on the right side of the road, you might end up dead!

When you read the Bible, you should expect to supernaturally experience God. So pray first for God to open your understanding to his supernatural truths, which otherwise would remain a mystery. Then expect the supernatural!

---❧---

You are the Big God, so I should have big expectations. You created the world, and you run the universe. You gave Jesus for my salvation. You love me and are committed to me. When I pray to you, may I expect you to be the Big God in my life too. Amen.

MAY

On the Fringes

———— ❦ ————

In the same way, was not even Rahab the prostitute
considered righteous for what she did?

James 2:25

I love God's sense of humor. He uses some of the most unusual examples and outrageous stories in the Bible to get our attention and illustrate his teachings. Some are about respectable, rich, and religious people, like Abraham. But some are like Rahab—on the fringes of society and looked down on by the mainstream. The story of Rahab, a prostitute, was written to a Jewish audience in a day when Jews didn't associate with Gentiles (non-Jews), nor did they hold women in high regard. It would have been unimaginable for an ancient Jew to think of Rahab, a pagan prostitute, as a good or righteous person.

Yet that's exactly how Rahab is described. With little or no teaching other than hearing news of how God had saved the Israelites at the Red Sea, Rahab declared her faith in the God of Israel. She was a person God loved and included—and the kind of raw material for the church today and heaven tomorrow. Whoever we are, from Abraham to Rahab, God is committed to doing something great in our lives!

———— ❧ ————

God of saints and sinners, you welcome the best and worst of us into your kingdom. Including me! By faith I desire to please you and live for you. Bring me from the fringes into the center of your will and your people. Amen.

Fight for What's Right!

————◆◆◆————

"Don't be afraid of them. Remember the Lord,
who is great and awesome, and fight for your brothers,
your sons and your daughters, your wives and your homes."
Nehemiah, in Nehemiah 4:14

Twenty-five centuries ago, in the far western reaches of the Persian Empire, Jerusalem lay in ruins. Nehemiah, a high-ranking official from King Artaxerxes' court, was sent to rebuild the city's walls. He rallied the local Jews to start building, and things went well until neighbors joined together, threatening to attack them. In response, Nehemiah prayed and set up guards. But with some of the laborers standing guard instead of working, the job got even harder. All were tired, discouraged, and, most of all, scared. Everyone was ready to quit until Nehemiah stepped in with a plan. He grouped all the workers into the open spaces of the wall, so they were visible to their enemies and looked mightier in number than they actually were.

The moral of this story? Focus on God—not on the threats getting you down. Do what God wants even if the odds are against you. When the enemy surrounds you, think of God and fight for what's right!

∽∾

*My eyes and thoughts are on you, Lord. If I look away, I get
scared. When I focus on you, I have courage and hope. My
desire is to watch you, listen to you, and do whatever you want
me to do, no matter how hard the assignment. Amen.*

Who's Sitting on the Throne?

Let the peace of Christ rule in your hearts.
Colossians 3:15

Imagine your life as a kingdom, and in the center is a room with a large, important-looking throne. The question to consider is, "Who is sitting on that throne, ruling your life?" When *we* rule our lives, we often get ourselves in trouble. We get upset when things don't go our way. But when Jesus Christ sits on the throne as King of our lives, he gives peace and strength to deal with whatever comes up.

But it's a day-to-day decision as to who will rule your life. It's all too easy to sneak into the throne room and to push Jesus aside so we can sit on the throne for a while. Pretty soon we're in trouble again.

Take a peek into your throne room. Who's sitting on the throne? If it's Jesus, ask him to help you never to rebel against his rule. If it's you, ask Jesus to take control over 100 percent of your life. Choose Jesus as your King!

King Jesus, I know you are the ruler of the universe. You are the King of all kings. Now I want you to be the King of my life. Too often I have pushed you aside and proudly sat on the throne of my own heart. It has never been good. Come into my heart. Sit on the throne. Be the sovereign King of me. Amen.

No More Sting!

———◦◦❧❦◦◦———

"Where, O death, is your sting?"... Thanks be to God!
He gives us the victory through our Lord Jesus Christ.
1 Corinthians 15:55–57

One of my favorite summer pastimes as a boy was bee-catching. We lived in an area filled with clover, and I used to catch bees in a jar. One day, proud of my success, I sat down on the lawn to count my collection through the glass. Unbeknownst to me, one of the bees I didn't capture was sitting on a clover beneath me and stung me—well, you know where. I was too embarrassed to seek help and, because of the strategic target selected by the bee, was unable to help myself. So I suffered the sting of the bee unaided. But at least that particular bee could no longer sting anyone else, because his stinger was in me.

And that's what Jesus Christ did for us when he died on the cross. He took the sting of death—the penalty for our sin. Death may continue to be a reality, but it is no longer a threat for those who have accepted Jesus Christ as their Savior.

———◦❧◦———

*Death is terrifying. Sin is terminal. If it were not for you, Jesus,
I would be so scared. However, you took the sting of sin and
death when you died on the cross for me. You have saved me
from the worst of sin and death. Thank you! Amen.*

Abba, Daddy!

———◦❦◦———

And by him we cry, "Abba, Father." The Spirit himself testifies
with our spirit that we are God's children. Now if we are children,
then we are heirs—heirs of God and co-heirs with Christ.

Romans 8:15–17

No one wants to be alone. We all desire to be part of a family—to belong to
someone. The Bible says that Jesus is God's "only son." But when Jesus was
teaching his followers how to pray, he said, "Our Father," not "My Father."
Jesus wanted us to be able to claim God as our Father too. In fact, the word
Jesus used for Father was *Abba,* the common word for "daddy."

By his death on the cross, Jesus paid the exorbitant fee for us to be adopted
into the forever family of God. When we become Christians by accepting
Jesus as our Savior, God adopts us as his sons and daughters—as brothers
and sisters of Jesus Christ. Then we can legitimately address him as "Our
Father, Our Daddy."

My friend, the next time you are scared, or need help, or want to share
some success or failure, pray to "Our Daddy." He's always there, listening.

———◦∾◦———

*Our Daddy who is in heaven…. Oh, Father, dare I really call you my
"Heavenly Daddy"? It sounds so familiar. So intimate. Yet, that's who you
are. You are the God who created and rules the heavens and the earth. And
you are my Lord, Father, and Dad. I love you. All through Jesus. Amen.*

Forever Changed

---◆◆◆---

I lift up my eyes to you,
to you whose throne is in heaven.

Psalm 123:1

American missionaries once traveled eleven days by canoe into the remote rain forest of the Congo. When they came to a clearing and sensed Pygmies (also known as Bambenga) hiding in the bushes, they began playing a taped message over and over: the gospel set to music in their language. They also set out salt as a gift—a rare and valuable commodity in that area. Gradually, a courageous few ventured out, then more and more.

Because many considered themselves inferior, they resisted looking into the eyes of others. But when they heard about Jesus Christ, how they could have their sins forgiven and receive eternal life, two thousand prayed aloud for Jesus to become their Savior. The missionaries reported, "They lift their eyes and look at you, and the biggest smile comes across their faces."

That's what faith in Jesus does, regardless of your culture. You are forever changed.

---◆---

Seeing you changes the way I see everything, Lord Jesus. When my eyes look to you, I receive forgiveness, hope, and joy. Through you I see myself and others in a new and healthy way. You change me as no one else ever could. You make me new. Amen.

Hope to Go On

Be strong and take heart, all you who hope in the Lord.
Psalm 31:24

Viktor Frankl, a Jewish psychiatrist from Vienna and a survivor of the Nazi death camp at Auschwitz, concluded that the survivors who endured and kept their sanity had hope. Many without hope committed suicide or gave in to death.

We all need hope to go on when we lose our jobs, when our marriages break apart, when our lives seem to go nowhere, and when our hearts are broken. Where can we find that hope? Through God, who gives us a second chance through new birth. When Jesus was dead and buried, God the Father raised him back to life again. If God can do this, he can give us a new beginning. No matter how bad our situation or how badly we've messed up, God is there for us. This possibility of a new beginning is what gives us hope for tomorrow and hope to go on.

*God and Father of our Lord Jesus Christ, I need hope. On days
when I am discouraged I fear that tomorrow will be either more
of the same or even worse. You are the God of mercy, new birth,
and living hope. I will trust you for a better tomorrow. Amen.*

Stopping the Skid

———◆⟨☙☙⟩◆———

Repent, then, and turn to God, so that your sins may be wiped out,
that times of refreshing may come from the Lord.
Acts 3:19

When people move to northern states like Minnesota, we long-timers of
the state try to explain how to safely drive on slippery roads. One of the
basic principles is to turn into a skid. It's counterintuitive—experience and
instinct tell you that if the car is skidding right, you should turn the car
hard left. But that's the worst thing you can do. You get control by turning
into the skid. We may not understand the technical explanation for that
maneuver but, bottom line, it works.

It's the same with finding meaning in life. Our instincts tell us to turn
inward and take care of ourselves and *then* life will have meaning. But that's
the worst thing we can do. It's by turning toward God and toward others that
we find meaning in life. We may not understand the theological explanation
for this but, bottom line, it works. So love God—and love others. It's the key
to a meaningful life.

———⟨☙⟩———

*There are days when I am skidding out of control. I grab the wheel and
intuitively turn to my old ways to get back on the road. It doesn't work, Lord.
I keep skidding in the wrong direction. Today I repent of my old selfish ways
and turn to you. Get me going in the right direction as I follow Jesus. Amen.*

A Secure Reservation

One of the seven angels...showed me the Holy City, Jerusalem,
coming down out of heaven from God. It shone with the glory of
God, and its brilliance was like that of a very precious jewel, like
a jasper, clear as crystal. It had a great, high wall with twelve gates,
and with twelve angels at the gates.

Revelation 21:9–12

Have you ever received a beautiful postcard from Hawaii, the Grand Canyon, the Oregon coast, or the Florida Keys? Perhaps your friend hastily scrawled a note: *Having a great time. This place is fantastic. Wish you were here.* Pictures show you a little of what those places are like, but they are far more spectacular than any picture can communicate. At least they let you know that Hawaii or the Grand Canyon is far different from where you live!

The Bible is like a postcard from heaven—a glimpse, a snapshot addressed to each one of us and signed by Jesus himself, who writes, *This place is spectacular. Wish you were here!* But you have to experience it for yourself to really understand what it's like.

The good news is that we can make guaranteed reservations for heaven by believing on Jesus Christ as Savior and Lord. He is our ticket to eternal life. In the meantime, there's great comfort in knowing your reservation in heaven is secure.

*Your heaven is beautiful. God, I accept your invitation and will come.
With my faith in Jesus, I pray. Amen.*

How Much Is Enough?

"Where your treasure is, there your heart will be also."
Jesus, in Luke 12:34

A reporter once asked John D. Rockefeller, "How much money is enough?" That extraordinarily rich man answered, "A little bit more."

The Bible gives a very different answer to the question of how much is enough. Jesus said, "Watch out! Be on your guard against all kinds of greed; a man's life does not consist in the abundance of his possessions" (Luke 12:15). These words contradict the monetary message of our society. We are constantly told through advertisements, magazines, and conversations that life *does* consist in the abundance of possessions. Our worth as persons is defined in terms of what we've got.

Never underestimate the influence the world's values have on you. We each need to ask ourselves, "Am I living for this world, or am I living for Christ's kingdom?" God calls us to find life's meaning in terms of spiritual things, not material things.

Give me a heart for you, dear God. Satisfy my soul with what I already have. Make me content to give up rather than to get more. Make me zealous for Christ and his kingdom. May I always want more of Jesus. Amen.

Overwhelmed with Jesus

———— ❧ ————

"Your sins are forgiven.... Your faith has saved you. Go in peace."
Jesus, in Luke 7:48, 50

When a woman known for living a life of sin approached Jesus, she shocked the people watching by washing his feet with her tears. Then she loosened her long hair and used it to dry his feet. Why was this so shocking? In those days, loose, flowing hair on an adult woman was a sign of sexual impropriety. If that were not enough, she kissed Jesus' feet and poured expensive perfume on them. Such flasks of perfume were both adornment and served as emergency savings accounts, as the perfume was worth a lot of money.

But this woman lost track of what was acceptable and what was unacceptable. Being in the presence of Jesus was all that mattered. She loved Jesus and was overwhelmed with who Jesus was. She didn't care what anyone else thought of her actions. She gave him the perfume, her most precious and valuable possession.

How about you? What do you think of Jesus? What are you willing to give him?

———— ❧ ————

How exciting to come into your presence, Jesus. You are so good,
so holy, so divine, so wonderful...that I am overwhelmed. My
words don't make sense. My emotions are soaring. I forget there are
other people around. I love to give you my very best. Amen.

The Ideal Woman

———◆⟨⟨⟨⟨⟩⟩⟩◆———

She opens her arms to the poor and extends her hands
to the needy.... She speaks with wisdom, and faithful
instruction is on her tongue.

Proverbs 31:20, 26

Who wouldn't like to be described as "hard-working and successful"?

The Bible's "ideal woman" is depicted not only as diligent and hard-working but also as compassionate. She has eyes for the needs of others. When someone hurts, she hurts with them. When someone is hungry, she wants to feed them. When someone is lonely, she invites them over, whether or not her house is clean. Her first thought is meeting the other person's need, not her reputation as a hostess. Her words are kind, not critical. She's a person you can go to when you have a need or when you are burdened about what you have done wrong. She'll listen, try to understand, and respond with love.

How do you get to be this way? Put God first and let his love flow through you. People may forget accomplishments and hard work, but they'll never forget the compassion or kindness you show them.

———∽◦∾———

*That's the way I want to be. That's what I want to do. As a believer in God
and follower of Jesus, may I be wise in my decisions, compassionate to the
needy, kind in my words, understanding when I listen, and loving in all that I
say and do. Make me the kind of person you want me to be. Amen.*

God Is Faithful

—⟨⟩—

Yet this I call to mind and therefore I have hope: Because of the Lord's great love we are not consumed, for his compassions never fail. They are new every morning; great is your faithfulness.

Lamentations 3:21–23

Over and over in the Old Testament God rescued the Hebrew people from wars, from slavery, and from their own mistakes. Afterwards, he instructed their leaders to remind them of those deliverances on a regular basis. The whole idea was that experience should be their teacher, and peace of heart and mind would come from the memory of God's past care. And that's true for us today as well.

Through the years, I've heard countless stories of how God has taken care of Christians. He's given them peace in circumstances where, humanly speaking, you would expect them to be in fear and despair. Life is filled with crises, but God is always there. He sees you through. And once you have experienced God's care and peace in the past, your faith grows stronger, making it easier to trust him for his care and peace in the present and future. Great is his faithfulness!

—⟨⟩—

God of compassion, protect me from danger and evil. Rescue me from the mess I'm in. Get me through today's problems and into a better tomorrow. You've done this so many times before. You are always faithful, and I am always grateful. I am totally counting on you. Amen.

Straight-Shooting Jesus

———◆◆◆———

"After I have risen, I will go ahead of you."
Jesus, in Mark 14:28

There's no easy way to handle life's inevitable tough situations. But we can learn a lot from the way Jesus handled a tough situation with his disciples.

When Jesus told his disciples he was about to die, he also said they would fail him in his darkest hour. He knew they didn't have what it would take to make it through the difficulties ahead. He knew they would crumble under the pressure and run away.

Jesus could have kept his disciples in the dark or promised them everything would turn out fine, but he chose to be a realist. He told them the truth, even if it hurt—and warned them of what was to come. I like Jesus' straight-shooting style. But then he looked *beyond* their failure and *beyond* his crucifixion to his resurrection and to their restoration.

If Jesus were here today, he would speak frankly about our problems and sufferings. But he would also point to the better times to come—to our future with him.

∽◆∾

Tell me like it is, Lord Jesus. Show me my sin. Let me know what to expect. And give me the hope, promises, and encouragement that you are famous for. I need to see myself through your eyes. Amen.

Be a Lifeline

If you really keep the royal law found in Scripture,
"Love your neighbor as yourself," you are doing right.

James 2:8

On the phenomenally successful TV program *Who Wants to Be a Millionaire?* the original contestants were allowed three lifelines: 50/50, Phone-a-Friend, and Ask the Audience. That way the contestant stuck on a question could get the help necessary to move on toward winning the prize of a million dollars. The lifeline people got nothing in return for their assistance. They didn't share the million-dollar prize. Their reward was in helping someone else win who might otherwise lose.

When Jesus told us to love our neighbors as ourselves, he was, in effect, asking us to be lifelines to our neighbors. We give them the love they need to win. We tell them what they need to know about Jesus Christ. We are there for them whenever they need help—not because we will share their prize, but simply because we love them like God loves them.

---

*God of love and help, you want me to love you and love my neighbor.
That's what I want to do. Choose which neighbors you want me to
love first and love most. Show me ways to help them. Motivate me
with your love so that I don't need to be thanked or expect any reward
in return. Make me a lifeline to some neighbor today. Amen.*

Set Free

It is for freedom that Christ has set us free.
Galatians 5:1

There is a story that some have attributed to Abraham Lincoln—that he once watched the unspeakable indignities of selling and buying human beings at a slave auction. His response was a mixture of disgust, sadness, and outrage.

A young woman was brought to the block, her eyes and body language screaming defiance and hatred. She had been used and abused by her previous owners, and now it was going to happen all over again.

To everyone's amazement the man-against-slavery shouted a bid. As the price went up, so did his bids. Eventually he was declared the buyer. He paid the price, then told the young woman, "You're free."

With animosity and hatred she replied, "Yeah, free for what?"

"You're just free. Free to do anything you want to do; free to go anywhere you want to go."

Her appearance changed as she absorbed what this stranger had just told her. Then she replied, "Then I'm going with you."

Our gratitude should be even greater when we realize what Jesus did for us when he died on the cross. He has forgiven our sins and set us free to follow him.

---

*Jesus, my Savior, you have rescued me from sin and set me free.
I'm going with you. I'll follow you anywhere. Amen.*

When God Talks, Listen

"I will raise up for them a prophet...I will put my words in his
mouth, and he will tell them everything I command him."
The Lord, in Deuteronomy 18:17–18

We live in a literate society where we depend on written records. However,
other cultures are often amazingly careful and accurate in preserving and
passing along oral histories and information. The origins of the Bible began
long before the actual words of the Bible were written down.

God spoke with Adam and Eve; God told Moses how to free the Hebrew
people from slavery in Egypt. After giving Moses the Ten Commandments,
God gave him a long list of specific instructions about how the Hebrew people
were to live in a covenant relationship with God—everything from how to
cook food, to how to punish criminals, to setting political boundaries—and
it was all oral. Later Moses wrote it down so he could read it to the people.

Here's the point: God spoke and Moses wrote what God said. What started
out as spoken words became written words that were properly preserved and
passed forward into future generations. And God supervised the process so
the humans doing the writing didn't distort or change his message!

---

*I love to listen to what you say. Your words, my God, are wise and true. Teach
me your truth. Give me understanding. Hold me accountable. Just don't ever
be silent. I need to hear everything you have to say. Amen.*

A *Doulos* of Jesus

———•◆◆◆•———

Simon Peter, a *doulos* and apostle of Jesus Christ.
2 Peter 1:1

When a person describes himself, he chooses the words carefully. The apostle Peter described himself as a servant of God. He didn't use the word for a household servant but for a slave (*doulos*). In the Roman Empire a master owned a slave as a piece of property. Slaves owned nothing, had no holidays or days off, and their only law was their master's command.

Few people would choose to identify themselves as a slave, but Peter called himself a slave of Jesus. That meant he completely belonged to Jesus. His only law was Jesus' command. All of Peter's life was centered on Jesus, and he was proud to be the slave of Jesus Christ!

Are you willing to be the *doulos* of Jesus? Or do you want to keep the title to your life so you can chose when and if you obey Jesus? Peter trusted Jesus enough to be his slave. And being the slave of Jesus brought Peter to a deeper level of faith.

———◆◇◆———

May your name be my name, Jesus. May your will lead my life. May your mind fill my thoughts. Because I trust you, I willingly become your doulos. And as your slave, I learn to trust you more and more. Some may think it dangerous to give up their independence to you; I believe there is nothing safer or more exciting than belonging to Jesus. Amen.

Dinner from a Cauldron

———— ❦ ————

"When you enter a town and are welcomed,
eat what is set before you."
Jesus, in Luke 10:8

I once visited a small African village south of the Sahara Desert. Before World Relief provided a well for this village, the women had walked, with large clay jars on their heads, several miles to the closest source of water and then back with an amazing amount of weight. Now they had a deep well in their own village, and they wanted to express their gratitude. An unidentified animal was cooking in a large cauldron over an open fire. When it was my turn to eat, I was handed a grappling fork to hook whatever I could get out of the pot. I had no idea what animal this was and, worse yet, no idea what part I had hooked. But I'd been told these people ate meat only about once a year. They had significantly sacrificed to provide this meal. I ate what was served.

In Luke 10:8 Jesus was saying, "Don't be a complainer; don't be finicky. Be grateful for the food, clothes, and friends God has provided for you. Be content with what you get."

———— ❧ ————

Remind me, Lord, that others have so little when I have so much. Instead of wishing I had more, make me grateful for what I have. Forgive my words of complaint and hear my words of thanksgiving. May I desire to be clothed in loyal faithfulness more than in latest fashions. Amen.

Not Like Satan

—◦◦◦—

"I saw Satan fall like lightning from heaven. I have given
you authority to trample on snakes and scorpions and
to overcome all the powers of the enemy; nothing will harm
you. However, do not rejoice that the spirits submit to you
but rejoice that your names are written in heaven."
Jesus, in Luke 10:18–20

Satan started out as a magnificent angel, perhaps the highest in heaven—more powerful, intelligent, and beautiful than any other creature. But he became proud of his assets and rebelled against God, so God kicked him out of heaven forever.

Jesus warned his disciples to be careful about their attitude toward God's blessings. The danger was that they could confuse the source of their blessing and become proud. After all, that's why Satan fell "like lightning out of heaven."

Today our gifts from God may be good looks, money, an excellent education, or a powerful position rather than the authority to trample on snakes, but any of these things can become a source of pride. Take Jesus' advice: "If you want to be excited about something, rejoice if your name is written in heaven."

Now *that* is something to really get excited about.

—◦◦—

*You've blessed me with who I am and what I have. It's tempting to take credit
for your blessings and to abuse your gifts. Forgive me, Lord. I don't want
to fall like Satan. I want to rise and find my excitement in you. Amen.*

Sign Up Toll Free

❦

"Everyone who calls on the name of the Lord will be saved."
Paul, in Romans 10:13

Delta Airlines' frequent flyer program gives you Silver status if you fly 25,000 miles in a year, Gold status if you fly 50,000 miles a year, Platinum status if you fly 75,000 miles a year, and Diamond status for 125,000 or more miles per year. Each level brings increased benefits and rewards. Imagine you want to move up to a higher level, so you book a long flight from Los Angeles to London. Trouble is, you never signed up for the program. No enrollment date is recorded. Those miles don't count!

It's much the same with Christianity. To move up to the Silver, Gold, Platinum, or Diamond level of relationship with God, you have to sign up first—and that takes faith. If you're in doubt about your frequent flyer membership, you can call toll free and verify it. If you're in doubt whether you are signed up with God, call upon him in prayer. Say, "Yes, I believe in Jesus. I commit myself to him and want to be sure I am enrolled." It's as simple as that, but you have to make the call.

∽

*Hello, God?! I'm calling to make sure that I am enrolled in heaven.
I don't want any doubt that I am fully, totally, and completely a
Christian. I can't depend on anyone else to sign up for me. I call
for and claim my eternal salvation in Jesus' name. Amen.*

Everything We Need

---◆⟨◈⟩◆---

"Your Father knows what you need before you ask him."
Jesus, in Matthew 6:8

Twenty-four-year-old Danny Simpson really must have needed money to commit armed robbery for only $6,000. He was arrested, tried, convicted, and sentenced to six years in prison. After the trial was over, the gun he'd used for the robbery was donated to a museum. It was a .45 caliber Colt semi-automatic made by the Ross Rifle Company in Quebec City in 1918—and valued at $100,000! If Danny Simpson had realized what he had in his hand, he probably wouldn't have robbed that bank.

Not realizing what we've got is a common mistake. We desperately search for things we need to make it in life, failing to recognize what God has already given us. But the Bible says that God has already given us everything we need! Sometimes we live like paupers when we are endowed like royalty. If and when we grasp this truth, our lives can be truly transformed.

---⟨∿⟩---

Take my eyes off of what I don't have and let them see what
you have already put in my hand. Replace my lust with trust.
Guide me to use your blessings well. As you generously meet
my needs, may I faithfully serve you, Lord. Amen.

Worth-ship

❦

Sing to the Lord a new song; sing to the Lord, all the earth.
Sing to the Lord, praise his name; proclaim his salvation day after
day. Declare his glory among the nations, his marvelous deeds
among all peoples. For great is the Lord and most worthy
of praise...the Lord made the heavens. Splendor and majesty
are before him; strength and glory are in his sanctuary.

Psalm 96:1-6

Have you ever given much thought as to what people do in heaven? Do they
sit on clouds playing harps? The Bible tells us the primary occupation of
those in heaven is worship—the same as it is for those of us on earth who
believe in God.

Just what *is* worship? The word evolved from the Anglo-Saxon term *worth-
ship*. To worship anyone or anything is to recognize and affirm worth. When
we worship God, we are saying that he is worth it. He's worth worshipping.

In Psalm 96 the poet lists the worth of God in his attributes (who he is)
and in his acts (what he does). Have you seen the hair-color ad where the
actress says, "Because I'm worth it"? Well, I really don't know if she's worth
it or not, but God *is* worth it. He is worth worshipping, and it's our humble
privilege to worship him.

∽

*You are worth it, Magnificent God! You are worth everything.
I worship you in the name of Jesus Christ. Amen.*

Secret Sins

❧

Nothing in all creation is hidden from God's sight.
Everything is uncovered and laid bare before the eyes
of him to whom we must give account.

Hebrews 4:13

Have you ever noticed that sometimes when things seem to be going really well in your life, they take a turn for the worse? Back in Bible times the nation of Israel left their slavery in Egypt to enter the Promised Land, and God gave the army a great victory over the city-state of Jericho. But their next battle—against the far smaller and weaker city of Ai—was a humiliating defeat. Don't you hate it when that happens?

For Israel, it was all because Achan, one of their leaders, had secretly sinned. He'd stolen clothing, silver, and gold from a previous battle and had buried his loot under the floor of his tent. Because of his sin, God brought defeat to an entire nation.

Secret sins matter. They impact families, friends, churches, and nations. But the path to forgiveness and freedom begins with this realization: our secret sins aren't secret at all! God not only knows about our sins but has the power to forgive them and to help us move past them. And that's good news!

❧

There are reasons my sins are kept secret. I don't want anyone to know. This is so foolish. You know every sin, and you have offered full forgiveness. Come, Lord Jesus, see my secret sins and cleanse me from them all. Amen.

First Things First

———— ❧❧❧ ————

"Seek first God's kingdom and his righteousness."
Jesus, in Matthew 6:33

Pleasing God and putting God first is both a decision and a mindset. It affects everything we do and think. It can transform how we live life.

If we put money first, profit will be our greatest goal. If we put pride first, our concern will be preserving our reputations so we look good. If we put career first, all relationships and situations will be evaluated as to how they will further our careers. But if we put God first, our concern is always: *what would God like me to do in my current situation?*

Seeking God and his kingdom first may not answer every question or solve every problem, but it will put our hearts, our motives, and our faith in the right place. And when we do so, God will meet our needs abundantly. We won't have to worry about tomorrow. That's why "Seek God first" is such a powerful principle!

❧

You first, Lord! You first. My family, health, job, money, relationships, and a lot of other things are really important to me, but you are Number One. More than anything else I choose to love you, live for you, seek your kingdom, and be righteous. Just like Jesus! Amen.

The Customizer

—◆⟨⟨⟨⟩⟩⟩◆—

Thomas said to them, "Unless I see the nail marks
in his hands and put my finger where the nails were,
and put my hand into his side, I will not believe it."
A week later…Jesus came…and said to Thomas,
"Put your finger here; see my hands. Reach out your
hand and put it into my side. Stop doubting and believe."
John 20:25-27

The disciple of Jesus we call "doubting Thomas" has certainly gotten a lot of bad press. But have you ever thought that maybe he was just wired that way? Some of us believe things easily. Others have a lot of questions. Thomas was wired to wonder. Belief did not come as easily to him as it did the others. He may have dated his girlfriend for years before he could get over his doubts about marriage. And he probably was a salesman's nightmare. You could never close a deal with Thomas. He always wanted more information.

Jesus did an amazing thing for Thomas—he customized his approach. He related to the other disciples one way but recognized he had to come to Thomas in a special way. And he did just the right thing to draw Thomas to faith.

Jesus does the same for us. He customizes. He meets us more than halfway. He does what he needs to do to turn our doubt into faith.

~⟨⟨⟩⟩~

Jesus, sometimes I have doubts like Thomas. Come and
take my doubts away. Help me believe. Amen.

Created for Love

---❦---

This is how God showed his love among us: He sent his
one and only Son into the world that we might live through
him. This is love: not that we loved God, but that he loved
us and sent his Son as an atoning sacrifice for our sins.

1 John 4:9-10

Management expert Peter Drucker was wealthy, successful, and remained
married to the wife of his youth his entire life. In an interview when he was
ninety-four years old, he said that people his age no longer pray for a long
life but for an easy death. His story is all of our stories—we always want
something. Our want list is long, but at every age and circumstance there is
one "want" that tops most lists. We all want love.

All of us have a deep need for love because we were created that way by God.
God created us in his likeness, and that included both the capacity for love
and the desire for love. Just as fish are made for water and birds are made
for the air, so we are made for love. Whenever we lack love, we instinctively
know something is missing from life. St. John was an old man when he
wrote 1 John 4:9-10, saying that just as our desire for love came from God,
the fulfillment of that desire is best found in God. Nothing—or no one
else—will do.

∽❧∾

God, you love me! I am loved by God! Amen.

Giving Beats Getting

———◦◦———

Remembering the words the Lord Jesus himself said:
"It is more blessed to give than to receive."
Acts 20:35

Observe small children and it's quite evident they would rather receive a gift than give one. Yet part of achieving maturity, both chronologically and spiritually, is discovering the joy in giving to others. And that's what God wants for us—to experience the joy of blessing others. God blesses us so we can be a blessing. When we handle God's blessings generously he trusts us with more blessings. It's almost like God is saying to us:

If I give you money, be generous with it to others.
If I've made you healthy and strong, volunteer to serve others.
If I've provided you with a house, entertain others.
If I've answered prayers for you, pray for the needs of others.
If I've blessed you with influence, use it to help the disadvantaged.
If I've made you smart, be a mentor or a tutor to someone else.

Jesus wants us to discover the greatest blessing of all: being used as a conduit through which blessings flow to others.

———◦◦———

*Make me a blessing to others. Create in me a generous heart, O Lord.
May I share, not accumulate; use power to help, not hurt; and take
more delight in meeting the needs of others than in meeting the wants
I have. May I give to others as Jesus has given to me. Amen.*

Getting ready for Jesus

---‹⸎›---

"Yes, I am coming soon."
Amen. Come, Lord Jesus.
Revelation 22:20

Imagine the headlines at the time of Jesus' birth and death! When he was born, an extraordinary star shone so brightly that astrologers from the East followed it all the way to Bethlehem. They had never seen anything like it. Angels appeared to ordinary shepherds on the outskirts of Bethlehem. Then, when Jesus was dying on the cross, the sky turned dark at noon. There was an earthquake, rocks split apart, tombs opened, and long-dead bodies came back to life and walked the streets of Jerusalem. Three days later Jesus himself came back to life. Forty days after that he ascended into heaven, promising he would return again.

Jesus described this future return by saying his followers will be caught up into the sky to meet him (1 Thessalonians 4:17). It will be just as sensational as his first visit to earth...but very sobering. Since no one but God the Father knows the day or the hour of his return, Jesus warned everyone to be ready.

What about you? Are you ready?

‹⸎›

Lord, I'm ready and getting ready. I'm prepared, and I'm preparing. Yes, I believe in Jesus and have pledged my faith in him. So I'm ready. Yet I want to live so that I have no regrets if this is the day I will meet Jesus. Amen.

Citizen of Heaven

———◦⟨⟨⟨⟩⟩⟩◦———

You are no longer foreigners and aliens, but fellow citizens
with God's people and members of God's household.

Ephesians 2:19

When I was a first grader, my family moved to a new house, not far from
our old house but in a different school district. I didn't want to go. My
parents said I would make new friends and I would love my new house, but
I was reluctant to believe them. Still, you don't have much choice as a first
grader, so we moved. To my great surprise, the new place was even better
than they promised. Soon I could hardly remember my life at the old house
and school.

This world is a marvelous place, created by God for us to enjoy. We can,
and should, be grateful for it and for the experiences we have, whether in
America or in a distant land. However, we must remember where our true
citizenship is—as followers of Jesus in heaven! Someday this life on earth will
seem so distant amid the fullness of heaven in the presence of God.

◦⟨⟨⟩⟩◦

*God, I've had my share of ups and downs in this world, but it is still
home for me, and I'm reluctant to ever leave. Then I remember that
you created this earth and that you created heaven to be much better.
Heaven is where I really belong—that's where my eternal citizenship is
recorded. I'm looking forward to my new eternal home with you. Amen.*

Good News

—⚬⚬⚬—

Put…hope in God, who richly provides
us with everything for our enjoyment.
1 Timothy 6:17

When a young man asked his girlfriend's father for permission to marry her, the father asked the would-be son-in-law if he had a job. He didn't have a job. So the father asked how he expected to provide a home. The young man answered, "God will provide!"

The father said, "Well, if you don't have a job, how are you going to buy an engagement ring?" The young man said, "God will provide."

Then the father said, "How will you support my future grandchildren?" Predictably, the young man answered, "Don't worry, sir. God will provide."

Later that evening, the mother asked the father how the conversation with their future son-in-law had gone. The father said, "The bad news is, he has no job, no money, and no plans. The good news? He thinks I'm God."

In life there's both bad news and good news. The bad news is: we don't have what it takes to make it in life on our own. The good news? If we know Jesus, God will provide!

—⚬⚬—

*God, you are my generous provider. You delight to give what
I need. You even go beyond my needs to bless me with enjoyment.
Forgive me for those times I am self-reliant, and I don't trust
you as I should. You take such good care of me. Amen.*

JUNE

Hanging in There!

Therefore, since we are surrounded by such a great cloud
of witnesses, let us throw off everything that hinders and
the sin that so easily entangles, and let us run with perseverance
the race marked out for us.

Hebrews 12:1

Lance Armstrong, the world's best cyclist, has won the Tour de France multiple times. But being diagnosed with advanced cancer when he was twenty-five brought a sudden halt to his dreams of athletic accomplishment and filled his future with doubts. After months of chemotherapy he just lay on the couch. One day Kristin (now his ex-wife), told him, "You need to decide something. Are you going to be a golf-playing, beer-drinking, Mexican food-eating slob for the rest of your life?"

That conversation changed everything. "Within days I was back on my bicycle," Lance says. "For the first time in my life I rode with real strength and stamina and purpose. Without cancer, I never would have won a single Tour de France.... Pain and loss are great enhancers."

The Bible says suffering produces "perseverance," which means "hanging in there"—not giving up, remaining faithful. It's giving God time to help us and heal us. When we trust God, he settles our hearts and gives us the grace to hang on.

There are days I want to quit the race. Keep me going, Lord. Wake me up.
Give me the kick I need. Help me persevere like Jesus did. Amen.

Unthanked Hero

---❦---

One of the ten, when he saw he was healed, came back,
praising God in a loud voice. He threw himself at Jesus' feet
and thanked him—and he was a Samaritan.

Luke 17:15-16

On September 8, 1860, the steamer *Lady Elgin* started to sink, and the passengers and crew abandoned the ship. Standing on the shore of Lake Michigan was Edward W. Spencer, a student from Garrett Biblical Institute. He spotted a woman holding on to some wreckage, dove in to save her, and brought her safely back to shore.

Then he saw others, so he kept going back in, even when he was shaking from exhaustion. That day Edward saved seventeen people before he collapsed from exposure and fatigue. He never fully regained his health, and he was never strong enough to enter the ministry for which he was preparing. Years later, his obituary reported his heroism, adding that not one of those he saved ever came back to thank him.

Edward's life was forever altered by his selfless acts, but it was not in vain. Jesus taught that we are to do what is right, even if at great cost to us and appreciated by no one else.

---❧---

God of salvation, thank you for saving me! Thank you for loving and blessing me. Thank you for all you have done in the past, all you are doing today, and all you will do in the future. I am grateful beyond all words. Amen.

Jesus to Our Generation

If the whole body were an eye, where would the sense of
hearing be? If the whole body were an ear, where would the
sense of smell be? But in fact God has arranged the parts in
the body, every one of them, just as he wanted them to be....
As it is, there are many parts, but one body.... Now you are
the body of Christ, and each one of you is a part of it.

1 Corinthians 12:17–18, 20, 27

Almost two thousand years ago, God was represented on earth by Jesus.
You could see and touch his body and talk to him. But after he returned
to heaven, the replacement body on earth—the "body of Christ"—was the
collection of all Christians together making up the church. We are Jesus to
our generation.

The Bible makes it clear that a Christian trying to live independently of
the church is like having an eye or a hand that is totally independent of the
rest of the body. It simply doesn't work. The church is a body made up of
different parts with different talents and roles. God's plan is that we work
together as a body, for together we are able to do what individually we could
never come close to.

Jesus, you did amazing things in your body while here on earth.
Now you are doing amazing things through your church of believers
here on earth. That includes me! Amen.

Repayment Not Required

--- ❦ ---

The righteous give generously.
Psalm 37:21

A young Asian woman came to the U.S. to get her Ph.D. and asked Jan, a jewelry business owner, to buy her family jewelry so she could pay her tuition.

"How about if I simply give you the money," Jan said, "and after you get your Ph.D., if you are able to pay me back, that's great. But if you can't, then go back home and make your life count."

The girl was stunned. "Why would you do that?"

Jan said, "When I was buying this business, a friend believed in me enough to give me ten thousand dollars, saying he didn't care if I paid him back; but if I could, that would be great. Since then I've wanted to help someone else in a similar way. And also, even though this might seem like a big gift, it's nothing compared to the gift God gave us, through the death of his Son on the cross." You see, to Jan, the story was not about the money. It was about the opportunity to share who Jesus is. (Five months later the young woman returned with a check, and they have corresponded since!)

--- ❧ ---

My generous Lord, you have given so much to me. As you have blessed me, may you bless others through me. May I give wisely but without an expectation of receiving something in return. The future results are up to you. Amen.

Are You a Shouter?

———————⚬✦⚬———————

The whole crowd…began joyfully to praise God in loud voices.
Luke 19:37

Some people are shouters and some are not; and for the most part, I'm not a shouter. So it always fascinates me at professional football games to see people with painted faces yelling until they're hoarse. I just smile. Occasionally I get carried away and clap, but mostly I'm quiet. I've sometimes wondered what it would be like if the stadium were full of people like me—sixty thousand silent smiles. It wouldn't make for very good TV coverage! But I'm married to someone who can and will shout and cheer at sporting events.

My point is, when it comes to Jesus, you can shout if you like to shout, and you can worship quietly if that's what you want to do. But whatever you do, don't miss out on the ecstasy of worship. Focus so completely on Jesus that you are unaware of whether the person next to you is shouting or whispering, clapping or kneeling. Abandon your heart in praise to the Son of God.

———⚬✦⚬———

Yea, God! Hallelujah! Praise the Lord! God is great! God is good!
Jesus is Lord! I lift my voice in loud adoration. And, I bow in silence
to offer quiet worship. In solitude I come into your presence. Whatever
the circumstance or volume, you are worthy of all praise. Amen.

An Attitude of Gratitude

Give thanks to the Lord, for he is good. His love endures forever.

1 Chronicles 16:34

John Claypool, when a young Southern Baptist pastor in Kentucky, stopped to visit two middle-aged women in the same hospital.

The first woman was about to be discharged. She blasted him for not coming sooner, complained about the lousy food, criticized the staff for not taking better care of her, and complained that her children were late to pick her up.

The second woman was dying from cancer. When he entered her room, she greeted him. "You must be Pastor Claypool. Thanks for coming to see me, although you really didn't need to. There are others who need your time and attention more. I'm doing just fine. The doctors and nurses here are wonderful, and the food is great! Of course, I only have two teeth left to eat with, but praise God, they both meet in the middle!"

On his way home Pastor Claypool couldn't help but reflect on the difference between the two women. One had an attitude of gratitude and the other did not. How about you?

Blessed God, deliver me from my complaints. Forgive me for my bad attitudes. Create in me a grateful heart that is quick to see your goodness and anxious to give you thanks. I count every day of life as a gift from you and take joy in what you have given, without anger for what you have withheld. Thank you in Jesus' name. Amen.

That Day

——◦◦◦◦——

Do not boast about tomorrow,
for you do not know what a day may bring forth.
Proverbs 27:1

Sometimes, when I fly on a plane, I find myself thinking about crashes and dying. Truth is, none of us knows what our future holds. We must live as though any flight could crash, any car trip could end in disaster, and any day might bring a heart attack. We need to be ready all the time.

Jesus said he will come back to earth in a sensational way at a time when people are busy going about their normal lives, not thinking about him at all. It could be soon, or it could be years from now. But we need to be ready because when the time comes, there won't be enough time to do anything to get ready. Jesus is alerting us to keep our priorities straight because one day ordinary life, as we know it, will be interrupted and radically changed. May we live in a way here and now that we are ready to meet him when that day comes.

——◦◦——

*Life is short. Tomorrow is unknown. Uncertainties abound.
So I don't want to live as if I can control my life because I know
I can't. That's one of a million reasons I must trust you, O Faithful
One. You know tomorrow before it comes. You watch out for me
all the time. Your plan is best. My life is in your hands. Amen.*

Letting Go

Do not take revenge, my friends, but leave room for God's wrath,
for it is written: "It is mine to avenge; I will repay," says the Lord.
On the contrary: "If your enemy is hungry, feed him;
if he is thirsty, give him something to drink.
In doing this, you will heap burning coals on his head."

Romans 12:19–20

Jesus forgave others, and he wants us to do the same. But what exactly is forgiveness?

Forgiveness is letting go of revenge—being willing to move on when we are mistreated. You no longer expect the other person to make it right, and you're no longer trying to get even.

Jesus says we have a choice about getting even. We don't have to do it ourselves; we can let God take care of it. When we are kind and forgive someone instead of seeking revenge, the Bible describes it as *"heaping burning coals on his head."* That's a figure of speech meaning that the person might end up feeling embarrassed and guilty because we have been so nice when they were so wrong. They might even end up changing for the better!

But most of all, forgiveness means trusting God enough to let go and let him handle it.

---

*It's up to you, God. I don't want to carry the burden
of resentment or the need to get even. It's time to let go
and to move on. I give them to you, Lord. Amen.*

Heart and Mouth

———— ❦ ————

If you confess with your mouth, "Jesus is Lord," and believe in your heart that God raised him from the dead, you will be saved. For it is with your heart that you believe and are justified, and it is with your mouth that you confess and are saved.

Romans 10:9–10

I once worked at a summer camp where I did a lot of horseback riding. I remember the first time I put a bit in a horse's mouth. I thought I would lose my fingers! I soon learned that some horses have soft mouths and are sensitive to the slightest pull on the reins while others are so resistant that it takes a harsh bit and a strong pull to stop them.

Compared to the size of the horse, the bit is small, but its influence is considerable. The Bible compares it to the influence of the tongue on our bodies. Like the bit in the horse's mouth, the tongue can control the direction our entire bodies go. In many ways, Christianity begins with the mouth. In order to become a Christian, the tongue has to say so. Faith from the heart and words from the tongue change a person's life now and eternal destiny forever.

∽✦∾

May the faith of my heart and the words of my mouth declare my commitment to Jesus. You are my Savior and Lord whom I live to please and honor in all I say and do. Amen.

A Courageous Decision

I am still confident of this:
I will see the goodness of the Lord
in the land of the living.
Psalm 27:13

Having faith and confidence in God doesn't automatically chase away life's battles. David, God's chosen king of the ancient kingdom of Israel, expressed his doubts in the Psalms. But he also courageously decided to put his confidence in God. He decided to believe God for a good outcome, even if David didn't know what it might be. And that is exactly what faith is: deciding you'll no longer operate on the basis of apparent circumstances but on confidence in God.

What changed for David? Nothing! God didn't give him any new promises; God didn't change the battle; the dangers to David didn't disappear. The life-transforming difference? David courageously decided to depend upon God in confidence.

Like David, we must choose between doubts, which depend on us, and confidence, which depends on God. When you are crumbling under the weight of doubt is precisely the time to courageously decide to put your confidence in God.

Doubts don't disappear. I have uncertainties and worries. God, I don't promise not to doubt, but I deliberately choose to go beyond my doubts and place my confidence in you. You are trustworthy, and I believe in you. Amen.

The Joy of Giving

——❦——

Every good and perfect gift is from above,
coming down from the Father of the heavenly lights,
who does not change like shifting shadows.
James 1:17

Why is it happier to give than to receive? Because we have received so much. The Bible says, "Every good and perfect gift comes from above." There isn't anything good we have that God didn't give to us. The more we realize God's generosity to us, the more we are motivated to be generous to others. It is also happier to give than to receive because of the wonderful satisfaction that comes from blessing others. Frankly, it *feels* good.

Think of all the people who will cross your path this summer. Why not visualize yourself as a giver of encouragement to those who are down? As a supporter of those who are criticized? As a helper to those who are poor or lonely? May we all give generously and sacrificially of our resources and of our time because we have received so much from God.

——❦——

You like to give, and you like to bless. That's just who you are as God. Like you, I enjoy the feeling of giving to others, lightening their load, and making them feel better. Open my eyes to see every opportunity to bless others as you have blessed me. Amen.

Cooling the Conflict

———◦◦◦———

His speech persuaded them.
Acts 5:40

A huge conflict erupted in first-century Jerusalem between the followers of Jesus and the religious establishment. Change was in the wind, and the Sanhedrin was protective of the status quo. Several Christian leaders had been thrown into jail, only to be set free by an angel. They were then rearrested, and the Sanhedrin was called into session to determine what to do with them. Many of the Sanhedrin wanted the Christians killed to quell the movement.

Before the vote was taken, Gamaliel, a leading rabbi, advised, "Leave these men alone. Let them go. For if their purpose or activity is of human origin, it will fail. But if it is from God, you will not be able to stop these men. You will only find yourself fighting against God."

Good for Gamaliel. This veteran of conflict knew how to deescalate conflict. I want to be like him, understanding that while conflict is inevitable, it can be a force for good, if handled correctly.

◦◦◦

There is no shortage of conflict in our world—from wars between nations to family feuds. It's too easy to join the fight and make things worse. God, I want to be more like Gamaliel, who cooled the crowd and trusted you for the outcome. May I be the one who throws water, not fuel, on the fires of hostility. Amen.

To Be Like Jesus

❦

"Father, forgive them, for they do not know what they are doing."
Jesus, in Luke 23:34

When we think of Jesus, it's easy to dwell on his "perfect Son of God" side and forget about his human side. But he had relationships and relationship challenges just like we do. Shortly before Jesus died, Judas, one of his closest friends, tipped the soldiers off as to Jesus' whereabouts, then identified him with a kiss. Jesus knew exactly what was happening, yet he responded by calling Judas "friend."

After an illegal trial, soldiers nailed Jesus to a cross and placed it between two other men being executed for their crimes. The reactions of Jesus and the two criminals to their executioners couldn't have been more different. The criminals cursed them, but Jesus prayed, "Father, forgive them because they don't know what they are doing."

Jesus was amazing! His friend betrayed him, strangers crucified him, yet he didn't get angry, as we undoubtedly would have. Our goal should be to have an attitude toward others that is "the same as that of Christ Jesus" (Philippians 2:5).

❧

Jesus, I'll never face anything like your crucifixion. Nobody is going to nail me to a cross. Still, I sure do get attacked sometimes. People can be really mean. Teach me to be like you and give my attackers the benefit of the doubt and forgiveness for what they have done. Amen.

Start with Questions

They found him in the temple courts, sitting among the teachers,
listening to them and asking them questions.
Luke 2:46

When Jesus was twelve, his parents found him hanging out in the Temple courtyard, dialoging with the leading religious teachers of Judaism. Even at his young age, Jesus was *others centered*. He was a good listener and a good questioner. He focused his attention on others and was eager to learn from them.

Jesus was also a *continual learner*. He asked questions when he was twelve, and he was still asking questions when he was in his thirties. A graduate school professor of mine once said, "You can often tell more about a person from the questions asked than by the answers given." When Jesus talked with people, he usually started out with questions—finding out what they thought, where they were from, what they were interested in. Then he talked to them based on the information he learned about them.

The example of Jesus is powerful! Focus on others. Be an inquirer. Ask questions more than you give answers. Listen. Learn. And grow.

God of truth, what do you want me to learn today? Whom should I ask? What should I say? May I be quick to question and slow to answer, anxious to learn before I try to teach, and centered on others rather than on myself. If Jesus started with questions, then so will I. Amen.

Start the Smiles

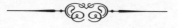

The memory of the righteous will be a blessing.
Proverbs 10:7

In a Volkswagen ad, a bunch of people are standing on a street corner. They open doors, smile, say "hello," and are the picture of friendliness. Their actions are sequential—one kind act leads to another. Then the camera runs in fast reverse to see where it all started. Seeing a VW Beetle convertible driving around the corner made one person smile and feel good enough to be nice to the next person and then to the next. Apparently the world would be a better place if a lot more Volkswagens drove by a lot more corners!

Imagine that a Christian takes the initiative to be nice to someone whether that person deserves it or not. That act of kindness starts a chain of events that changes another person's life.

When we take the initiative to bless someone else's life, that action often becomes sequential, and even contagious—making the world a better place, and making ourselves more like Jesus.

Start the chain of blessing with me. Actually, Lord, it started already with you. You have smiled at me and given me joy. Now it's my turn to spread the smiles. I'll start with the first ten people I see today even if I don't know who they are and will never see them again. I'll never know where the chain will go, but you will. Make me the agent of your joy. Amen.

Olympic Faith

———— ❧ ————

If only I may finish the race and complete the task the Lord Jesus
has given me—the task of testifying to the gospel of God's grace.

Acts 20:24

Eric Liddell was a very fast runner whose specialty was the 100-yard dash.
The trials for that event in the 1924 Olympic Games were held on a Sunday.
Because his Christian convictions prevented him from competing on
Sundays, Eric wouldn't run and was disqualified. Instead, he switched events
to compete in the 400-yard run, an event for which he had never trained. In
the race, he tripped, yet was able to recover and finish five yards ahead of his
closest competitor, setting a world record of 47.6 seconds!

Some would say missing your event in the Olympics hardly qualifies as a
tragedy. It's certainly not in the same league as a terminal brain tumor or
being imprisoned in a concentration camp. Actually, Eric Liddell qualifies
on all counts. After the Olympics, he became a missionary to China. In
World War II he was captured by the Japanese and interred in a concentration
camp, where he died of a brain tumor in 1945.

Eric Liddell knew tragedy firsthand, but he didn't let it define him. His faith
in God gave him peace.

❧

Life is a lot like a race. Sometimes it is on a smooth Olympic track, although
I can stumble anywhere. Sometimes there are wonderful trophies to win.
Sometimes the race is on rocky terrain. My Lord, may I run faithfully. Amen.

Get Good Advice

—————◦⟨✦⟩◦—————

Listen to advice and accept instruction,
and in the end you will be wise.
Proverbs 19:20

There's an old political saying about American presidents: a president cannot get close advisors after his inauguration. The idea behind it is that once a person becomes president of the United States he doesn't have time to figure out whose advice he can trust. He needs to know in advance. His closest advisors must be people he learned to trust long before he was seated in the Oval Office.

We too should pick our advisors before they are needed. We can't afford to wait until a crisis to figure out whom we can trust. We need to look around in advance for those who have experience and godliness and who speak the truth.

What if you unexpectedly faced one of the most difficult and important decisions of your life this week? Whom would you call to pray for you? Whom would you call for counsel? The best time to build those relationships is before the crisis comes.

⟿⟾

Wise God, you are my greatest source of wisdom. But, I know that you often direct me through the advice of others. Bring good friends who are wise counselors into my life before I need them. May I be transparent enough for them to correctly understand me. May they be godly enough to be conduits of your counsel. May I be discerning enough to know whose advice to take. Amen.

Jack the Cat

———— ❧ ————

Be completely humble and gentle; be patient,
bearing with one another in love.

Ephesians 4:2

Our family used to have a cat named Jack who was lean, quick, and equipped with sharp claws and a fast paw. He was more than capable of getting whatever he wanted—whether it was me or a bird. Our young children didn't always treat cats as cats ought to be treated. Sometimes they would grab too hard, carry him upside down, or even drop him. When Jack's patience ran out, he would swing quickly and accurately with his paw. He would always hit his target, but he'd never put out his claws. He never scratched our children even though he had every right.

Jack's gentleness in those situations is a good example of what the Bible means when it describes the followers of Jesus as being gentle. Living God's way means that even in situations where we might feel justified in lashing out with our claws, we choose instead to be kind to others…even if they don't deserve it.

———— ❧ ————

You know about my claws, God. You've heard me when my words are cutting. You know I am capable of scratching others. Make me gentle. Keep my claws in. When I could swing to hurt, may I reach to help. When I could be cruel, may I be kind. Just like Jesus. Amen.

The Cornerstone of History

—◈◈◈—

"See, I lay a stone in Zion,
a chosen and precious cornerstone,
and the one who trusts in him
will never be put to shame."

Peter, in 1 Peter 2:6

St. Peter quoted the prophet Isaiah to describe Jesus as a cornerstone. We often think of a cornerstone as a special stone, sometimes hollow inside to hold a time capsule to be opened in a hundred years. The cornerstone is laid in a dedication ceremony at the completion of a building. But, originally, a cornerstone had an architectural function. The cornerstone gave perfect right angles and was the first stone to be set. It became the basis for the entire building, and every stone and every brick was laid to align with the cornerstone. If the cornerstone was perfectly square, then the rest of the building was in alignment. But if the cornerstone was crooked, then everything was out of alignment.

Jesus is the cornerstone of history—the cornerstone of the church of God. He is the standard of truth and the basis for everything that God is doing in the world. Why not make Jesus your cornerstone and align your life with him today?

◈

Jesus, you are the cornerstone of my life. I completely depend on you. My goal is to line up everything I say and do with you. Whatever is out-of-line, I ask you to correct. May everything about me lead straight back to you. Amen.

A Striking Resemblance

Reckless words pierce like a sword,
but the tongue of the wise brings healing.
Proverbs 12:18

A Southern preacher took his wife to a restaurant overlooking the Smoky Mountains of Tennessee for a romantic dinner. An old man unexpectedly interrupted their meal to tell them his life story of growing up under a cloud of shame as an illegitimate child in a Tennessee mountain village. Townsfolk tried to guess who his daddy was.

As a preteen, he sneaked in to a country church to hear the music but found himself drawn even more to the preacher's words. He returned Sunday after Sunday. One Sunday, the preacher caught up with him before he left. "Son, you look a lot like…" The boy's heart sank. He didn't want to be hurt by this man too. But the preacher continued, "You have a striking resemblance to God. You must be a child of God."

"I was born again that day," the old man said. "I was forever changed by the blessing of those words."

As the old man turned to leave, the preacher and his wife asked his name. He was Ben Hooper—twice-elected governor of Tennessee.

You see, the words we speak have great power.

*Whatever my family history, I pray that others may see God in me.
May the family resemblance point them to you, Lord. May it be
obvious that you are my Father and I am your child. Amen.*

Like a Little Child

"Anyone who will not receive the kingdom
of God like a little child will never enter it."
Jesus, in Mark 10:15

Obviously Jesus isn't suggesting we literally become children again, nor did he mean we should behave childishly. He was letting us in on one of the great truths of all history—that anyone who wants to become a Christian must have faith like that of a child.

Children are dependent upon others for everything. They trust their parents to provide food, clothing, and shelter for them. It never occurs to them that they should provide for themselves unless they are forced into that thinking by inadequate parenting. Children are also believers. Faith comes easily. Doubt is something we learn as we grow older and become proud and sophisticated, thinking we are smarter than others.

Too many of us outgrow the simplicity of childhood—that ability to take God at his word and to admit our inadequacy and helplessness. We need to trust him to provide for our basic needs and to love him more than anything else in the world. Jesus says that unless we are childlike, we will never enter his kingdom.

Father God, in some ways I am so grown up; in many ways I am still a child. As your child, I reach my hands up to you. With simple faith I tell you "I love you" and depend on you. Take care of me, I ask. In Jesus' name, amen.

The Rest of the Story

---•❦•---

"This is what I told you while I was still with you.
Everything must be fulfilled that is written about me
in the Law of Moses, the Prophets and the Psalms."
Jesus, in Luke 24:44

The famous radio commentator Paul Harvey used to tell fascinating stories that led him to talk about "the rest of the story." Anyone who reads the Old Testament hears the inspired Word of God, but the rest of the story is in the New Testament and it's all about Jesus. The Old Testament is a start, not a finish. It begins with sin but never fully explains salvation. It starts with the Hebrew people but never includes the rest of humanity. It predicts that a Messiah will come and bring salvation. The New Testament picks up the story to explain that God sent his Son, Jesus, from heaven to earth to live a perfect life and to die on the cross to pay for our sin. Then God raised him to life again so that all who believe in Jesus can have their sins forgiven, go to heaven someday, and have the love of God transforming their lives right now.

The biggest point of both the Old and New Testaments is Jesus!

∼❧∼

*God, you knew Jesus was coming and had him in mind when you
inspired your holy Scriptures. Jesus, let me see you in the Old
and New Testaments. Let me see you today, too. Amen.*

God's Agents

───❦───

"Ask and it will be given to you; seek and you will find;
knock and the door will be opened to you."

Jesus, in Matthew 7:7

Imagine you take an overseas job with a major company. Since you are new and unproven, your authority is limited at first, and you need approval for any expenditure over a hundred dollars. After a while you gain a reputation with the home office as a loyal and trustworthy employee. The boss knows that all of your requests for authorization have been in the company's best interests and that you won't use your position for your own self-interests.

We Christians, as God's agents here on earth, have the privilege of prayer to ask anything of the home office in heaven. When God knows that we are absolutely loyal to him and that our requests seek his priorities and policies rather than our own, he increasingly puts his power at our disposal through prayer.

Do your prayers put God first? Do they seek *his* will and reflect *his* thinking?

───❦───

*I'm not sure I've thought of prayer this way before. But it makes
sense, Lord. You aren't going to automatically give me everything
I ask for. You love me too much to give the bad stuff I sometimes seek.
You want to know that you can trust me to ask for what is good and
right. Today I ask that you will guide me to ask as I should. Amen.*

Different Destinies

"I tell you that the tax collector, rather than the Pharisee, went home justified before God. For everyone who exalts himself will be humbled, and he who humbles himself will be exalted."

Jesus, in Luke 18:14

Two men came to the Temple to pray. The Pharisee, a religious leader, stood in a prominent place and prayed loudly, thanking God he was not like other men who did evil. Then he recited all the good he had done. The tax collector, despised by his fellow Jews because of his profession, stood off inconspicuously to the side, beating his chest in despair. He prayed the only prayer he dared to pray: "God, have mercy on me, a sinner."

The Pharisee compared himself to others and felt he came out pretty good. The tax collector compared himself to God and came out a hopeless disaster. He knew he was a sinner, and he needed help. He didn't try to impress anyone; he just asked God for mercy.

The two men went home that day with different destinies. The Pharisee, the good guy, left a sinner—disconnected from God. The tax collector, the bad guy, left a saint—connected to God. Which one is most like you?

On the outside I can look pretty good. I try to give the impression I'm a really righteous person. But you know what I'm like on the inside, don't you, God? I am a sinner who needs your mercy. God, have mercy on me, for Jesus' sake. Amen.

A Cheerful Giver

Each man should give what he has decided in his heart to give, not reluctantly or under compulsion, for God loves a cheerful giver.

2 Corinthians 9:7

A fourth-grade class sent a get-well card to their teacher when she was in the hospital. The card read: *Dear Miss Jones, Your fourth-grade students wish you a quick recovery from your operation by a vote of 13 to 12.* The card was a nice idea, but the attitude was certainly lacking in cheerfulness!

Or, what if your child gives you a birthday gift and then says, "Dad told me I would be grounded for six months if I didn't give this to you." Knowing about the motivation for the gift changes your idea of the gesture, doesn't it?

Now imagine getting a gift from someone who is just bubbling with excitement to see you open it. That's the kind of giving God loves. With him, the issue is not so much the *actual* gift but the attitude with which we give it. Our giving is transformed when we are truly cheerful givers.

Look at me, God. I'm the one with the happy face. I'm the one with the bubbly laugh. I'm the one who is cheerful. Want to know why? It's because I decided to give to you and now I'm doing it. My gift isn't because of pressure, guilt, legalism, or fear. I give out of love, gratitude, and delight. What fun! Amen.

God's Calendar

With the Lord a day is like a thousand years, and a thousand years
are like a day. The Lord is not slow in keeping his promise, as some
understand slowness. He is patient with you, not wanting anyone to
perish, but everyone to come to repentance.

2 Peter 3:8–9

Many people are disappointed or angry with God and are close to concluding
that he isn't as good as he claims to be. Let's think about that for a moment.
If God is not good, then evil prevails and we have no hope—in this life or
in the next. Those who interpret God by their difficult circumstances are
traveling down a dangerous road toward disaster.

I prefer to go with Jesus' explanation. He said that God is good and that
those who pray to him get justice and get it quickly. But how does that fit with
our unanswered prayers?

I think the answer lies within these words in the Bible. God isn't tardy; he
just measures time by a different scale than we do. From our perspective it
might seem like God is slow in helping, when, in reality, he is allowing time
for the other person's repentance. God's decisions are rooted in his love and
compassion for everyone. Not just for you and for me, but for the other guy
as well.

*God, forgive my impatience. I forget that your calendar isn't the same
as mine. I will trust you for the best timing for me. Amen.*

Answers to Prayer

———◦⊱⊰◦———

So Jesus left them and went away once more and prayed
the third time, saying the same thing.
Matthew 26:44

Nobody likes getting "no" for an answer—especially when you're praying.
The night before Jesus was crucified he prayed three times that his death be
called off. And three times God the Father said no. Even though Jesus was
without sin and had good motives for his request, God still said no.

Sometimes the most committed of Christians pray with fervency, asking
God to heal their illness, to reverse their financial difficulties, or to repair
their broken relationships. We think that if we get our prayer exactly right,
if we have enough faith, or if enough people are praying with us, God will
do as we request.

But answers to prayer are up to God, not us. The final decision on our
prayers is his decision. Our faith is in him, not in the expectation that
everything will be as we choose it to be. Faith is the belief that God will do
what is right and best, not that we will get the answer we want.

∼⦿∼

Jesus, like you, I've prayed and gotten no for an answer. So I went back and
prayed the same thing again and again. It's hard to take no for God's answer
even when I believe that God knows best. I need to pray what you prayed:
"Not my will but your will be done." Amen

Brenda's Miracle

❦

Hannah was praying in her heart, and her lips were moving but
her voice was not heard. "I am a woman who is deeply troubled....
I was pouring out my soul to the Lord."
1 Samuel 1:13, 15

This is the story of Brenda, a divorced single mom. Her former husband
had accidentally dropped their baby, Zachary, while bathing him, causing
damage to his brain and rupturing his retinas. The doctors said that if the
baby survived, he would never see, walk, talk, or sit up. The young mother
prayed for a miracle.

Ten years later a story appeared in *USA Today*, saying: "Brenda's prayers have
been answered. Zachary is partially blind, able to read words and see objects
that are held within inches of his face, and he gets around fairly well. He's
a rambunctious fifth grader, mainstreamed in many classes, and enrolled
in special education classes to learn math, spelling, and how to tell time."
Brenda's persistence in prayer and faith in God so touched the life of a man
named Kurt that he too became a Christian. Today Brenda's husband and
Zachary's adoptive father is Kurt Warner, the quarterback for the St. Louis
Rams when they won the Super Bowl.

Brenda prayed a long time. Her prayer was not answered exactly as she asked
it, but she is convinced she got her miracle!

❧

Hear my repeated prayers. I pour out my heart to you.
Answer in your miraculous way, Lord. Amen.

The Parts Car

You have taken off your old self with its practices and have
put on the new self, which is being renewed in knowledge
in the image of its Creator.
Colossians 3:9-10

Take a look at the classic car ads sometime in the Sunday newspaper or
on the Internet. They start out with those described as "mint condition,
show ready, fully restored." The price is staggering—tens of thousands of
dollars. Then there are those that say "good condition," and they're a little
less money. The next group is described as "runs well." Below that, with the
price rapidly dropping, is "repairable." At the bottom of the pecking order
is the "parts car"—the one that's far enough past dreaming and past driving
that all you can do is haul it home and store it in the garage. Then, when
you're making a dream come true in another car, you take parts off the parts
car to put into the dream car to make *that* one into a classic.

God takes the pieces out of dreams that we'll never drive again and puts
them into new dreams that he turns into classics. If you feel life has dealt
you only unfulfilled dreams, why not give them to God to use for parts?

Will you do this, Lord? Will you take the broken pieces
of my old dreams and make them new? By your grace I will
dream new dreams with hope and faith. Amen.

The Best Kind of Faith

Now faith is being sure of what we hope for and certain of what
we do not see. By faith the prostitute Rahab, because she welcomed
the spies, was not killed with those who were disobedient.

Hebrew 11:1, 31

One of the people featured in *LIFE* magazine's "The Power of Prayer" cover
story was a young prostitute from White Pine County, Nevada. It caught my
attention because it seemed inappropriate, even embarrassing, to give so
much space to a prostitute's prayer life.

Yet the Bible does the same thing with a woman named Rahab. Forty years
after the nation of Israel escaped slavery in Egypt, they were ready to invade
the promised land of Canaan. But before beginning the conquest, two spies
were sent to check things out. They found lodging in the house of Rahab the
prostitute. She believed in the God of Israel and agreed to hide the spies and
aid their escape.

In the New Testament Rahab is brought up as an example of the best kind of
faith in God, which results in acts of righteousness. At first it seems a little
inappropriate to think of a prostitute as an example of faith. But Rahab's
story is a great encouragement. It shows that nothing is too embarrassing or
too sinful for God to handle. He delights in loving us and changing us into
his best.

God of mercy and grace, you welcome all with faith.
Even me. I believe. I have faith in Jesus. Amen.

JULY

My Beloved Dumbo

"Man looks at the outward appearance,
but the Lord looks at the heart."
The Lord, in 1 Samuel 16:7

As a little boy, I had a beloved stuffed elephant named Dumbo. Over the years, he lost an eye, his color faded, and I sort of lost interest. But after my daughter, Jill, came along, I gave Dumbo to her, and it was love all over again.

Jill is now grown with a daughter of her own, but Dumbo is prominently displayed in her living room. He doesn't look as good as he once did; in fact, his market value is probably zero. But I doubt Jill would sell him for any price. Dumbo is still loved—not because of his looks, but because of his value to her. She values Dumbo because of his relationship to her father.

Isn't that the way we want to be loved? Not because of our looks, but for ourselves? It is our relationship to God the Father that gives us value. It was while we were at our worst, with nothing to offer, that God loved us and sent his Son to die for us.

Loving Lord, I live in a world where I am continually judged by the way I look. My heart yearns to be loved and accepted just as I am—not because of clothes, age, or appearance. That's the way you love me. You see me exactly the way I am and you love me completely. I am so grateful. Amen.

You Are What You Speak

> "The things that come out of the mouth come from
> the heart, and these make a person 'unclean.'"
> *Jesus, in Matthew 15:18*

You know the popular slogan, "You are what you eat"? It's used to encourage people to eat more healthful foods, which is a good thing. However, I find it interesting that Jesus taught quite the opposite: you are what you speak. We know we can control what goes into our mouths, but controlling what comes out is a lot harder. In fact, Jesus put it this way: "No one can tame the tongue. It is a restless evil, full of deadly poison" (James 3:8).

Have you ever asked yourself in disgust, "Why did I say that? Why do I always stick my foot in my mouth?" When we want to be different, but we just can't pull it off, we need God's help. It's not that tongues can't be tamed; it's that we can't tame our *own* tongues. Only God can transform us from the inside out so that what we say will be good.

*My Creator, you designed my tongue. Forgive me for all my sinful talk.
Hear my speech and help me keep my tongue under control. Reign
it in. May I speak words of truth and grace. When tempted to speak
lies, gossip, profanity, or injury, keep my tongue still and quiet. May
your words be my words, and may my words speak for you. Amen.*

Seriously Seeking Jesus

---❦---

Without faith it is impossible to please God, because
anyone who comes to him must believe that he exists
and that he rewards those who earnestly seek him.
Hebrews 11:6

Lew Wallace was so convinced Jesus Christ never existed that he told his
wife he was going to write a book debunking the Jesus myth. It was hard for
her to hear, for she was a Christian. Several years into his research, Wallace
struggled with some of his own conclusions:

"I was in an uncomfortable position...face to face with the fact that he was just
as historic a personage as Julius Caesar, Mark Antony, Virgil, or Dante.... I
asked myself candidly, 'If he was a real person, (and there was no doubt), was
he not then also the son of God, and the Savior of the world?'...I fell on my
knees to pray for the first time in my life, and I asked God to reveal Himself
to me, forgive my sins, and help me to become a follower of Christ."

And with that, Lew Wallace abandoned his book but used his research to
write another book. It became one of the all-time classic movies—*Ben-Hur*—
a story punctuated with references to, and belief in, Jesus.

---❦---

*Jesus, count me as a seeker after you. Sometimes with gigantic faith and
sometimes with teetering doubt, I search for your truth. The more I learn,
the closer I come. The better I know you, the more I believe. Amen.*

The Right Map

---·◈◈·---

Direct me in the path of your commands,
for there I find delight…. I will walk about in freedom,
for I have sought out your precepts.
Psalm 119:35, 45

There are many different maps of the United States. One charts the land's topography with the most lines along north/south longitudes from Montana to Arizona, because the Rocky Mountains are there. A demography map shows most of the activity along the coasts and in the northeast, because that's where most of the people live. A meteorology map shows airflow lines across the top of the nation, because that's where the jet stream is. All of these maps are helpful—if you are making decisions about altitude, population density, or weather movements. But if you're looking for an interstate highway to get you from St. Louis to St. Paul, none of them will help. You have to read the right map!

When you are looking for direction in life, you need to read the right map. The Bible is different from typical maps. It gives lots of advice on how to drive through life but says very little about the actual highways. God's map is more about the way you travel than the route you take.

∽୧∾

Guide me, God of the Bible. Show me the way to go. Keep me off
the wrong roads. But, more than finding the name of the road to
take, help me follow the name of the Lord I trust. Amen.

Saints and Sinners

A record of the genealogy of Jesus Christ the son of David,
the son of Abraham...there were fourteen generations in all from
Abraham to David, fourteen from David to the exile to Babylon,
and fourteen from the exile to the Christ.

Matthew 1:1, 17

Most of us have someone in our extended family or ancestry that we'd rather not own up to. It's like the old saying, "You can pick your friends, but not your family." And Jesus was no exception. His ancestry, traced in the Bible, was quite a mixed bag of saints and sinners.

David, a brilliant musician, military strategist, and "a man after God's own heart," seduced his neighbor's wife and had her husband killed to cover up his adultery.

Abraham, the father of all Jews and a great man of faith, lied to protect his own skin.

Noah, famous for building the ark, had a problem with alcohol.

The fact that Jesus descended from Adam, just like every other human being, shows that he shares all our humanity, and that he's not only a Jew, but the Savior of Jews, Gentiles, Europeans, Africans, Asians, Latin Americans, males, and females. He came to be one of us so he could be the Savior for all of us.

---

*From Adam to Noah to Abraham to David...Jesus, you have quite a
family history. So you understand about my own family. We have quite
a history of our own. Thank you for being a Savior for us all. Amen.*

Worth Fixing

❧

From the beginning God chose you to be saved
through the sanctifying work of the Spirit.
2 Thessalonians 2:13

Whenever I read classic car ads, I'm tempted to buy an old car and restore it to its original condition. Then I realize that when the ad says "needs work," what the words really mean is that it would take $30,000 and the next thirty years of my life to make the beat-up old wreck into the car it ought to be. I've always decided it wouldn't be worth it.

That's why I'm so impressed with God's plan to fix us up through the Holy Spirit's work in our lives. When God looks at us and sees the battered shape we're in, it's amazing that he still wants us! But he assigns the Holy Spirit to sanctify us—to restore us to the way we ought to be. And we're not cheap. To buy us back and fix us up cost God his Son's life. Jesus died as the price for God to reclaim us and make us Christians.

Aren't you glad God decided we are worth it?

❧

Holy Spirit, you took on a major project when you chose me. Thank you for investing your sanctifying grace in my life. I remember the way I was when you started—like one of those "before" pictures. I see the difference you already have made, and I look forward to all you are going to do to restore me. Amen.

Balance Sheet Benefits

In this you greatly rejoice, though now for a little while
you may have had to suffer grief in all kinds of trials.
1 Peter 1:6

A former star of the National Football League once reported in an e-mail to me that he had just been diagnosed with cancer. He said he was "totally pumped" by this diagnosis and couldn't wait to see how God was going to use this in his life. I thought, *Either he is out of his mind, or he's really on to something that the rest of us need to find out about.* Then I remembered the words of St. Peter.

Take a minute to make a "balance sheet." List all your problems, pains, and difficulties in one column and add them up. Are they real? Yes! Is the total high? Sometimes it's staggering. Then list the benefits of being a Christian in the next column: new birth, eternal inheritance, divine protection, and a faith that works. Add them up. Are they real? Yes! Is the total high? It's higher by far than the total of troubles. That's why the Bible tells us to "greatly rejoice." Celebrate the blessings. Rejoice during troubles!

Suffering is real. Pain hurts. Grief is hard to describe. Yet, I will rejoice—not because of the uninvited circumstances but because you are with me and your goodness is greater than my trials. Help me to see your grace as clearly as I feel my problems. In Jesus' name, amen.

Holy Different

But just as he who called you is holy, so be holy in all you do;
for it is written: "Be holy, because I am holy."
1 Peter 1:15-16

I spent a summer studying in Europe while in college. Several Europeans walked up to me and said, "You're an American, aren't you?" I asked how they knew, and they laughed. "It's obvious!" one said. Others said it was the way I talked, the clothes I wore, and the style of my glasses. I was different. I looked like an American.

In the Old Testament God wanted the Hebrew people to stand out as different from other nations...as uniquely belonging to God. So God gave them a thousand rules to live by—how to dress, eat, worship, and behave— in order to make them different from everyone around them.

God wants us to be different. He wants our lives to be peaceful, our families to be strong, our treatment of others to be fair and honest, and our language to be clean. He wants us to be holy—to look like we belong to him.

---

*Holy, holy, holy, Lord God Almighty. You are so different, so good,
so beautiful, so gracious...so holy! Make me holy as you are holy.
When people analyze how I walk, talk, dress, work, and play,
may it be obvious that I belong to you. In a world where so many
want to go along with the crowd, help me to be holy. Amen.*

Tank Up!

———❦———

You believe in God, who raised him from the dead and
glorified him, and so your faith and hope are in God.

1 Peter 1:21

Imagine a U.S. military plane on a mission running out of aviation fuel. It's
going to crash. Through a radio signal, the pilot is told to hook up to a flying
tanker. He can't see the dispatcher, and he can't see the tanker. He simply
takes it on faith—going where he needs to go and doing what he needs to do.
At just the right moment he aligns the nose of the plane with the basket and
fuel line from the tanker. The tanks are filled, and the flight continues to
distances impossible without the refueling.

As Christians, we are on a mission for God. Sometimes we feel lost in the
clouds. We run dangerously low on fuel and fear crashing. Then we get a
message from the God we cannot see telling us he will refuel us and keep us
going. He asks us to come to him in faith.

If you are running low on fuel, today is the perfect time for you to tank up
and top off with faith and hope in God!

∼✇∽

Fill me, God. I am running low and don't know what to do.
Replenish my empty soul. Renew my weary spirit. Rest my
tired body. Download your thoughts into my spinning mind.
Stabilize and strengthen me for the journey ahead. Amen.

Forever Changed

—⁂—

Those who belong to Christ Jesus have crucified the
sinful nature with its passions and desires.
Galatians 5:24

The movie *The Doctor* is based on the true story of a surgeon who was arrogant and insensitive to coworkers, patients, family members, and everybody else. He developed a cough that didn't get better and discovered he had cancer. Suddenly the tables were turned, and the doctor became the patient. He underwent surgery, was cured, and eventually returned to the practice of medicine. But he was forever changed by his experience. It changed the way he related to his wife and family. It changed the way he treated patients and the way he spoke to nurses and fellow physicians. His life was revolutionized because he thought he was lost, and his life was saved.

If you have chosen to put your trust in God to save you from your sins, and you are living by faith, you are forever changed. And your life will show it!

May our faith always affect our lifestyle so that the way we live reflects our gratitude for being saved.

—⁂—

*Dear Lord who saves me from sin, you have forever changed me.
I remember when my mixture of insecurity and arrogance bubbled
out in the ways I mistreated others. That's not the way I want to
be. My prayer is for a disposition like Jesus. My plea is that you
will treat everyone with love and kindness through me. Amen.*

Just Be You

For you created my inmost being;
you knit me together in my mother's womb.
I praise you because I am fearfully and wonderfully made;
your works are wonderful,
I know that full well.

Psalm 139:13

Wayne Gretsky, the retired hockey star, is nicknamed "The Great One" because of his amazing ability to play hockey like no one else. But did you know that when Gretsky was growing up, he wanted to be a baseball player, not a hockey player? Fortunately, he was smart enough to play the sport God designed him to play rather than the one he first wanted to play.

If I announced to you, "Everybody is different," you would say, "Well, that's pretty obvious." But it's really a significant truth. God made each of us to be different both in our bodies and in our souls. Have you asked God who you are? What task has he designed you to do well? Are you living that out by being you?

Don't compare yourself to others. Don't try to be Wayne Gretsky or Bill Gates or your cousin Pete. Be the best teacher, salesman, counselor, or business consultant you can be for God. Just be you.

Thank you for making me the way you did. Even though there are things about me I would like to change, I trust you, Lord. I am unique. Help me to love myself as you love me and to be myself as you made me. Amen.

First, Last, and Forever

"Father,
hallowed be your name,
your kingdom come."
Jesus, in Luke 11:2

When Jesus' followers asked him to teach them to pray, he began with a sample prayer. Why? Because the most important lesson of effective praying is to start with God! Some of us start with ourselves: "I need this—I want your help—I want you, God, to do the following." Instead, the prayer that gets God's attention is the one beginning with his name. We are told to address him as "Father." That is stunning. In other religions God is portrayed as distant and difficult. But Jesus is telling his followers that we are to talk to him as our father.

When we start with God, we acknowledge up front that prayer is on his terms and not our terms. Starting our prayers with God means we are agreeing in advance to submit to God's will. It means we are agreeing that he is good and right—even when his will is different from ours.

Our Father, you are first. Prayer is not about me; it's about you. You have asked me to pray to you. Prayer to anyone else makes no sense. You are God and can hear the simultaneous prayers of millions of us and answer every one. You are bigger and better than all my best and highest words… so I'm not very good at offering adequate praise. Therefore, I'll just say simply, Our Father, you are God—first, last, and forever. Amen.

Free to Speak My Mind

Let us then approach the throne of grace with confidence, so that we may receive mercy and find grace to help us in our time of need.

Hebrews 4:16

Sooner or later it happens to all of us. Life's pressures build up, and we find ourselves facing extraordinary problems. Suddenly the needs are greater than ordinary people can bear. Is it really possible to have confidence in God during such times?

Hebrews 4:16 says yes. We are to approach God with confidence. The original Greek word *parresia* meant "the freedom to say whatever you want to say." When we have confidence, we have the freedom to stand in front of a group and give a speech or to ask the boss for a raise.

But it goes further than that. Whatever your need is, you have the freedom to speak directly to God himself and know that he will hear your need. You have the confidence to go right to the top, to talk to the boss, to speak to God himself!

Through Jesus Christ my Savior, I come into your presence, Lord God. I am a sinner and know I am not worthy to speak to you or ask for anything. When I should be shaking before your throne, I have confidence because I come at your invitation. I tell you boldly all that is on my heart and dare to ask you to hear my pleas and meet my needs. Amen.

Same Sermon Rerun

———❧❧———

Do not merely listen to the word,
and so deceive yourselves. Do what it says.

James 1:22

Everyone liked the new young pastor. They were impressed with the mature insights in his first sermon. He used interesting illustrations and made relevant applications. All in all, it was an excellent sermon, and they looked forward to the next one.

To their great surprise, the next Sunday he preached pretty much the same sermon. People thought it a bit odd, but they didn't want to be critical. After all, as a new pastor, he was really busy.

The third Sunday brought yet another rerun. The church board held an emergency session. They called in the new pastor and asked if he anticipated having any other sermons in the years to come. He said, "Yes, of course."

"Then why do you keep preaching the same sermon?"

With a warm naiveté the young pastor said, "I figured that when you got around to doing what I said in the first sermon, then I would preach the second sermon."

It isn't enough to just listen to what God says. We need to actually do it!

———❧———

Speak to me, God of wisdom and truth. Speak and I will listen. Speak and I will obey. May I never be content with truth that is only academic. Grow the seeds of your words into the fruit of righteousness in my life today. I want to be like Jesus, in whose name I pray. Amen.

Good Gifts

—◦◦◦—

"Which of you fathers, if your son asks for a fish, will give him
a snake instead? Or if he asks for an egg, will give him a scorpion?
If you then, though you are evil, know how to give good gifts
to your children, how much more will your Father in heaven give the
Holy Spirit to those who ask him!"

Jesus, in Luke 11:11-13

Did you know God welcomes our requests and desires to give us good gifts?
He wants to answer our prayers, and he desires to say "yes."

Jesus uses human fathers as an example. Most fathers are good to their
children. What dad takes his child to McDonalds, and when the child asks
for a fish sandwich, he gives him a McSnake? Or, if he says, "I want an Egg
McMuffin," he gives him a McScorpion instead? No father would do that.
And if human fathers are good, God is a million times better. He gives us
the best of the best.

Listen to this! At the moment a person becomes a Christian, God gives the
Holy Spirit to come and live inside that person. This is the best gift God has
to give—and proof he is the kind of father who is generous and good.

◦◦◦

*Father! (I love to call you my Father!) How good you are—always
protecting from the worst and giving the best. Thank you for your Holy
Spirit living in me. And thank you for every other gift as well. Amen.*

Learning Contentment

—⟨⟨⟨⟨◈⟩⟩⟩⟩—

I know what it is to be in need, and I know what it is to have plenty.
I have learned the secret of being content in any and every situation,
whether well fed or hungry, whether living in plenty or in want.

Philippians 4:12

Some people in our culture have lived with very little. Henry David Thoreau moved into a shack by Walden Pond to enjoy the contentment of living with little. His experience was immortalized in his book *Walden*. During the Great Depression in the 1930s many people lost everything and were forced to live in poverty.

Few of us today live at the baseline minimum, but all of us struggle with achieving contentment. What is contentment? The acceptance of a situation with peace and without regret.

The apostle Paul suffered persecution throughout his ministry, yet he wrote, "I have *learned*...to be content." And that's the secret: contentment is learned; it doesn't come naturally.

True contentment is adjusting what we *want* to fit what we have, instead of trying to adjust what we *have* to fit what we want. Have you, like St. Paul, learned contentment? It can change your life!

∽✑∾

*My Rock, I rely on you. You alone can meet my needs and make me
content. I am still learning to be content with what I have instead of
discontent with what I want. Often I think that I need more to make
me okay. Satisfy my soul to be content with little or much. Amen.*

Love That Does

——◆⟨✿⟩◆——

Dear children, let us not love with words
or tongue but with actions and truth.
1 John 3:18

On July 29, 2002, nine coal miners were rescued from 240 feet under the ground near Somerset, Pennsylvania. They had been trapped for 77 hours. During those three full days underground, all were aware they would likely die down there. They shared the one sandwich they had and, before their batteries ran out, wrote good-bye notes to their families. They tied themselves together so they could die together and be found together. When forty-three-year-old Randy Fogel started to shiver and experienced tightness in his chest, the other eight men, fearing he was suffering from hypothermia, surrounded him and took turns hugging him and each other.

As these rugged miners huddled together in the darkness, I doubt they whispered the words, "I love you," to each other. But they did love each other—with actions more than words.

And that's how the Bible tells us to love...as God loved us. And his love took the ultimate action. He sent his Son to die, so we may live!

——◆◇◆——

Loving Lord, I know you love me—because you say so and because you show so. As much as I love to hear you say you love me, I know your love from the way you treat me. You hold me. You heal me. You feed me. You keep me warm. But, most of all, you gave me Jesus. Amen.

The Main Message

—⚬◈◈⚬—

God so loved the world that he gave his one and only Son, that
whoever believes in him shall not perish but have eternal life.
John 3:16

Did you know that many of our common everyday expressions come from
the New Testament? We hear people talk about someone being a "good
Samaritan" or a "prodigal son." Or, someone is described as being willing
to "go the second mile" or "turn the other cheek." We say, "Isn't she the salt
of the earth?" or, "That's a case of the blind leading the blind." The Bible
has had a greater impact on our country and culture than many people
realize.

But the Bible is far more than that. We must never forget the main message
of the Bible—that God sent his Son to die for us. God invites us to believe
in Jesus as our Savior and Lord and promises that he will forgive our sin
and give us eternal life. The Bible is like a Gift Certificate of Eternal Life.
But like all gift certificates, it needs to be accepted and cashed in to get the
benefits.

⚬◈⚬

*Author of the Bible, your book is the lamp to my feet and the light
to my path. Encourage me to read and remember your words. I
love the Bible's stories and truth. I want the vocabulary of the Bible
woven into my thoughts and conversations. Most of all, I believe the
message of salvation and receive your gift of eternal life. Amen.*

Jesus Shining Like the Sun

———◆⊙⊙◆———

As Jesus was praying, the appearance of his face changed,
and his clothes became as bright as a flash of lightning.
Luke 9:29

One day Jesus took his three best friends up on a mountain for a prayer retreat. What happened on that mountaintop astounded Peter, John, and James. They had seen him perform spectacular miracles, but nothing prepared them for what they saw that day on the mountain. It was almost as if Jesus had been wearing a human disguise that was suddenly stripped away and they saw him the way he looks in heaven. The Bible says that Jesus' face "shone like the sun" (Matthew 17:2). They could still recognize him, but the change was startling!

Think of it this way. One day you're lying on a hospital bed awaiting surgery. In walks a doctor who seems vaguely familiar. He introduces himself as your former newspaper boy. You're shocked. You see the resemblance, but you can hardly imagine it's the same person.

That's nothing compared to Jesus' transformation. His friends saw a preview of heaven itself. They were in the glorious presence of Jesus!

∼⧼∽

*My Brilliant Lord, I have read about you in the Bible and
experienced you in my life. I have seen artists' pictures and dreamed
of your appearance. I can only imagine what you will look like when
I see you in heaven. You will be brighter than the sun. I know I will
be amazed. I will be thrilled to see you face to face, Jesus. Amen.*

What's Your Number One?

"You still lack one thing. Sell everything you have and give to the poor, and you will have treasure in heaven. Then come, follow me."

Luke 18:22

A rich young man once came to Jesus, asking what he had to do to inherit eternal life. He had kept all the Ten Commandments, he said, but he felt something was missing.

Jesus' answer was shocking then, and it still is today. Was Jesus saying we must sell everything we have to go to heaven? If so, many of us would rather not go. The usual response to this teaching is to suggest that Jesus didn't mean what he said. But I think he did. The reason was simple. The young man said he kept the Ten Commandments, but he really didn't. Money was his god—his number one. If it came down to a choice between God and money, money won out.

For many of us, it's the same. Money is our god. For others it's a job; for some it's a relationship. The principle is simple. In order for us to have treasure in heaven, *anything* more important than God has to go.

You are my Leader; I am your follower. You are the Boss; I work for you. You own everything; I am your manager. Jesus, it would be hard to sell everything. I really like what I have. But whatever it costs; whatever you ask. You are Number One. Amen.

A Satisfied Soul

❦

"I tell you the truth…no one who has left home or wife or brothers or parents or children for the sake of the kingdom of God will fail to receive many times as much in this age and, in the age to come, eternal life."
Jesus, in Luke 18:29-30

David Livingstone was a successful English physician who left a lucrative career to explore Africa and open the continent for Christian missionaries. The price was huge. He never became rich. He was mauled by a lion, leaving him with a crippled arm. He suffered tropical diseases and was away from his family for long periods.

When no one had heard from him for a long time, the English journalist Henry Stanley traveled to Africa to locate Livingstone and to ask him about the sacrifices he had made. Dr. Livingstone responded by saying, "Sacrifices? I never made a sacrifice in all my life."

God had done something supernatural in Livingstone's life, giving him something better than money and fame. God satisfied his soul and made him happy.

If you ever visit Westminster Abbey in London, you will see the tombs of kings and queens and hundreds of other great English heroes. But the most famous tomb of all, located in the most prominent place, is the tomb of David Livingstone.

God takes care of those who live for him.

❦

Satisfy me, Great God, so that no sacrifice seems sacrificial.
Grant the delight of giving everything I am and have to you. Amen.

Better Every Day

---◆◆◆---

Make every effort to add to your faith goodness; and to
goodness, knowledge; and to knowledge, self-control; and to
self-control, perseverance; and to perseverance, godliness;
and to godliness, brotherly kindness; and to brotherly
kindness, love. For if you possess these qualities in increasing
measure, they will keep you from being ineffective and
unproductive in your knowledge of our Lord Jesus Christ.

2 Peter 1:5–8

After World War II, the words *Made in Japan* became synonymous with junk.
But in the decades to follow, a revolution took place until *Made in Japan*
became synonymous with the highest quality of automobiles, cameras, and
electronics. How did that transformation take place? There's a Japanese
word, *kaizen,* that refers to a manufacturing approach called "Total Quality
Control." *Kaizen* calls for constant improvement. Every day brings at least
one tiny improvement. Every day increases the quality of a product. Over
years and decades the results can be revolutionary.

St. Peter's wise advice suggests that we can *kaizen* our Christian lives bit by bit
and day by day as we practice "Total Quality Control." If we do, I think we'll
find that over years and decades the results in our lives will be as revolutionary
as the turnaround in manufacturing quality was to Japanese products.

~∽⌖∽~

*Today, Holy Spirit, work your grace in my life to make me better than
yesterday. Show your goodness, knowledge, self-control, perseverance,
godliness, kindness, and love in my words and deeds. Amen.*

Peace in the Storm

———◆◆◆———

"Peace I leave with you, my peace I give you....
Do not let your hearts be troubled and do not be afraid."
John 14:27

There's a wonderful old story about an art contest for the painting best depicting peace. The judges narrowed it down to two finalists. One picture was a serene lake, tranquil and idyllic...the kind of picture that calms your emotions as you look at it. But that painting came in second in the contest. The winner was a painting of a raging storm. Looking at it, you could almost hear the wind howling and feel the driving rain. Everything was bleak and tumultuous. But if you looked closely, there in the midst of the storm was a bird sitting on a nest tucked in a crevice of a cliff. The little bird was completely at peace.

The point of the painting was simple: peace is not the absence of problems or conflict; peace is calm in the midst of the storm.

We all have a shot at personal peace in our lives. Jesus said we will always have storms in this life. But peace can be ours in the storm.

◆◆◆

Lord of nature and all of life, the storm has been howling. Between the winds that blow me over and the rain that soaks me through, I wonder if I will even survive. I need peace. I'm looking for that quiet place. Bring me to that crevice in the rock and surround me with yourself. Amen.

Evil Out; Good In

❦

"When an evil spirit comes out of a man, it goes…seeking rest
and does not find it. Then it says, 'I will return to the house
I left.' Then it goes and takes seven other spirits more wicked
than itself, and they go in and live there. And the final condition
of that man is worse than the first."

Jesus, in Luke 11:24, 26

For every problem, weakness, or addiction that causes us to suffer, there
seems to be a self-help book or support group to help us deal with it. Most
of us believe that getting rid of the bad stuff will solve most of our problems.
If we can stop gambling, cease lying, or conquer our addictions, then life
will be good.

But will getting rid of the bad stuff solve anything? Jesus' point was plain
and simple: bad must be replaced by good. Getting rid of bad friends is not
enough. If you don't replace them with good friends, you risk getting the
bad friends back with even more bad buddies. The principle is to kick Satan
out, but let Jesus in. When hatred leaves, love must enter. When addiction
is kicked out, loyalty and zeal for God must take its place.

Solving our problems and getting rid of evil are not enough in themselves.
God and good must fill and control our lives in their place.

❦

Almighty God, deliver me from evil.
Fill me with good. In Jesus' name, amen.

In Balance

———◦❀❀◦———

So then, let us not be like others, who are asleep,
but let us be alert and self-controlled.

1 Thessalonians 5:6

Columbia University did an interesting experiment a generation ago to test the self-control of four-year-olds. Children were seated at a table with two pieces of candy in front of them and were told to wait ten minutes for the teacher to return. They were also told that if they didn't eat the candy during those ten minutes, when the teacher returned, they would be given five pieces of candy. During the ten-minute wait, some of the children touched the candy, some looked anxious and frustrated, and some gave in and ate the two pieces even though it meant they wouldn't be given the five pieces later.

The children were followed over the next thirty years, and interesting facts emerged. Those who demonstrated the greatest self-control had higher SAT scores, the boys had fewer run-ins with the law, and the girls were less likely to become pregnant as teenagers.

Having the self-discipline to subject our passions to God, the Bible, and to the healthy influence of others will help keep our passions focused and in balance.

———◦❀◦———

Preserve me from carelessness. Strengthen my discipline and self-control so I don't sacrifice tomorrow on the altar of today. You are the God who always thinks things through and wants us to pray and think about the future before we act in the present. Give me balance like Jesus. Amen.

The Long Haul Perspective

"Blessed is the man whom God corrects;
so do not despise the discipline of the Almighty.
For he wounds, but he also binds up;
he injures, but his hands also heal."

Job 5:17–18

The annoying thing about the crooked Russian olive trees we planted in our backyard was that their trunks grew more sideways than upward. Some were so low to the ground that I could hardly mow under them. I remember thinking, *Why can't you grow straight like an oak?* I tried trimming them, but that didn't help. The only way to change a naturally crooked Russian olive is to rope it and stake it for a very long time, perhaps for the whole life of the tree.

People are even harder to straighten out than crooked trees. We are born with a natural bent toward sin. God may chop off a few branches from time to time (which hurts), but without the slow, long-term training of roping and staking, we won't grow in the right direction. We'll spring right back to our crooked shape.

That's why we need to persevere and hang in there for the long haul, remembering that God disciplines and trains us because he loves us. Give God the time to get the job done right!

Straighten me out, God. Grow me tall. Trim my branches. Bend my limbs. Be gentle so I will not snap but be firm to shape me as you want me to be. Amen.

Grabbing the Hand of God

―――◦✦◦―――

It is by grace you have been saved, through faith.
Ephesians 2:8

Imagine what it would be like to fall off a ship and be drowning in the North Atlantic. Someone sees you, calls the Coast Guard, and they send a rescue helicopter. You can hear the beating sound getting closer and closer until the helicopter is directly overhead. As you frantically tread water, you see a line drop out of the side of it, and a diver is lowered to within a few feet of you. He reaches down to you and says, "Grab my hand."

Do you hesitate and wonder if he has the proper diving credentials? Do you worry whether the helicopter is air worthy or the pilot is qualified to conduct ocean rescues? You don't know these things, but there is no time to find out. You have to make an instant judgment. If you believe and trust the diver, you reach up and grab his hand and are lifted to safety.

That's what faith is. Faith is grabbing the hand of God. Faith is taking him at his word. Faith trusts him. It's the only way to be saved.

―◦✦◦―

Savior of sinners, there is no doubt you are fully qualified. There is no one else in the universe who can rescue us from sin and eternal death but you. I trust you. I reach out and grab your hand to save me from today's problems and for eternity in heaven. All through Jesus. Amen.

Worried and Upset

———◆❀◆———

"Martha, Martha...you are worried and upset about many things,
but only one thing is needed. Mary has chosen what is better."
Jesus, in Luke 10:41–42

On his way to Jerusalem, Jesus stopped at the home of his friends Mary and
Martha. Mary sat listening at Jesus' feet, while Martha busied herself in the
kitchen. Then Martha complained to Jesus, "Don't you care that my sister
has left me with all of the work? Tell her to help me!"

Martha was a good person trying to do the right thing. She meant well, but
she had lost focus. The pressure of being overwhelmed with all there was to
do built until she burst out in anger. Jesus explained that Martha needed to
put first things first. There was only one priority, and that was Jesus.

This prescription applies to us. We need to stop rushing around and spend
time with Jesus. If we make Jesus our highest priority, our lives will have
purpose and focus, and we can trust *him* with the things and the people we
cannot control.

———❧———

*Jesus, you can call me "Martha" because I get worried and upset. It's not
that I don't care or don't want to listen to you...I'm just so busy. Help
me to slow down, stop what I'm doing, and trust you more. Amen.*

More than Tinkering

❧

Men of Issachar, who understood the times
and knew what Israel should do.
1 Chronicles 12:32

Charles Steinmetz, a brilliant electrical engineer, designed and built the electrical generators for Henry Ford's first factory in Dearborn, Michigan, making the automobile assembly line possible and profitable and Henry Ford a very rich man.

One day the power went down. The plant mechanics worked frantically but couldn't fix the problem. Finally Henry Ford himself called in Charles Steinmetz. For the next several hours, Steinmetz tinkered with motors, switches, and wires. Then he threw the switch, power was restored, and the assembly line resumed production.

Steinmetz sent Henry Ford a bill for $10,000—an astonishing amount of money in those days. Henry Ford was offended and refused to pay it. "Why would I pay you $10,000 for a few hours of tinkering around?" Steinmetz revised his invoice and resubmitted it: *For tinkering around on the motors, $10. For knowing where to tinker, $9,990. Total: $10,000.* Henry Ford paid the bill.

Exercising our talents and doing what we're good at is worth about $10. But knowing how to do what we are good at in such a way that it brings glory to God, *that's* worth $9,990.

∽

It's wisdom that I need. You've taught me much in life, my Lord. I've learned a lot, and I know a lot. But those around me need wisdom more than knowledge. Guide me to know what to do and to do what is right and good. Amen.

Faith. Faith. And More Faith.

For in the gospel a righteousness from God is revealed,
a righteousness that is by faith from first to last,
just as it is written: "The righteous will live by faith."

Romans 1:17

Without faith there's no such thing as being a Christian. Faith is the foundation. It's a personal belief in Jesus. Faith is committing to Jesus as the Boss and the Leader of our lives.

Think of it this way. If you need a knee replacement, you go to an orthopedic surgeon who performs the surgery necessary to give you a new knee. Afterwards, the surgeon prescribes physical therapy that will enable you to take full advantage of the new joint. If you try to live the Christian life but don't start with faith, it would be like going for physical therapy but skipping the surgery. Without the surgery first, the exercises won't be of much help. Without faith, going through the motions of the Christian life won't make much difference.

God has given us all we need to live a life of godliness, but we have to take advantage of what God has given. It all begins with faith!

Giver of salvation, faith is believing you and believing in you. Faith is first. Faith is last. And faith must permeate everything in between. Look into my heart. Read my lips. Feel my faith. My trust in you is first and last and always. Everything in my life is founded on faith. Amen.

God on My Side

---•◦⟨⟨⟩⟩◦•---

Let us throw off everything that hinders and the sin that
so easily entangles, and let us run with perseverance the
race marked out for us. Let us fix our eyes on Jesus, the author
and perfecter of our faith, who for the joy that was set before
him endured the cross, scorning its shame, and sat down
at the right hand of the throne of God.

Hebrews 12:1–2

Did you know God wants us to be winners? He sees life as a race, and he is
determined to make all those who believe in him into winners.

Some people think God is an enemy and he works against us. They envision
him as some terrible ogre up in the sky who is always trying to trip us up.
When something good happens they keep looking around the corner,
wondering when God is going to turn the good into evil. How alien that is
to the words of the Bible.

The truth is, God is always on the side of those who have put their faith
and trust in Jesus. When you believe that, you see all of life differently. It's
a transforming truth to know that God is continually committed to your
success, and he will do what is necessary to make you into a winner.

∾⟨⟩∾

*Jesus, I'm running with your name on my jersey. Give me strength
and endurance to keep going to the finish line. Keep me focused
on you and my eyes off unworthy distractions. Amen.*

AUGUST

An Investment in Eternity

❧

There before me was a great multitude that
no one could count, from every nation, tribe, people
and language, standing before the throne.
Revelation 7:9

Imagine if someone were to whisper in your ear what the Security Exchange people call "insider information." It's information that says if you purchase a certain stock, it will skyrocket in value in the weeks ahead. Your informant tells you it's a sure thing. In fact, it's predicted that within ten years you will get a thousand dollars' return for every dollar you invest. What would you do? If you trust the informant, you could scrounge up every dollar possible and invest it in that stock.

Compare that to God's dream of people coming to him by trusting in his Son, Jesus, for the forgiveness of their sins. The difference is that God can actually see and know the future. The Bible gives us "insider information" that God will win millions of people to Jesus Christ and that he's going to do it whether we invest or not.

So why not be a participant in an investment that will last for all eternity?

❧

God of the future and Lord of the universe, you have shown us a glimpse of tomorrow when you will gather into heaven speakers of every language, persons of every race, and citizens of every country. What a grand inclusive gathering that will be. Today I will live with tomorrow in mind, investing in those who will populate eternity. Amen.

Who Is Jesus?

"But what about you?" he asked. "Who do you say I am?" Simon
Peter answered, "You are the Christ, the Son of the living God."
Matthew 16:15-16

"Who is this Jesus?" was a question on the lips of many who observed him.
In some ways he seemed so ordinary—a local boy from Nazareth, a man
whose appearance didn't stand out in the crowd. He laughed and cried, ate
and slept like everyone else. Yet he also was completely out of the ordinary
with his amazing miracles, articulate arguments, and keen intellect. Some
days he looked and sounded like a Jewish carpenter. Other days he acted
and talked like God himself. When asked to identify himself or give an
explanation, his answers were often hard to understand.

Jesus revealed himself little by little. He had a plan and a timeline. He knew
he had come to earth with a purpose. As the time for his crucifixion grew
nearer, he revealed himself more clearly to those closest to him. But even
they had trouble grasping what he was telling them.

Today we can read the whole story in the Bible, so we have the benefit of
hindsight. Who do you believe Jesus is?

---

*I know who you are! You are Jesus, my Savior, my Lord, and my
Friend. Every day I yearn to know you more. May I be closer to
you today than ever before. May I understand you more fully.
You are the Christ, the Son of the Living God. Amen.*

Childlike Faith

—◦⦅֎⦆◦—

"I tell you the truth, unless you change and become like little
children, you will never enter the kingdom of heaven. Therefore,
whoever humbles himself like this child is the greatest in the
kingdom of heaven."
Matthew 18:3–4

Jesus had the amazing ability to turn ordinary situations into teaching
opportunities. One day his disciples asked him who was the greatest in the
kingdom of heaven. When a small neighbor boy wandered into the house
where they were talking, Jesus knew they were thinking, *Get this child out of here!
We're having an important conversation with our teacher.*

But Jesus called the child over to him and sat the little boy down immediately
to his right, clearly communicating that the place of honor went to the
child. Jesus' answer wasn't difficult to grasp. If they wanted to be great, they
shouldn't seek the place of honor but should instead become like children
who couldn't care less about social prestige. Jesus was telling them to become
like the neighbor boy in his simplicity and humility.

Unless we humble ourselves and come to Jesus in simple childlike faith, we
will never enter the kingdom of heaven.

～◦～

*Lord Jesus, you are the greatest. I'm a nobody. Most people in my town don't
know who I am. My ambition is not to be famous but to be near you. Like
a child, I come to you with love and devotion. Whether you call me to be
world-famous or world-forgotten is totally up to you. Amen.*

Living with Regret

———— ✦ ————

"Forget the former things;
do not dwell on the past.
See, I am doing a new thing!...
I am making a way in the desert
and streams in the wasteland."
Isaiah 43:18–19

Everyone has regrets. Prisons are full of inmates who regret the crimes they committed...or at least regret getting caught. Divorce courts echo with the stories of marriages people wish they had never entered.

There are plenty of examples of regrets in the Bible. Moses regretted his disobedience to God that prevented him from entering the Promised Land. King David regretted his adultery. Peter regretted his denial of Jesus.

The reality is that our past is always part of our present. We must deal with our yesterdays by acknowledging who we are, what we've done, and then live the life we have for God from now on. A rabbi once said, "At the end of your life God will not ask you why you weren't Moses. He'll ask you why you weren't you."

Who you are includes all of your abilities, your successes, *and* your regrets. No one can change yesterday. But we do have a choice about tomorrow!

———— ✦ ————

My God, you know what I've said. You know what I've done.
You know all that I am. There are lots of regrets. I wish I could
go back and do things over again. But I am who I am, and you
believe in me. Let me be all you want me to be today. Amen.

What I Am Worth

You are not your own; you were bought at a price.
Therefore honor God with your body.
1 Corinthians 6:19-20

What if I held up a pen and asked you, "What do you think this is worth?" If it's a Bic, you might say, "One dollar." If it's a Mont Blanc, it would be worth hundreds of dollars. If I then added that this pen used to belong to Abraham Lincoln or John Kennedy and was used to sign one of the most important documents in American history, you might guess it was worth ten thousand dollars. What's the difference? All are used to write. The value is in who owned the pen.

The Bible tells us that those who believe in Jesus belong to God. When you are owned by God, your value is transformed. You are something special— even if you don't always feel that way. If you have accepted Jesus Christ as your Savior and Lord, you are a Christian. You belong to God, and that is a very good thing!

Owner of all things, your wealth is infinitely beyond my comprehension. You created the heavens and the earth. The galaxies are counted among your possessions. I am so small and insignificant. There are times when I feel so worthless and completely unimportant. To think you valued me enough to send your Son and to realize I am your prized relationship—it is wonderful beyond words. Today I acknowledge that I belong to you! Amen.

Gifted!

There are different kinds of gifts, but the same Spirit. There are different kinds of service, but the same Lord. There are different kinds of working, but the same God works all of them.

1 Corinthians 12:4–6

God gives gifts to every one of his followers. These gifts fit into two basic categories: speaking and serving. Some people have both kinds of gifts. Some only have one kind of gift. But we all are gifted!

What is your gift? What are you good at? Teaching? Helping? Giving? Leading? Whatever God has made you good at is what you should do to bless others in the name of Jesus. Maybe your gift is teaching Sunday school or tutoring children struggling in school. Maybe your gift is advocating for the poor, helping the unemployed find jobs, or running a corporation.

Whatever you are good at, whatever God has gifted you to do, put your gift to use. Jesus blessed and helped the thief on the cross next to him right up until he took his last breath. Use your gift to serve others—and make it a way of life.

Giver of gifts, thank you for those you have given to me. Protect me from envy of the gifts of others and encourage me to delight in the gifts you have chosen just for me. My desire is to grow the gifts you have given and use them to honor you and serve others in Jesus' name. Amen.

A Miraculous Outcome

—⟡—

Be merciful to me, Lord, for I am faint;
O Lord, heal me, for my bones are in agony.
My soul is in anguish.
How long, O Lord, how long?
Psalm 6:2-3

Nathan Christiansen, a Wisconsin high school student, lost control of the family car trying to avoid a deer. At the hospital he was diagnosed with a broken leg, spinal cord damage, a collapsed lung, numerous body lacerations, and a fracture to the C-4 vertebra, putting him in danger of at least partial, if not full, paralysis. His chances of survival were 1 in 100.

For two weeks, Nathan prayed daily that God would heal him. One night, as he lay in bed, he sensed a popping in his neck. The next day X-rays showed the vertebrae to be healed. Three months later Nathan was cleared to resume participation in football, wrestling, track, and field!

Sometimes God says yes through a miracle and sometimes through the skills of a surgeon. Other times he says no. But we are still invited to ask for healing. Just as we trust the surgeon when consenting to an operation, so we trust God when praying for healing. But our faith must be in God—not the outcome.

—⟡—

Great Physician, restore me with your supernatural touch. Cure the disease. Relieve the pain. Make me whole. Knowing that you may say yes or no and trusting your final decision, I pray for your divine healing in the powerful name of Jesus Christ. Amen.

The Other Side of Suffering

❧

To this you were called, because Christ suffered for you, leaving you
an example, that you should follow in his steps.

1 Peter 2:21

I have visited the church in China and fellowshipped with these dear fellow
Christians. Because they have gone through such great suffering, they have
much to teach us. One of the most profound lessons I've learned is that
suffering is an inevitable, essential part of the Christian life. And while that
seems to be bleak news, it reminds me of the way Jesus faced his death on
the cross—with unflinching realism. There's something else our Chinese
friends say: that on the other side of suffering and difficulty, God gives us
a new chapter, a new season of good, of peace, of comfort, of special gifts
and blessings.

We all experience suffering. But Jesus offers hope—that he will go through
it with us and guarantee his presence and goodness on the other side. God's
perfect ending will be added to every Christian's true story.

❧

*Savior who suffered for me, help me to understand what it means to suffer
for you. Not that I desire problems or pain. My inclinations are toward a
life of comfort and ease. But I will not run from suffering to which you call
me or pain which you approve for me to experience. Just keep me strong
and faithful until you bring me safely to peace on the other side. Amen.*

All of Us Who Stumble

We all stumble in many ways.
James 3:2

I have a little note in my desk drawer that says, *Babe Ruth struck out thirteen hundred thirty times.* And that doesn't include another thirty strikeouts during World Series games. It's a reminder to me that striking out is not a disqualification for coming back to the plate. If the standard for teaching was perfection, there wouldn't be a single teacher.

James the Bible writer wants us to know that even though we make mistakes, we aren't disqualified from influencing the lives of others for God. In fact, most of us learn best from teachers who admit their mistakes. We can't identify with teachers who pretend they always get everything right and are far superior to their students. We want to learn from people who are like us—teachers who walk where we walk and stumble where we stumble. A wise teacher explains, "This is the way you stumble, and this is the way God helps you to go on."

I have stumbled, Lord. My strikeouts are so many that I've lost count. Getting up and trying again seems silly if not dangerous when I trip so often. Pick me up, loving God. Set me on my feet. Point me in the right direction. Hold my hand and help me keep my balance. In you I have hope to walk steadfastly, serve effectively, and believe wholeheartedly. This I pray in the name of Jesus, who walks by my side. Amen.

A Heart for God

❧❧❧

The Lord has sought out a man after his own heart
and appointed him leader of his people.
1 Samuel 13:14

God wants us to be women and men of faith. Not faith that is tacked on to the rest of life, but faith that controls everything and leaves old beliefs behind. Faith that is convinced God is the God of everything—from the big stories in the news to the smallest details of our lives. People who have that kind of faith are easy to spot. It shows in the way they live.

Unfortunately, people who have a heart for God don't always do what is right. They can disappoint or disillusion us. That's how I've always felt about King David in the Bible. It irritates me that David committed adultery, lied, and murdered to cover up what he did, yet the Bible describes him as "a man after God's own heart."

But I think I finally have it figured out. David's heart for God was greater than his sin. He was overwhelmed with sorrow when he failed the God he loved. Not only did he repent, but he learned his lesson and didn't do it again.

That's the kind of heart for God I want to have!

❧

*I love you with all my heart, Father God. More than words can
say, I am committed to you. When my devotion dwindles or my love
loses passion, I rush back to you—with all of my heart. Amen.*

Following Jesus

———◦❧❧◦———

As Jesus was walking beside the Sea of Galilee, he saw two brothers,
Simon called Peter and his brother Andrew. They were casting a net
into the lake, for they were fishermen. "Come, follow me," Jesus
said, "and I will make you fishers of men." At once they left their
nets and followed him.

Matthew 4:18-20

Peter was a fisherman in first-century Palestine, just as his father and
grandfather had been before him. Peter had always expected to be a
fisherman. But he wanted something more. When Jesus extended his
invitation to "Follow me," how did Peter go about making that decision?

First, Peter was keenly aware of what others had to say about Jesus. He had
already checked out Jesus' references. But even more important was the
virtue, genuineness, and integrity Peter could see when he looked Jesus in
the eye. He knew that in Jesus he'd found someone he could follow for the
rest of his life.

When Jesus calls us and asks us to believe in him and follow him, it's only
natural for us to check out his references—to read the Bible and to ask others
about their encounter with Jesus. But it's not until we look Jesus in the eye
and see for ourselves the astonishing power and presence of God that we can
say yes to his call to follow him.

——◦❧◦——

Jesus, I hear your call. I am following you! Amen.

Choosing Contentment

————◦◦◦————

Godliness with contentment is great gain. For we brought nothing into the world, and we can take nothing out of it. But if we have food and clothing, we will be content with that. People who want to get rich fall into temptation and a trap and into many foolish and harmful desires that plunge men into ruin and destruction.

1 Timothy 6:6–9

The American president Calvin Coolidge said, "There is no dignity quite so impressive and no independence quite so important as living within your means." But being content with your means, and living within them, can be very difficult in our culture. For instance, one out of every three American high school students has credit cards, half of them in their own names. And, in one year alone, 94,000 Americans under the age of twenty-five declared bankruptcy.

Contentment, on the other hand, is being able to say, "I may have more or less than others, but I will be content with what I have and live within those limits." It's choosing to enjoy the gifts God gives us, and choosing *not* to constantly compare what we have with what somebody else has.

Choosing contentment can make your life happier and give you a better attitude toward life in general.

————◦◦————

Thank you, Generous God. It is so much more than most people have even if it is less than others have. Shrink my wants to fit your blessings. Free me from debt and greed. Make me content. Amen.

Tapping Into the Power

> May the God of hope fill you with all joy and peace
> as you trust in him, so that you may overflow with hope
> by the power of the Holy Spirit.
>
> *Romans 15:13*

Before Jesus returned to heaven, he told his followers that he would send them help to live the way God wanted them to live. That power source was the Holy Spirit. Ever since, some Christians have tapped into his power, and some have tried to live without it.

Think of it this way. You can run an air conditioner with just the fan, or with the fan and the compressor. If it's a hot day and you only run the fan, all you do is stir up the hot air. The fan can't cool by itself. But if you turn on the compressor with the fan, the air will cool. You need the power of the compressor to change the temperature.

So it is with us. We can live by our own power—just moving the hot air around—or we can tap into the power of the Holy Spirit to get the help we need.

Holy Spirit, fill me with yourself. Let your spiritual power flow in and through me. Deliver me from my weakness and empower me with your strength. I enthusiastically open every part of my life to your presence, boldness, courage, wisdom, and power. As you have poured the life of heaven into saints on earth throughout history, now pour into me. Amen.

The Dream

We have this hope as an anchor for the soul, firm and secure.
Hebrews 6:19

In August 1963 Martin Luther King, Jr., spoke to 250,000 people at the Lincoln Memorial in Washington at the peak of the American Civil Rights Movement. The president's advisers had asked King to tone down the rhetoric so people wouldn't get too riled up, so Dr. King read a carefully prepared speech. As Dr. King turned to sit down, Mahalia Jackson, the famous singer, shouted to him, "The dream, Martin. Tell them about the dream!"

King turned back to the microphone and spoke stirring words of hope in his now famous "I have a dream" speech: "I have a dream that my four little children will one day live in a nation where they will not be judged by the color of their skin but by the content of their character...."

What is your dream? A better job? That you will survive cancer? That someday you will marry? That you will be able to birth a child?

If you base your hope on Jesus, he will not disappoint.

God of dreamers, thank you for the dreams you have given to and fulfilled through leaders of past generations. Now you are giving new dreams to my generation. May I dream big. May my hopes run high. May my thoughts and words come from you. May your dreams be my dreams and then may you make these dreams come true. Amen.

The Mighty Men

———— ·◦◦◦· ————

As one of the three mighty men, Eleazar was with David when they
taunted the Philistines gathered at Pas Dammim for battle. Then
the men of Israel retreated, but he stood his ground and struck
down the Philistines till his hand grew tired and froze to the sword.
The Lord brought about a great victory that day.

2 Samuel 23:9-10

Around 1000 BC King David recognized thirty of his best soldiers as an
elite corps. These "Mighty Men" were competent, godly, and fiercely loyal
to their king. Three of them were identified in the Bible as being the most
courageous soldiers of all. Eleazar was one of the three.

One day, while facing their Philistine enemies, brave Eleazar stood alone
and fought the Philistines until they were defeated and he was exhausted.
Eleazar's fellow soldiers, who had run away, didn't return to the battlefield
until it was all over and the Philistines lay dead.

It takes great courage to stay when others leave. It takes great courage to stay
when you are outnumbered. It takes great courage to keep going when you
are ready to drop from exhaustion. God honored Eleazar's courage with a
military victory that was humanly impossible.

We need people like Eleazar today: people who will stand and courageously
fight for the cause of God, even if everyone else retreats.

∽◦∾

Lord of all life's battles, give me strength when my hand grows tired.
Grant courage to stay in the fight. Win a great victory this day. Amen.

Giving That Costs

❧

"I will not sacrifice to the Lord my God
burnt offerings that cost me nothing."
King David, in 2 Samuel 24:24

King David once tried to buy a piece of property in Israel that he wanted to use as an offering to God. The owner of the property saw it as an opportunity to get in the good graces of his king, so he told him to just take it. But David refused to accept the property without paying for it. He knew that the only truly meaningful gift is one in which you are giving away something that has real value to you.

My father-in-law used to spend one week every summer driving a bus so children could attend Vacation Bible School. You're probably thinking, *Big deal. A lot of people do volunteer work.* But let me explain. My father-in-law got only two weeks of vacation a year, and he gave up half of it to serve others.

Every once in a while, it's a good thing to take something that you consider really valuable and give it away—not for a tax deduction and not for thanks. Doing so might just change your life...for the good.

∼❧∼

*You have sacrificed so much for me, what could I sacrifice for you,
my God? I want to give to you something of value that costs me.
Not to win your favor; not to impress others; not to get anything in
return—I just want to give out of love and gratitude. Amen.*

Grown-Up Birth

"I tell you the truth, no one can see the kingdom
of God unless he is born again."
Jesus, in John 3:3

Nicodemus, a prominent religious leader, was fascinated by Jesus. But he couldn't make sense of Jesus' metaphors and teachings. Just how could a grown-up be reborn? he wanted to know.

Jesus seized the opportunity to teach Nicodemus some profound concepts about a person's relationship with God. He answered, "The truth is that there are two births. The first one is physical and the second one is spiritual. Our mothers give physical birth and the Spirit gives spiritual birth. So don't be surprised when I tell you that you need to be born a second time."

Nicodemus still didn't grasp what Jesus was telling him, but he went home that night with Jesus' words seared into his memory. Nicodemus would be back for more.

And that's how Jesus often works in our lives. He teaches us things along the way, bit by bit. But down the line, we will be able to look back and say, "Wow! So that's what he was teaching me!"

Teacher, sometimes I am slow to understand what you are talking about. But that can be good because I am forced to listen and think to comprehend. May I have the persistence of Nicodemus and keep coming back to you, Jesus, until I know and live all your teachings. Amen.

The Bricks of God

As you come to him, the living Stone—rejected by men but chosen
by God and precious to him—you also, like living stones, are
being built into a spiritual house to be a holy priesthood, offering
spiritual sacrifices acceptable to God through Jesus Christ.

1 Peter 2:4–5

The city of Sparta, one of the city-states of ancient Greece, was one of
the most formidable military powers of its day. To have Sparta as an ally
was a wonderful asset, but to face Sparta as an enemy was a frightening
prospect. A Spartan king once boasted to a visiting monarch that his city was
invincible because the protective walls could not be conquered. The visiting
king couldn't see any walls, so he asked, "Where are the walls that you have
been boasting about?"

The king of Sparta proudly pointed to his soldiers. "These are the walls of
Sparta, every man a brick."

Similarly, the strength of the cause and the church of Jesus Christ is not in
buildings or walls, but in people. We are the ones God uses and counts on
to do his work and accomplish his will in our world. We are the bricks of
God—the church of Jesus Christ.

*Architect of the Church, your design is eternal, and your building
blocks are most unusual. You have chosen me and my Christian
friends. You are building the church of Jesus Christ out of us
ordinary believers. May we be strong and faithful. Amen.*

Tie a Yellow Ribbon

You did not treat me with contempt or scorn. Instead,
you welcomed me as if I were an angel of God.
Galatians 4:14

The song "Tie a Yellow Ribbon 'Round the Old Oak Tree" is based on the story of a man returning home from prison. Unsure whether the woman he loves will accept or reject him, he writes to her. If she can forgive him and welcome him home, he asks her to tie a yellow ribbon around the old oak tree at the entrance to town. That way, when he arrives on the bus, he'll know instantly. If there is no ribbon, he'll just stay on the bus and ride on. When the bus finally pulls into town, the old oak tree not only has one yellow ribbon, but a hundred yellow ribbons tied around it! Not only does she forgive him, she wants him home with all of her heart.

And that's what it will be like for those of us who have given our hearts to Jesus Christ and asked for his forgiveness. Someday he'll welcome us into heaven with a million yellow ribbons!

You haven't told me when I will go to heaven, Lord Jesus. I know it could be today or a long time from now. What you have promised is that you will welcome all who believe in you into your magnificent eternal home. That's me! I believe. I can imagine your welcome. I am looking for those yellow ribbons of heaven. Amen.

Applying the Bible

---◆◈◈◆---

Now the Bereans were of more noble character than
the Thessalonians, for they received the message with great
eagerness and examined the Scriptures every day.

Acts 17:11

When you read a newspaper, you tend to skip over information that doesn't relate to you. You may not read the articles about cars being recalled, typhoons in the Philippines, or earthquakes in China—unless it's the car you own, someone you love is in the Philippines, or your company does business in the earthquake area of China.

That's how it is when we read the Bible. We naturally pay more attention when the words personally apply to our everyday lives.

I recently heard about a couple with a very high percent home mortgage interest rate. Their payment is twice what it would be if they refinanced, but they say they just don't have the time to apply for a lower rate mortgage. They could save tens of thousands of dollars—if they would only apply.

The Bible is powerful, practical, true, and supernatural, but in order to get good from it, we must apply its truths. Don't miss out on God's best. Take the time to apply the Bible to your life.

---◈◈---

*Draw me to your holy Scriptures, Author of the Bible. Give me a mind
and heart for your teaching. May I understand the truth, practice
the principles, and experience the power of your words. My goal is to
recall the lines of the Bible and live them out every day. Amen.*

Dependable Bible

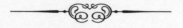

"Heaven and earth will pass away, but my words will never pass away."
Jesus, in Mark 13:31

Since the Bible was written thousands of years ago, how can we trust what we read to really be the Bible? We don't have the original manuscripts. And if our Bibles are translations from other languages, isn't there a danger that there have been a lot of distortions between where God started and what we have today?

These are good questions, but they shouldn't be a reason for worry. Centuries of scholars have worked very hard to get as close to the original as possible, and there are literally thousands of ancient manuscripts. We have every reasonable confidence that our Hebrew and Greek biblical texts today are very, very close to what was originally written.

Besides, if God revealed and inspired his truth in the first place, wouldn't it make sense that he would protect the transmission of that truth so we get the message he wants us to have? We can trust the Bible to be God's inerrant, inspired Word.

There are so many changes going on. Eternal God, I need something that is dependable, sure, predictable, and consistent. Your Bible is exactly what I need. Your words are enduring. Your truth is absolute. Your relevance fits every generation, culture, language, and personal need. May my faith and doctrine, my principles and practices, and my hope and assurance all be based on your holy Scriptures. Amen.

Living Forward

After Job had prayed for his friends, the Lord made him prosperous again and gave him twice as much as he had before. All his brothers and sisters and everyone who had known him before…comforted and consoled him over all the trouble the Lord had brought upon him.…The Lord blessed the latter part of Job's life more than the first.

Job 42:10-12

Many people pray for healing at some point in their lives. But have you ever given much thought as to what it means to be healed?

Job was healthy, wealthy, and wise until Satan tried to take him down. He lost his business, health, friends, and all ten of his children. Then God healed Job. His relationships were reconciled, his business prospered, and he fathered ten more children. But God didn't take him back to the way things used to be. Job suffered unspeakable loss—ten children he loved had died. Healing took him forward but did not restore everything as it had been.

Those who are healed of a thirty-year addiction today don't get to live those years over again. When we experience healing, our wounds are healed, but our scars remain. Healing is not about yesterday—it's about tomorrow. It's about living the life God wants us to live from now on.

God of Yesterday, you have carried me through past troubles. God of Today, you sustain here and now. God of Tomorrow, I look to the future with hope. Amen.

168 Hours Per Week

So whether you eat or drink or whatever you do,
do it all for the glory of God.

1 Corinthians 10:31

There's a huge diversity in people, but there's one thing we all share in common: 168 hours per week. No one has more time than anyone else. Sleep 50-60 hours. Work at least 40 hours. Add in commute time, lunch time, overtime, and extra minutes here and there along the way, and our work-related hours may be as much as a third of all our available hours. A good and healthy attitude toward the work we do will go a long way toward a good and healthy attitude toward all of life.

The Christian attitude is to work with excellence. Doing a good job is good for everyone. Enormous personal satisfaction comes from giving your best—whether others recognize the quality of your work or not. A job well done is good for your employer. But the ultimate reason to do a good job is to make God look good.

*God Who Created All, you are the hardest worker in the universe.
Now you have invited me to my work in your creation, and I desire
to serve you well. May my focus be on you and not on my status or my
title. Sharpen my skills, strengthen my endurance, and give me wisdom
to make good decisions. My highest pay is your pleasure. Amen.*

Doing Good

❦

We are God's workmanship, created in Christ Jesus to do good
works, which God prepared in advance for us to do.

Ephesians 2:10

One of the most important teachings in the Bible is that we cannot rescue
ourselves from sin and eternal death by being good. Receiving salvation
from sin and becoming a Christian is only possible because of the generosity
of God and not because of anything good that we do. In Ephesians 2:8-9
we learn that no matter how hard we try, we can never *earn* an eternal
relationship with God. Salvation comes not by good works, but by faith in
Jesus, who paid the penalty for our sins by his death on the cross.

However, we can't stop there. Ephesians 2:10 says that we are created to
do good works. In fact, one of the proofs that we are really following Jesus
is the presence of good works in our lives. As followers of Jesus, it is our
privilege to demonstrate our faith by the good things we do. Doing good will
never make anyone a Christian, but real Christians will do good.

❦

*After all you've done for me, I delight to do good for you! Lord, I'm not
trying to win your favor or earn forgiveness of sins—I know that's all
from your generous gifts. Now the good I do flows out of your goodness
inside of me. You have so many blessings you want to give through me.
I'm ready and anxious to work hard for you today. In Jesus' name, amen.*

A God for Everyone

This grace was given me: to preach...the unsearchable
riches of Christ, and to make plain to everyone the
administration of this mystery, which for ages past was
kept hidden in God, who created all things.

Ephesians 3:8–9

In the ancient world every nation and tribe had their own gods. The Egyptians had Isis; the Greeks had Zeus; the Romans had Jupiter; and Israel had Yahweh, or Jehovah. Everybody thought their god was better and more powerful than everybody else's god. Most ethnic and religious groups considered themselves superior and everyone else inferior. As a result, ancient religions didn't look for converts. To the contrary, they were exclusive.

That's why it was such a shock when God revealed himself in Jesus as not only the God of Israel, but the God of *all* nations. Paul was stunned when he received the call to preach to *everyone.* God wasn't a local god; he is the Creator of all things. He sent his Son to rescue humans from sin and death. And he offers this salvation to everyone—Jews and Gentiles, rich and poor, Asians, Africans, Europeans, Latin Americans, North Americans, and Native Americans. Everyone who believes and accepts Jesus as Savior receives the rich and eternal blessings of God.

---

*You are the one true God. All others are really not gods at all. You are the
God of all kinds of people. The God of everybody. And, most wonderfully,
you are my God through faith in Jesus Christ my Savior. Amen.*

Say "I Love You"

"Love the Lord your God with all your heart and with all your
soul and with all your strength and with all your mind."
Jesus, in Luke 10:27

There's something powerful and intimate about the words "I love you." And
just as we like to hear those three wonderful words spoken to us, God likes
to hear us say them to him.

You've probably heard the story of the husband who never told his wife that
he loved her. After thirty-eight years of marriage, she finally confronted him.
His explanation? "I told you that I loved you the day we were married. I'll
let you know if anything changes." But that's not good enough in a personal
relationship. And it's not good enough in our relationship with God, either.

When I pray in the morning, I tell God, "I love you!" When I take part in
communion, I silently pray and say, "I love you." When I'm driving alone,
I pray and tell God that I love him.

Telling God that we love him is important. It not only pleases him, it
reminds us of our commitment to him. So why not tell him often? In fact,
why not tell him right now?

Lord God, I love you with all my heart!
I love you with all my soul.
I love you with all my strength.
I love you with all my mind.
Amen.

A Love of Strangers

———◆◆◆◆◆———

Share with God's people who are in need. Practice hospitality.

Romans 12:13

In the first century, there were no hotels as we know them today. Public inns were filthy, dangerous, and immoral. Consequently, Christians opened their homes to other traveling Christians. The Greek word for hospitality combines two words meaning "love of strangers." In other words, we are to be nice to others, whether we know them or not.

This was brought home to me in a personal way one cold, wintry day. My wife, Charleen, and I were driving through a troubled inner-city neighborhood when we spotted a lonely-looking man holding a sign asking for money. As we approached the street corner, all the other cars just drove past. We stopped, and I gave him a ten-dollar bill. When he said, "God bless you," Charleen immediately responded with, "He already has."

That's why we should willingly show hospitality, because God has already blessed us. He has shown love to us, even when we were strangers to God, and he calls us to do the same.

———◆———

Make me a blessing to those in need, just as you have blessed me in all of my needs. O God of love and generosity to the widow, orphan, stranger, and alien, may I see the opportunities to help rather than the dangers of being taken advantage of. May my home, my car, my money, and all I own be instruments of your grace in the journey of others. Just like Jesus. Amen.

The Writing Finger of Jesus

Jesus bent down and started to write on the ground with his finger. When they kept on questioning him, he straightened up and said to them, "If any one of you is without sin, let him be the first to throw a stone at her." Again he stooped down and wrote on the ground.

John 8:6–8

I find it interesting that, even though the New Testament is the story of Jesus, Jesus didn't write any of it himself. However, we know Jesus was literate.

Perhaps you remember a story in the Bible of a woman caught in the act of adultery. The people were about to stone her to death, according to the law of that day. They were standing there, stones in hand, when Jesus intervened. He bent down and started to write on the ground with his finger. When the woman's accusers saw what he wrote, they all just walked away. That meant Jesus was literate. In fact, history tells us there was a surprisingly high level of literacy in first-century Israel. We also know Jesus gathered around himself followers who could read and write and therefore record Christian history for future generations to read. It's called *The New Testament*, and we can trust its words.

Jesus, you spoke so much more than you wrote. When you wrote, they were words to show compassion and save a life. Whether a note or a book, an e-mail or a text message, may my words honor you and bless others. Amen.

Changing for Good

—◆⟨⟨⟩⟩◆—

Now the Lord is the Spirit, and where the Spirit of the Lord is, there is freedom. And we, who...all reflect the Lord's glory, are being transformed into his likeness with ever-increasing glory.

2 Corinthians 3:17–18

Perhaps no other generation in history has faced as many changes as ours. In the past one hundred years we have moved from an agricultural economy to an industrial economy and now to an information and services economy. Travel across the globe has been reduced from months to hours. We routinely use inventions we could not have imagined even twenty-five years ago.

There are days I want to stop all the changes so I can relax and catch up. But too much comfort has its dangers as well. When scientists at the University of California-Berkeley placed an amoeba in a perfect, stress-free, unchanging environment with just the right temperature, food, and moisture, it died. There were no changes to deal with!

Dealing with change may be difficult, but those of us who trust in Jesus as our Savior needn't fear change. The Bible promises that we "are being transformed into his likeness." With that truth, change certainly loses its threat, doesn't it?

∽◈◡

God, you don't change but there are loads of other changes
swirling into my life every day. Some I welcome; some I hate.
Bless me with peace amidst change. Transform me to be more
like Jesus through everything new I experience. Amen.

Situation Excellent

✦❧☙✦

Though an army besiege me,
my heart will not fear;
though war break out against me,
even then will I be confident.
Be strong and take heart
and wait for the Lord.
Psalm 27:3, 14

Marshall Ferdinand Foch was the commander of the French Ninth Army on September 8, 1914, at the Battle of Marne. The Germans outnumbered the French 200,000 to 120,000, and the French were suffering a punishing defeat. Then Foch declared: "My center is giving way. My right is pushed back. Situation excellent—I am attacking!" And attack they did. Even though outnumbered almost two to one, that night the French Ninth Army routed the German forces, advancing toward the eventual Allied victory of World War I.

Marshall Foch had confidence. Even though they were losing, he had confidence in himself, his men, his weapons, and his strategy.

How much greater should our confidence in God be: in his power, in his promises, and in his goodness and his grace, even though we may appear to be losing. Like Foch, may we say, "My center is giving way. My right is pushed back. Situation excellent—I am attacking!"

❧☙

My Victorious God, I would rather fight a difficult battle with you on my side than an easy battle on my own. Thank you for every skill, strength, and weapon for spiritual warfare you have given to me. But my confidence is in you, not me. With God on my side, the worst becomes eternally excellent. Amen.

Crossword

———◆❦❧◆———

God made known to us the mystery of his will...which he
purposed in Christ...to bring all things in heaven and earth
together under one head, even Christ.

Ephesians 1:9–10

I have to admit something. I've started crossword puzzles, but I've never
actually finished one on my own. I always get stuck on some obscure reference
to science, history, or music that I've never heard of. And I think, *If you just
give me a few of these words, then I could finish the whole puzzle.* But without them, it
remains a mystery.

And that's the way it was with the mystery of God. Over the years the prophets
gave hints of what was to come. Earlier generations could fill in a lot of blanks
but couldn't finish the puzzle. And then came Jesus: "In the beginning was
the Word" (John 1:1), referring to Jesus. Jesus was and is the word that finishes
God's crossword puzzle. Without Jesus, no one ever could have figured out
the mystery of God. But with Jesus, it becomes amazingly easy.

When God solved the mystery with Jesus, the crossword puzzle of eternity
came together!

∿

*Jesus, you are the word to solve the puzzles of life. You are the
password to access all I need. Without you I am lost. Come to me
with your wisdom. Show me your mysteries. Fill me with your love.
Guide me to understanding. Today I need you and look to you
with admiration, hope, and complete commitment. Amen.*

SEPTEMBER

Getting the Job Done

---◆⟨⟨⟨⟩⟩⟩◆---

When our enemies heard that we were aware of their plot and that God
had frustrated it, we all returned to the wall, each to his own work.

Nehemiah 4:15

Woody Allen once said, "Eighty percent of success is showing up." I think
he's got something there. Lack of perseverance is a major reason for defeat
in many people's lives. We get a job half done, become discouraged, and
then walk away. People bail out of all kinds of things they could accomplish
if they would just hang in there.

Long ago, enemies were trying to stop the Jews from rebuilding the wall
around Jerusalem. It would have been easiest to quit, but Nehemiah, their
leader, encouraged them to persevere. It wasn't until they "returned to the
wall" and stood ready to fight that their enemies retreated.

There have been lots of times I've felt like quitting. But I'd hate to miss out
on God's grace just because I quit too soon.

Our responsibility is to stay in the fight—to show up to work. That's the only
way to make sure we'll be there when God brings the victory!

∾⊘∾

*Faithful God, don't let me quit too soon. Even when I face opposition,
discouragement, and difficulty, may I press on to do all you want
me to do. Protect me from stopping just short of victory. Keep
my eyes on you, not just the changing circumstances surrounding
me. May the work to which you call me be complete. Amen.*

Coming Out the Other Side

—◦❦◦—

By his power God raised the Lord from the dead,
and he will raise us also.

1 Corinthians 6:14

When I was a little boy, a friend and I noticed a large storm sewer that went under the street. My friend suggested we walk through it to the other side, but I was more timid than he was. As he disappeared from sight, I genuinely thought that was the last time I'd ever see him. I just knew horrible things would happen—he'd get stuck and drown and rats would eat him.

But to my surprise, he appeared on the other side of the road and called back, "It's not as scary as it looks. You can make it." I was still apprehensive, but he'd already proved it could be done, and I trusted him. So I did it! And it was far less difficult than I ever could have guessed.

Death can seem like a long, frightening tunnel, but Jesus Christ has said, "I'll go ahead." And he did. Now he stands above us, saying, "It's not as scary as you think. You can do it."

—◦❧◦—

Death looks so scary. It is such unfamiliar territory and seems so final. Then, Jesus, I remember that when you died on the cross, you entered the tunnel of death. You went ahead. Three days later you came out alive. Now when I face death I know you will be waiting, and I'll come out alive on the other side. Amen.

Know-It-All God

For God is greater than our hearts, and he knows everything.

1 John 3:20

Everyone wonders about the future. *Will I marry? Will I have children? Will I be rich? Will I be healthy? Will I be happy?* Most of these questions are not answered in advance. But there are some things God chooses to tell us about the future, through the prophecies of the Bible, to show us that he controls history and that it has a purpose.

God was the Lord of yesterday; God is the Lord of today; and God is the Lord of tomorrow. He is the sovereign king of the past, present, and future. They are all connected. Sometimes human history appears to be chaotic nonsense that is going nowhere. But history is the working out of God's plan, even if it all doesn't make sense to us. That's why biblical prophecy gives us great hope and comfort. Even though we cannot control the future, we can trust God to make everything work together for good in the end.

All-knowing God, I often wish I could know what tomorrow will bring. The uncertainty about what is ahead can fill me with worry. Yet I prefer trust over knowledge. I really don't want to fret over what is to come. Today has enough to think about without adding future years. So I simply and fully trust you to know what I cannot know, do what I cannot do, and love me through whatever is coming. Amen.

Joy Deep Down

———◆◦❀◦◆———

The disciples were filled with joy and with the Holy Spirit.
Acts 13:52

Did you know that *joy* is one of the most frequent words written within the Bible? It occurs 218 times in the Old and New Testaments!

While many religions are based upon fear and guilt and threat, grace and joy are central to the message of the Bible. Joy is a distinctive of Christianity. But understand that there is a difference between joy and happiness. Happiness may come and go in our lives, depending on our circumstances. But just as an ocean can have great turbulence on the surface and tranquility on the bottom, joy remains unchanged by storms raging on the top. It is the "deep down inside" controlling factor of the Christian's life that determines how we respond to the circumstances on the outside. The Christian's joy essentially comes from knowing what is really important. And the most important thing of all is God and his relationship to us.

∽◦∾

My joy comes from you, Lord. When the storms rage and my days are swamped with rain and illumined by lightning, I turn to you for peace at the foundation of my soul. You give a deep-down satisfaction that I cannot describe but delight to experience. Even when unhappiness roars, I feel that deep-down joy. In you I know that all is well. With you I am certain I am safe. My joy is in Jesus. Amen.

God at Work

—◆◈◆—

Now to him who is able to do immeasurably more than all we
ask or imagine, according to his power that is at work within us,
to him be glory in the church and in Christ Jesus throughout all
generations, for ever and ever! Amen.

Ephesians 3:20–21

You're probably familiar with those signs that say MEN AT WORK. Well, picture a sign around your neck that says GOD AT WORK. Some of us welcome God's changes, but probably more of us fight every change. Either way, God never gives up on us. He never quits. He works and works and works to change us...for our good.

Transformation comes easier for some than for others. Some of us are like soft, pliable clay that only needs gentle molding. Others of us are like hardened rock that needs a hammer and chisel. The point is that God is absolutely determined to do whatever needs to be done to make his children like Jesus.

God doesn't promise that every detail of our lives will work out the way we want it to work out. Rather, he promises to do whatever he needs to do in order to accomplish his good purpose in our lives.

—◈—

*Lord, I am a lifelong work in progress! Thank you for working so
well in my life. I see the difference you are making. I remember
the broken parts you have now repaired and the ugly parts you
have made beautiful. Keep up your good work in me! Amen.*

Thanks—or Praise?

———❦———

Now, our God, we give you thanks,
and praise your glorious name.

1 Chronicles 29:13

The Bible tells us to both give thanks to God and praise his name. What's the difference? God has done lots of good things for us and given lots of great gifts to us. If we were to each make a list of God's gifts to us, no two lists would be alike, but we all have plenty to be thankful for.

All of us want to be loved and respected for who we are, not just what we do, and God is no different. Have you ever stood outside on a dark cloudless night and admired the number, the beauty, and the great expanse of the stars? Yet they've never really done anything for you. They don't feed your children or heat your house. You just admire them for themselves.

That's what praising God is supposed to be: admiring him for who he is. He is loving. He is truthful. He is kind. And he deserves our praise!

———❧———

To you I sing the words of the Doxology Hymn: Praise God from whom all blessings flow. I praise you for who you are—the great, holy, loving, all-knowing, and all-powerful God. I thank you for all you give and do. You have given me so much when so many have so little. God, I praise and thank you in Jesus' name. Amen.

The 80/20 Principle

From Christ the whole body, joined and held together
by every supporting ligament, grows and builds itself up in love,
as each part does its work.
Ephesians 4:16

It's often said that 20 percent of the people do 80 percent of the work. That means 80 percent do little or nothing!

We've all experienced this gap in participation. At work, there are people who carry more than their share of the load while others arrive late, leave early, and spend time talking and doing personal stuff. At home, one person rakes the leaves, washes the dishes, and vacuums while other family members sit and watch TV.

All kinds of people say they are Christians and just don't do their part. And it's not merely individuals. There are thousands of churches that are content to ignore the rest of the world. So we have a choice to make. We can be either discouraged or motivated. As for me, I'm convinced that God is doing more to reach the world for Jesus Christ in our generation than ever before, and I delight in the opportunity to be a partner with him! How about you?

---

*Lord of this day, you have work for me to do. With your strength I will
do my part. Count on me to show up, labor with zeal, not complain, and
seize your opportunities for today. Help me to get your job done. Amen.*

Knowing Your Limits

—⚜—

Jesus made the disciples get into the boat and go on ahead of him to the other side while he dismissed the crowd. After he had dismissed them, he went up on a mountainside by himself to pray. And when evening came, he was there alone.

Matthew 14:22–23

One day was particularly stressful for Jesus. It began with the news that his cousin John had been beheaded as a party favor for King Herod's wife. Jesus must have been deeply grieved. Then he spent the major part of the day preaching, which can be exhausting and draining. He healed multiple people, then miraculously provided for the feeding of five-thousand-plus people. The crowds continued to come—they wanted to be healed and to learn about God. At the end of that stressful day, Jesus went away by himself. He knew his limits. He knew when he needed to be alone, away from the stresses.

What can we learn from Jesus' example? We need to know our own limits—to look at the demands on our lives, even the good things that need to be done, and realize when we need to back off and give the rest to God.

∽∾

When I am exhausted, I must remember that you have been there, Jesus. There is so much I want to do; so much I need to do. But there's only so much I'm able to do. Show me the time and place to unstress, to slow down, and to be renewed. Amen.

The Peace of God

———❦———

Do not be anxious about anything, but in everything, by prayer and petition, with thanksgiving, present your requests to God. And the peace of God, which transcends all understanding, will guard your hearts and your minds in Christ Jesus.

Philippians 4:6–7

What does it feel like to have God's peace? Peace is that inner calm that gives you confidence that God is in charge and that you don't have anything to worry about. He takes all your worries on himself.

It's not that we are to lay back and become irresponsible. We are still to serve him faithfully, but with peace and purpose rather than with worry and anxiety.

But what do we do if we pray and peace doesn't come? Keep on praying! Maybe you need to take a day off just to pray. Pray for hours instead of minutes. Pray until peace replaces worry.

The nineteenth century German-Lutheran theologian Johann Bengel wrote: "Anxiety and prayer are more opposed to each other than fire and water." Are your anxieties and worries burning out of control? Pour on loads of prayer! Then "the peace of God...will guard your hearts and your minds in Christ Jesus."

∿

God Above, I pray for peace. Lift my worries and settle my soul. Hold my pounding heart in your gentle hands and calm me down. I pause to feel your presence, listen for your voice, and experience your touch. Amen.

Our Destiny

In the beginning God created the heavens and the earth.
Genesis 1:1

The biblical account of creation distinctly differs from other ancient accounts of the beginning of the world and humanity. Absent are reports of battles between deities or gods having offspring. There are no hints that the sun, moon, or stars are deities to be worshiped. The Bible starts with God alone. Then it goes on to describe the different days of creation and says that every day God stopped to review what he had done and observed that it was good. On the seventh day God stopped what he was doing, for he was finished. He had done a marvelous job!

The last book of the Bible describes a magnificent scene in heaven where angels laid their crowns before the throne of God saying, "You are worthy, our Lord and God, to receive glory and honor and power, for you created all things, and by your will they were created" (Revelation 4:11).

From beginning to end, the Bible demonstrates that our design, our destiny, and our privilege are to worship our Creator!

From before the beginning, you are God. You are my Creator—I am not the result of some random process, nor did I make myself. You shaped me in love and gave to me eternal worth and immediate purpose. Today and for the rest of my life, I love you and will live for you! Amen.

Let's Roll!

———❦———

Who shall separate us from the love of Christ?
Shall trouble or hardship or persecution or famine
or nakedness or danger or sword?
Romans 8:35

Lisa Beamer was catapulted into tragedy and fame on September 11, 2001, when her husband, Todd, phoned from United Flight 93. He reported that the plane was hijacked, and the passengers were going to fight back. His last words—"Let's roll!"—are etched on our minds.

But this was not the first tragedy in Lisa's life. When she was fifteen, her father suffered an aneurysm and died. At first this rattled the teenager's Christian faith. Eventually, she was able to say, "I hit an understanding that God knew what was going to happen to my father but, for whatever reason, chose not to change it." In hindsight Lisa could see how God used one circumstance in her life to prepare her for another circumstance—Todd's death. We may not understand why we are going through what we are going through, but we can, like Lisa, choose to live in faith and hope that God is working his perfect plan for us.

———❦———

Make me ready, my God, for whatever this day will bring. If it is
so routine that I will not remember anything that happened, may
I be faithful in routine. If today brings great challenges I could never
have expected, make me brave to act with wisdom and courage. May
nothing shake my eternal faith in your love and goodness. Amen.

Cure for Pessimism

Our citizenship is in heaven. And we eagerly await a Savior from there, the Lord Jesus Christ, who, by the power that enables him to bring everything under his control, will transform our lowly bodies so that they will be like his glorious body.

Philippians 3:20-21

If you want to change a pessimist into an optimist, just have that person read Philippians 3:20-21! Jesus Christ promises he's coming back again to take everyone who has put faith and trust in him out of this world and into a heaven he's prepared for us. Whatever ill health we have now will be gone, and we will have resurrection bodies like Jesus Christ. Our lives and our destinies are safely in the hands of him who has the power to do absolutely *anything*.

No matter how bad things are now, we need never despair or be discouraged. Jesus will return to correct every injustice, cure every disease, and right every wrong. In other words, if things are bad, Jesus will make them good. And if things are good, Jesus will make them even better.

These words are more than hope for heaven someday. They are hope for living triumphantly right now!

Yes, I get discouraged. I get pretty pessimistic. Lift my thoughts, Lord Jesus. Since you have the power to bring everything under your control...well, that includes everything that gets me down. With your power I want to live triumphantly through my present problems until they are gone forever in heaven. Amen.

An Instant Faith

—◦⟨ co ⟩◦—

"Silver or gold I do not have, but what I have I give you.
In the name of Jesus Christ of Nazareth, walk."
Peter, in Acts 3:6

One day a paraplegic who had never walked shouted a request for money to Peter and John, Jesus' disciples. He must have been totally surprised by Peter's response—disappointed that he wasn't going to get money, but flabbergasted by the prospect of walking. After all, he had asked for money, not a miracle, but when he heard the offer, saw the faith of his benefactors, and heard the name of Jesus of Nazareth, the beggar grew an instant faith.

And a miracle occurred! For the first time in his life, this poor man stood erect. Feet that had never felt full weight were firm on the ground, and with a helping hand from Peter, he took his first steps. Without training or therapy he walked…then ran and jumped and shouted praises to God.

Peter made it clear that he and John didn't have money for alms or power for a miracle. It was all by the power of the God of Abraham, Isaac, and Jacob. This wasn't about Peter and John. This was about God's Son, Jesus.

⟨∽∾⟩

Our requests are often too small. We ask for money when you
want to give us a miracle. Surprise me, God, with miracles
I never requested. Go beyond anything money can buy. Jump-
start my faith. In the name of Jesus of Nazareth, amen.

Grace in the Midst

—◦⟨ℰ⟩◦—

"My grace is sufficient for you,
for my power is made perfect in weakness."
The Lord, in 2 Corinthians 12:9

While my wife and I visited missionaries in Bogotá, Columbia, we stayed in the house from which another missionary had been kidnapped and brutally killed four years earlier. I was amazed by the confidence displayed by the missionaries still at that same address. Once again they were facing similar threats, yet they were at peace when you would have expected them to live in fear. God had given them what they needed to face their situation.

Another example of "grace-in-the-midst" is in the apostle Paul's life. After his third request for relief from a physical malady, God said no to a cure but yes to the grace to cope and be victorious. You see, God guarantees us sufficient grace for whatever we face. Now, he does not give us grace for old age when we are still young, nor does he give grace to face calamity until we experience calamity. But we can be absolutely confident he will give all the grace we need, when we need it!

∼◦∽

To be really honest, I prefer that you take my problems away rather than give me the grace to live with them. And I prefer prepayment on your grace rather than waiting until the last minute. But, Wise God, I trust you to decide. Your grace and the timing of your grace are always good enough for me. Amen.

Coach Jesus

————————⟨≪⟩————————

Resist the devil, and he will flee from you.
James 4:7

Most football teams gather in the locker room before heading out to the field. The coach gives a somewhat predictable speech, warning the team never to underestimate their opponent. He reviews the game plan, telling them how to resist the other team's offense and how to send them running in the opposite direction.

Imagine that we're the team, and the coach is Jesus Christ. Our coach tells us this game called Life is the most important one we will ever play. The competition we face is stronger than any National Football League team and smarter than any NFL line. Our enemy is Satan, and his offensive line is huge. He is 100 percent bad and has superhuman powers. But he is not God. He can't be in more than one place at the same time the way God can, and although he is powerful, he is not equal to God. He is a terrible enemy, but he is not irresistible with Jesus as our Savior, Lord, and Coach. Now that's encouragement you can take to the field for a winning victory!

∽⟨∾

Satan is scary—so evil, so mean, so strong. I don't seem to have much
of a chance if he is after me. Then, Almighty God, I turn to you. You
are so good, so kind, so infinitely strong. In the name of Jesus I can face
down the devil, who will turn and run away. Thank you! Amen.

Grounded!

---❦---

No one has ever seen God; but if we love one another,
God lives in us and his love is made complete in us.
1 John 4:12

When I was fifteen, I bought an old Plymouth for fifty dollars. Eventually I got it running, but it wasn't always consistent. One day it wouldn't start, even though the battery was charged and there was gas in the tank.

My father asked if he could help. I figured he didn't know much because he was in his forties and really old, but since the car was in his garage, I was respectful. He took a look under the hood and said, "The ground wire isn't connected to the coil." I had no idea what he was talking about and assumed he didn't either. But after he drove away, I connected the ground wire to the coil. When I got back behind the steering wheel, that old Plymouth started immediately. Dad was smarter than I thought! He knew electrical systems need to be grounded to work.

It's the same way with love. The circuit starts with God's love for us. When we love others, the circuit is complete—we are grounded, and the system works.

---❦---

God of love, ground me in love. Not just good feelings, but actions in the best interests of others. Cause me to love you as you love me and to love others as you love them. May your love be the motivation of my heart. Amen.

A Living Masterpiece

---&-----

"The stone the builders rejected
has become the capstone;
the Lord has done this,
and it is marvelous in our eyes."
Mark 12:10–11

The magnificent artist Michelangelo, who gave the world the carved masterpieces of Moses, David, and others, was known for choosing large pieces of marble rejected by other artists. He could see the finished masterpiece inside the flawed stone and felt it was his calling to let it out. He would carve along the fault lines and use the discolorations in the stone to add wonderful elements of design. I wonder what the other artists thought when they saw his finished work—his masterpieces created out of what they had rejected?

While Jesus was on earth, many rejected him. They said he was flawed. They saw neither good nor a future in him. What would they think now if they could see him as the Masterpiece of God, the King of kings, and Lord of lords, the One whose birth defines the calendars of the world? Jesus is the living stone—chosen by God and precious to God.

~~~

God and Father of our Lord Jesus Christ, show me the beauty and majesty of your Son. Where others see an ordinary man, may I see the extraordinary Savior. When others say he is unattractive, may I see his beauty. What others hear as words from history, may I hear as holy revelation. Whom others reject, may I acknowledge as the Lord of all. Amen.

A Supernatural Combination

———◦❦◦———

You have known the holy Scriptures, which are able to make
you wise for salvation through faith in Christ Jesus.
2 Timothy 3:15

Do you ever wonder what the Bible means when it talks about "prophets"?
Prophets are those who speak God's truth to humans. As the authors of the
Bible, they didn't think up what they wrote all by themselves, nor did they
spin their own interpretation of history. They didn't make up a religion.
They simply spoke the words God gave them and wrote with the authority
and accuracy of the Holy Spirit.

The Bible is the most studied and documented book in history. What it says
has been dissected, analyzed, attacked, criticized, and verified for almost
two thousand years. Bottom line: the Bible is the Word of God. When you
put your personal experience of faith together with the truth of the Bible,
you have the two pillars upon which Christianity stands—faith and the Bible;
personal encounter and truth. Christianity is not just your own experience,
and it's not merely the truth of the Bible. It's a supernatural combination of
faith and facts. And, together, they are life transforming.

❧

*Sharpen my mind to read and understand the spiritual teachings
of the Word of God. Soften my heart to experience Jesus through a
personal relationship with him. Fuse together my heart and mind so
I will have neither cold intellectualism nor hot emotionalism. Amen.*

An Entire Library in One Book

———◈———

Everything that was written in the past was written
to teach us, so that through endurance and the
encouragement of the Scriptures we might have hope.

Romans 15:4

The word *Bible* comes from the Latin word *biblia* that means "books." And that's exactly what it is—a library of sixty-six books bound together into a single volume.

The Old Testament's thirty-nine books are organized into four sections: Law, History, Poetry and Wisdom, and Prophecy. Some of the books are named for content. For example, Genesis means "beginnings," and Exodus is about "exiting Egypt." Most of the books are named for people like Ruth, Esther, Jonah, and Isaiah.

The New Testament's library of twenty-seven books is also organized into four sections: the Gospels, History, Letters, and Prophecy. Most of the New Testament books are named for either the author or the recipients and are pretty much in chronological order.

Some people think the Bible is like a novel—you read it straight through to get the story. But it's actually organized more like a daily newspaper: topically, not chronologically. The more time you spend reading it, the more comfortable you will be with its organization. The important thing is to start reading!

———◈———

*Although the Bible is your written Word, God, I have read
too little of your book. The busyness of life and my difficulty of
understanding have been my excuses. Now I resolve to make the time
to hear you speak and to apply your words each day. Amen.*

The Biographies of Jesus

Jesus did many other miraculous signs...which are not recorded in this book. But these are written that you may believe that Jesus is the Christ, the Son of God, and that by believing you may have life in his name.

John 20:30-31

If you want to know all you can about Jesus, study all four of his biographies—the four Gospels. Mark wrote the first and shortest biography of Jesus, using Peter as his primary source. He wrote in a style especially appealing to non-Jews, minimizing references to the Old Testament.

Matthew included most of what Mark wrote but added lots of Old Testament references to target a Jewish audience.

Luke, a physician by training whose style reflects his Greek literary education, wanted to fill out some of the empty spots in the other biographies, so he wrote a longer biography. He wasn't an eyewitness, but he interviewed multiple eyewitness sources.

John, the disciple who lived the longest, wrote the last biography. He was closer to Jesus than anyone else and included previously unrecorded information. Not even John could include everything. What was written was enough for us to believe!

Jesus, you lived an amazing life—from virgin birth in Bethlehem to spectacular miracles across Israel to crucifixion and resurrection at Jerusalem. You healed the sick, empowered the poor, raised the dead, and forgave the sinners. I've read all about you in the Bible. And I believe and have eternal life through your name. Amen.

Eternally Grateful

———————◆⟨⟨⟨○⟩⟩⟩◆———————

As far as the east is from the west,
so far has he removed our transgressions from us.
As a father has compassion on his children,
so the Lord has compassion on those who fear him.

Psalm 103:12–13

One of my most memorable teenage experiences was driving my dad's brand-new red Chevrolet convertible to a friend's house down a twisting mountainous road and crossing the center line because I thought I could maintain the 45 mph speed limit. I sideswiped another car from headlight to taillight and smashed up the front of my father's convertible. The police came, I called home, and my father came immediately. He sent me on to my friend's house in the Volkswagen Beetle he was driving and said he would deal with the police and the car.

My dad never mentioned the accident to me again. Years later I found out it had doubled his insurance rates for the next three years. But he never criticized me for what I had done, nor told me of the cost. I was grateful for his forgiveness. I'm still grateful. But I'm even more grateful to God. Because the more you're forgiven, the more your gratitude and love overflow.

———∞———

*You are such a good father, Father God—loving, kind, generous,
and forgiving. You forgive sins I knowingly commit. You forgive the
good I knew to do but didn't do. You forgive me and move me on to
a better tomorrow. I am so honored to be your child. Amen.*

Doing What's Right

---·❧❧·---

"If we are thrown into the blazing furnace, the God we serve
is able to save us from it, and he will rescue us from your hand, O
king. But even if he does not...we will not serve your gods
or worship the image of gold you have set up."
Shadrach, Meshach, and Abednego, in Daniel 3:17–18

Hananiah, Mishael, and Azariah were kidnapped and brought to Babylon
in the sixth-century BC under the reign of Nebuchadnezzar. Although
born Jewish, the three boys were raised to be pagans. They were taught a
new language and given Babylonian names.

The emperor Nebuchadnezzar was very powerful, but he was also a nut.
Increasingly convinced he was a god, Nebuchadnezzar built a huge statue and
ordered everyone in Babylon to bow down and worship it. But Hananiah,
Mishael, and Azariah remembered that the Ten Commandments forbade
worshipping idols and held fast to the truth of God.

Did they want to be rescued from being cremated alive for disobeying
the emperor? Of course! Did they believe God was stronger than
Nebuchadnezzar or the flames of the furnace? Absolutely! If these three
men of faith could speak to us today, they would say, "Faithfulness to God
is the right thing to do even if it costs you your job, your friends, or your
life. God can save you from anything. But even if God doesn't intervene,
still do what is right!"

❧

*God of the blazing furnace, I will serve you and
no other—whatever happens. Amen.*

Using Conflict for Good

---·❦·---

Surely it was for my benefit that I suffered such anguish.
In your love you kept me from the pit of destruction;
you have put all my sins behind your back.
Isaiah 38:17

God is the master of using conflict for good. Early Christian missionaries Paul, Barnabas, and Mark couldn't get along and had to split up. But they had more effective ministries apart than they ever had together.

When the Watergate scandal took down President Nixon, his special counsel, Chuck Colson, was sent to prison for his part in the illegal activities. But out of this experience Colson came to faith in Jesus Christ and eventually founded Prison Fellowship, a Christian ministry that has transformed the lives of many prisoners around the world.

At what turning point in your life has conflict produced good results? Maybe it was being fired from your job that led to pursuing a whole new career. Or perhaps the heartbreak of a broken engagement led to a new relationship that resulted in a far better marriage.

God can take the worst of conflict and use it for good in our lives.

∽❧∾

Some people are so hard to get along with. Sometimes everything goes so wrong. Okay, Lord—I admit I can be hard to get along with and I make things go wrong. Please forgive me and then, in your grace, take the rubble of bad relationships and broken plans and build something new and better than before. I pray in Jesus' name, amen.

From a Distance

—◦⟨✦⟩◦—

But as for me, it is good to be near God.
I have made the Sovereign Lord my refuge.
Psalm 73:28

When you are a child, you think your father can do anything. You may even offer his services to beat up someone else's father. But when you grow up, you begin to realize that your father is as limited as you are.

Not so with our heavenly Father. He has no limitations. He can do anything. He is the God of the heavens.

But he is also infinitely personal. Bette Midler popularized the song "From a Distance," claiming that "God is watching us from a distance." Yet, is that what Jesus meant when he prayed to "our Father in heaven"? It's easy to imagine that God is far away from us—too far for us to reach. But the Bible clearly teaches that God is everywhere. He is with us in the car; he goes with us to work and school; and he is also there on his celestial throne in far-away heaven. He is the infinite God who is both here and there at the same time. He is beyond us—greater than our widest horizon.

—◦⟨✦⟩◦—

You are the God of Everywhere—from the highest heights to the lowest depths; from the farthest distance to inside of our souls. I worship you as the Sovereign on the distant throne of heaven. I talk with you as my closest Friend who is always near. Amen.

A Matter of Faith

—◦❦◦—

"What good will it be for a man if he gains the whole world, yet forfeits his soul? Or what can a man give in exchange for his soul?"
Jesus, in Matthew 16:26

Imagine for a moment you have to make an immediate financial plan for your assets—house, car, savings, pension, whatever. You can invest any way you choose. First, you have to decide whether or not you have confidence in the U.S. dollar. But there are other choices. You could put your life savings into Albanian leks, Burundi francs, or Mexican pesos. It's a matter of which currency you most trust. If your faith is right, you'll come out ahead. If your faith is misplaced, you risk losing everything.

Being a Christian means you have invested your life and soul in Jesus Christ alone. But it's your decision and a matter of faith. You may choose to invest your soul in Buddha or Muhammad; or you may choose, as many Americans do, to invest your soul in yourself. As for me, I choose to invest my soul in Jesus Christ alone. If faith is right, we've got it made for this life and forever. But if faith is misplaced, the loss is tragic and eternal.

—◦❧◦—

Jesus, I invest everything in you—not in religion, career, relationship, possessions, or anything else. Not that these other things aren't part of my life, but my faith is in you, not them. I am totally counting on you now and forever. Amen.

God Wins!

Then I heard what sounded like a great multitude, like the roar
of rushing waters and like loud peals of thunder, shouting:
"Hallelujah! For our Lord God Almighty reigns.
Let us rejoice and be glad and give him glory!"
Revelation 19:6-7

Revelation, the last book of the Bible, begins with the words, "The revelation
of Jesus Christ." A revelation shows or reveals something we wouldn't and
couldn't have figured out by ourselves. Revelation is not primarily a book
about what will happen someday in the future; it is primarily a book about
Jesus Christ. It tells about the great conflict between good and evil, the
great battle between God and Satan. The thesis of the book is that God wins
through Jesus Christ. If you get that, you've got Revelation. If you miss that,
you miss God's message.

When we read today's newspapers or watch the news and wonder if things
can possibly get worse, we may be tempted to give up and think that Satan
will ultimately triumph. It's then we especially need to hear the resounding
message of Revelation: God wins. God always wins!

*Jesus, you are the ultimate and final victor in the war against sin and death.
Even though there are events today that make it look like evil will triumph,
I don't believe it. You are on the way to conquer every enemy once and for
all. I'm on your side. You are the Eternal Winner. Amen.*

The Heart of Jesus

———✦❦✦———

When Jesus heard what had happened [the death of John],
he withdrew by boat privately to a solitary place. Hearing
of this, the crowds followed him on foot from the towns.
When Jesus landed and saw a large crowd, he had compassion
on them and healed their sick.
Matthew 14:13–14

It's easy to say in theory that God knows and cares about our suffering, but it's not so easy when we are in the midst of pain. The clear message of the New Testament, though, is that Jesus personally understands suffering. He's been there. He knows what it is like to go through the tortures of pain, humiliation, loneliness, and death. One of the greatest snapshots of the character and the heart of Jesus is when he was informed of the brutal execution of John the Baptist. Jesus and John had shared a special relationship since birth. Jesus loved John and their relationship was unique and powerful. When Jesus heard about John's death, he was deeply grieved. Yet, in the midst of his own grief and suffering, he saw the needs of others and cared enough to say, "Yes, my heart's breaking, but so are theirs." Putting his own pain aside, he ministered to others.

Yes, God knows about your needs. And he not only knows, he cares and he heals.

∿

Compassionate Jesus, thank you for your care for all who suffer.
Even in your own grief you are concerned for me. Amen.

Getting Close to Jesus

———◦◦◦———

Grace and peace be yours in abundance through
the knowledge of God and of Jesus our Lord.

2 Peter 1:2

In a life of uncertainty and turmoil, we particularly need grace and peace. *Grace* refers to the gifts God gives us to make it through life. *Peace* is the inner calm of heart that God gives us in the storms of life. I can't tell you how many times I've prayed, "Oh God, please help me," and he has given his grace. When my heart is pounding with fear and worry, he settles my soul and supernaturally calms me down.

So how do we get grace and peace? "Through the knowledge of God and of Jesus our Lord." The word *knowledge* in the Bible is sometimes used to describe the intimacy between a husband and wife. Our relationship with Jesus should be the closest of all connections. Knowing Jesus means sharing all of your life with him: your successes and your heartbreaks, your joys and your needs. Knowledge of both head and heart is the source of grace and peace for the Christian.

———◦◦◦———

I want to know you better, Lord. And I want you to know me. I realize you are the all-knowing God, but I want you to be the one to whom I tell all—my happiness and sadness, my questions and answers, my jokes and my memories. Every day may our knowledge of one another draw us closer as I experience your grace and peace. Amen.

Is God Good—or Not?

※

When the woman saw that the fruit of the tree was good
for food and pleasing to the eye, and also desirable for gaining
wisdom, she took some and ate it. She also gave some to her
husband, who was with her, and he ate it.

Genesis 3:6

Adam and Eve literally had it made. They lived in paradise and lacked nothing. But they decided perfection wasn't good enough. They thought Eden would be a better place and their lives would be much happier if they could add just one more fruit to their breakfast menu.

Most significant, they decided God wasn't as good as he made himself out to be and really didn't know what was best for them. God had warned them that if they ate the forbidden fruit, they'd get sick and miserable and die as a result. But they wouldn't listen. They took the fruit and tragically discovered that God was right and they were wrong. They changed the whole world and our entire human family ever since.

It's been thousands of years since Adam and Eve and the collapse of Paradise, but we still face the same decision every day. Is God really good or not? What we decide about the goodness of God shapes every detail of our lives and determines our interpretation of every circumstance.

※

*God of the Garden, you blessed our foreparents with
paradise and they wanted more. Deliver me and my family
from ever thinking you are not good enough. Amen.*

Where Are You Going?

❧

I press on toward the goal to win the prize for which
God has called me heavenward in Christ Jesus.
Philippians 3:14

Albert Einstein, the great physicist, was once traveling from Princeton on a train when the conductor came down the aisle, punching the ticket of each passenger. When he came to him, Einstein reached into his vest pocket. His ticket wasn't there, so he reached into his other pocket. It wasn't there, either, so he looked in his briefcase. Then he searched the seat. He still couldn't find it. At last the conductor said, "Dr. Einstein, I know who you are. I'm sure you bought a ticket. Don't worry about it." Einstein nodded appreciatively.

When the conductor was ready to move to the next car, he noticed the great physicist down on his hands and knees, looking under his seat. The conductor rushed back. "Dr. Einstein, I know who you are. You don't need a ticket."

Einstein looked at him. "Young man, I too know who I am. What I don't know is where I'm going."

Do you know where you are going? Are you trusting in Jesus?

❧

My destination? I'm headed to heaven. That's where Jesus is
preparing a place for me to live. God of heaven, during today's
journey to my final destination may I behave as a follower of Jesus.
My goal is the prize of pleasing you. In Jesus' name, amen.

OCTOBER

Shout for Joy!

❈

Shout for joy to the Lord, all the earth.
Worship the Lord with gladness;
come before him with joyful songs.
Enter his gates with thanksgiving
and his courts with praise;
give thanks to him and praise his name.
Psalm 100:1-4

About three thousand years ago an unknown songwriter wrote words about happiness and joy that are now among the most famous musical lines ever written. They have been translated into hundreds of different languages and have spun off hundreds of different songs. Called the 100th Psalm, it was originally sung by Jewish worshippers as they marched through the streets during festivals of celebration and worship.

The words are so good that they transcend time and culture to be as relevant today as they were three millennia ago. Even if you're not a shouter or a singer, praising God with other Christians will lift your heart. Anyone who has the joy of the Lord wants to shout about it and to do it with others. You want friends, family, and even the whole earth to join the celebration. Together, let's "shout for joy to the Lord, all the earth"!

❧

For the Lord is good and his love endures forever;
his faithfulness continues through all generations. Amen.
Psalm 100:5

Ten Thousand Points of Light

❧❧❧

Lift your eyes and look to the heavens:
Who created all these?
He who brings out the starry host one by one,
and calls them each by name.
Because of his great power and mighty strength,
not one of them is missing.
Isaiah 40:26

On a clear night you can see ten thousand points of light. A few are nearby planets of our solar system, and thousands are the stars of the Milky Way. Thousands more are far distant galaxies in the universe. The heavens are huge and magnificent, far beyond our comprehension.

The Bible says that when God created the heavens, he also created the earth. In a sequence of creative acts God changed that which was formless and empty into the world we know with light; atmosphere; land and plants; the sun, moon, and stars; birds and fish; animals and humans.

When we contemplate those ten thousand points of light in the sky, we see how insignificant each of us is in a universe so vast. But this same God who created the heavens and the earth loved us enough to sacrifice his beloved Son on our behalf. The very vastness of creation serves as a reminder of the vastness of God's love for us.

❧

Creator God, you are amazing in artistry and sensational in science. Your power is incomprehensible, and your love is wonderful. From the microscope to the telescope, I am in awe of all you have made. Amen.

It Takes Time

I have labored and toiled and have often gone without sleep;
I have known hunger and thirst and have often gone without food;
I have been cold and naked.

2 Corinthians 11:27

St. Paul lived a life of contrasts. He received the best possible education available in his generation. He traveled the empire, conversed with the rich and powerful, and was God's leader in bringing the gospel to Europe. He also wrote much of the New Testament.

But Paul also did and said stupid things. He made bad mistakes, suffered serious illness, and knew poverty and distress firsthand. He was run out of town on several occasions, beaten, imprisoned, shipwrecked, and misunderstood. Yet through all his successes and difficulties Paul learned that every difficulty in life is a lesson from God in how to be content even if things go wrong.

Learning contentment takes time, just as a mighty oak requires time to mature. It takes the combination of winter's cold, the budding of spring, summer's warmth, and the falling leaves of autumn over a cycle of many years to make a mighty oak tree that can stand solid in a storm.

Contentment doesn't come in a day or in one lesson. It's learned over a lifetime.

*Be patient with me, God. I am slow to learn from life's
experiences. Use my difficulties for good. Use them all and let
none go to waste. May defeats, discouragements, and difficulties
all teach me contentment and shape me for good. Amen.*

Filling an Empty Life

—————————⟨☙⟩—————————

It was not with perishable things such as silver or gold that
you were redeemed from the empty way of life handed down to you
from your forefathers, but with the precious blood of Christ....
Through him you believe in God, who raised him from the dead
and glorified him, and so your faith and hope are in God.

1 Peter 1:18-19, 21

Life can be very busy—we can be on the run from early morning until late at night. But if we're really honest, we have to admit that, in all our busyness, life sometimes can be pretty empty. There is a profound sadness to a life that hasn't been anywhere and isn't going anywhere. It lacks meaning. Some people come from a long heritage of such sadness—their parents' and grandparents' lives didn't matter much, either.

That's the way it once was for first-century Peter. He was married and had a job as a fisherman, but he still wasn't fulfilled. His soul was hollow. Then he met Jesus, and suddenly his life overflowed with purpose and meaning. He wanted to tell others with empty lives how to fill up with faith and hope. Peter wanted everyone to know that Jesus is the answer to emptiness in your life.

∿☙∿

*Fill me, Lord. And, if you must first purge the worthless out
of me to make me ready for filling, I give you permission.
Fill me with your Spirit, purpose, and joy. Amen.*

Career Changes

Since then, no prophet has risen in Israel like Moses,
whom the Lord knew face to face, who did all those miraculous
signs and wonders the Lord sent him to do in Egypt—to Pharaoh
and to all his officials and to his whole land. For no one has ever
shown the mighty power or performed the awesome deeds that
Moses did in the sight of all Israel.

Deuteronomy 34:10-12

Over thirty-five hundred years ago, the Egyptian Pharaoh commanded that all Hebrew baby boys were to be killed. But God supernaturally intervened and saved the life of a particular baby boy. He was adopted by the daughter of Pharaoh, who named him Moses. He grew up in Pharaoh's court as an aristocrat. Then, when he was forty, he had a career change. Leaving the comfort of the court, he moved into the desert and became a shepherd. He spent forty years in this second career, which many would consider to be beneath the lofty position he first held. When he was eighty—an age when many people would say, "Time to retire!"—he changed careers again. God made him into the leader of the nation of Israel. Moses became the lawgiver of Sinai, God's own spokesman to his people.

Just as God directed Moses, God directs, changes, molds, and uses us—whether at twenty, forty, or eighty. And he does it for our good and for his glory.

God, I'm open to any change you have for me. Amen.

The Mark of a
Truly Great Person

———◆◆◆———

"For even the Son of Man did not come to be served,
but to serve, and to give his life as a ransom for many."
Jesus, in Mark 10:45

If you were to scan the shelves of the self-help section of any bookstore, you probably wouldn't find too many books on how to be ready to sacrifice.

But that's a skill Jesus wants us to develop. There never has been and never will be anyone greater than Jesus. And there never has been and never will be a greater sacrifice than Jesus giving up his life to die on the cross to ransom us sinners from eternal death.

Jesus wants us to know that greatness through service always has a price. The cost is often time: serving others takes many hours. The cost may be lack of recognition: servants are seldom famous or adequately honored. And the cost may be criticism: often the best servants are criticized for what they do.

Sacrifice is giving up something that you have every right to keep. It's the mark of a truly great person!

∼◆∽

Son of God, you gave up heaven for earth. You surrendered life for death. You sacrificed so much for me. You are truly great. And now you have called me to your greatness. Grow a servant's heart in me. Show me the satisfaction of sacrifice. Teach me to honor others above myself. Make me generous to others. May I find greatness in being like you, Jesus. Amen.

Choosing Joy

"In this world you will have trouble.
But take heart! I have overcome the world."
Jesus, in John 16:33

Troubles are an inevitable part of our world. And until we figure that out, we're never going to enjoy life as God intended for life to be enjoyed.

We often try to eliminate trouble. We exercise and eat right to stay healthy. We save money and buy insurance to protect ourselves from poverty. We do everything we can to protect our children from difficulties. We believe that if we work hard enough and long enough, we can get over the hurdles of troubles and be home free.

But there's nothing we can do to completely eliminate trouble. Vegetarians get sick. Billionaires go broke. Children raised by terrific parents turn out wrong. When troubles arise, we can choose to delight in the Lord and choose to live the joy of Jesus Christ in the midst of those difficulties. The apostle Paul said it well: "Rejoice in the Lord always. I'll say it again: Rejoice!" (Philippians 4:4).

Help me to understand this, Holy Spirit. I struggle to get my thinking wrapped around the idea of rejoicing in trouble. Keep reminding me that problems are part of life and that everyone has them. Strengthen me to handle difficulties with wisdom and grace. Convince me that I can rejoice in God even when circumstances are bad. Bless me with feelings rooted in my Eternal Lord rather than in my temporary traumas. Amen.

Hope for Tough Times

❧

Have you not heard? The Lord is the everlasting God.... He will not grow tired or weary, and his understanding no one can fathom. He gives strength to the weary and increases the power of the weak. Even youths grow tired and weary...but those who hope in the Lord will renew their strength. They will soar on wings like eagles; they will run and not grow weary, they will walk and not be faint.

Isaiah 40:28-31

After the Hebrews had been carried into captivity in Babylon and were far from their Jerusalem home, they were deeply discouraged...desperate, even. When the captives turned back to God, Isaiah the prophet offered them hope. He offered them comfort. And, regardless of their circumstances, Isaiah always pointed the people back to God. He wrote, "Comfort my people, says your God. Speak tenderly to Jerusalem, and proclaim to her that her hard service has been completed, that her sin has been paid for."

Isaiah's words of encouragement were not just for people thousands of years ago in captivity by a foreign power, but for Christians who, for thousands of years, have memorized and quoted Isaiah's words through difficult circumstances. What a reminder of God's goodness and love for tough times!

❧

*God of Israel, you are my God. When I grow weary, give
me strength. When I am upset, settle me down. When I am
discouraged, show me the end of this struggle. Amen.*

Simple Strategies

---❦❧---

They read from the Book of the Law of God,
making it clear and giving the meaning so that the
people could understand what was being read.
Nehemiah 8:8

A friend and I once rented a car at Chicago's O'Hare Airport. The key was in the ignition, so I started it up and drove to our appointment. But when I turned off the ignition, I couldn't pull out the key. For fifteen minutes we tried to get that key out. Finally, the parking lot attendant told us there's a button behind the key. Push that button, and the key comes out. It was simple...if you knew what to do.

In some ways, the Bible can be like that. Some people can't make sense of what it says, so they park it on a shelf and walk away, leaving it for someone else to figure out.

But God didn't send us the Bible in code to keep it a secret. We just need a few "buttons to push" to make sense out of it: (1) look for the original meaning when it was written; (2) let the Bible explain itself; (3) pay attention to the context. Try these, and you'll be amazed at how the Bible comes to life!

---❧---

Teach me your truths, God of the Bible. Make me anxious to read.
Replace my ignorance with your knowledge. Help me interpret
correctly, understand fully, and apply wholeheartedly. Amen.

Owners—or Stewards?

By him all things were created: things in heaven and on earth,
visible and invisible, whether thrones or powers or rulers or
authorities; all things were created by him and for him.

Colossians 1:16

Every time the verb *create* appears in the Old Testament, the reference is always about what God does—never about what humans do. As much as we may be impressed with our human ability to invent machines and medicines, we are not creators. We are merely stewards of what God has already created. Even the most innovative science fiction filmmakers can only fashion variations of creatures we already know. Only God can speak a universe into existence.

One of the most basic questions of life is that of ownership. Does everything belong to God, or do we own it? Is it our world and our environment to treat as we please? Are these our bodies so we can determine our own destiny? The answer to this question of ownership is the essential difference between being a believer and an unbeliever. Psalm 24:1 says, "The earth is the Lord's, and everything in it." If God created the world, then he owns it, and we are accountable to him.

---

*Good job, God the Creator! You can make anything you want,
and your workmanship is superb. You are the author of all
and the owner of everything. May we, your creatures, be wise
and careful to manage well all that is yours. Amen.*

Only the Beginning

————◦◦◦————

I wrote about all that Jesus began to do and teach.

Acts 1:1

Luke, a first-century historian and physician, wrote a two-volume set—the books of Luke and Acts—to tell the story of Jesus. The first line of Acts is truly amazing. It says the story of Jesus—from heaven to earth, from miracles to teaching—was only beginning. That means when the Gospel of Luke ends, Jesus is just getting started! There would be more miracles, more transformed lives, more of everything he began.

The story of Jesus is not limited to thirty-three years in an ancient strip of land along the eastern shore of the Mediterranean Sea. It did not end two thousand years ago. Jesus is still at work in our world. I find this to be breathtakingly exciting, because you and I are part of the story. We couldn't be there when Jesus walked on water, healed the sick, and raised the dead, but we can experience the presence and power, the teaching and ministry of Jesus right here and now. The story isn't over yet!

————◦◦————

Keep going, Jesus. What you began in Bethlehem, Galilee, and Jerusalem, continue today. Call us to be your disciples. Teach us your divine truths. Tell us your memorable stories. Show us your powerful miracles. What began then with dozens has already multiplied to billions. Keep doing and teaching in our generation. And let me be part of the gospel of Jesus Christ today. Amen.

A Confirmed Reservation

Therefore, my brothers, be all the more eager
to make your calling and election sure.
2 Peter 1:10

There's nothing quite like a free trip! Recently I cashed in some frequent flyer miles online. I was issued a confirmation number, but I wanted to talk to a real person to make sure. So I called the toll-free number. The agent said, "You've got an e-ticket." Well, I wanted something more tangible, so she offered further confirmation by e-mail, fax, or mail. I asked for all three. I wanted to be sure I was getting that trip!

Peter wasn't writing about an airline destination, but about our eternal destination. He was talking to those who have called up God in prayer and asked for a reservation to go to heaven. God gives two confirmations of that reservation. First, "If you confess with your mouth 'Jesus is Lord,' and believe in your heart that God raised him from the dead, you will be saved" (Romans 10:9). Second, becoming a Christian changes your desires and behavior. It makes you live a better life.

So why not confirm your eternal destiny today? Then you can joyfully anticipate the benefits of your reservation!

God, I'm calling to confirm. My prayer confesses that Jesus is my Lord. Please confirm my salvation with your good changes in me. Amen.

Pecking Order

———— ◆⟨◎◎⟩◆ ————

"Whoever welcomes this little child in my name welcomes me;
and whoever welcomes me welcomes the one who sent me.
For he who is least among you all—he is the greatest."
Jesus, in Luke 9:48

What's the difference between driving a Mercedes, Lexus, Hyundai, or Honda? They are all European or Asian brand cars that transport you from point A to point B. But in our minds, the car you drive says a lot about your position in society. Everything today seems to be about who is great and who is not. From street gangs to the United States Senate, we are constantly positioning ourselves in the proverbial pecking order.

Even Jesus' disciples were not above jockeying for position. When they were arguing among themselves as to who was the greatest, Jesus placed a little child at his side in the position of honor. What was Jesus saying by his action? He didn't need to rub shoulders with the rich and the famous or the powerful. He was glad to be associated with this little child who occupied a humble position in society and wasn't impressed with greatness or pecking order.

Jesus identifies with those who are less important. Do you?

———— ⟨◎⟩ ————

*Father, Son, Holy Spirit, your names are the highest. And, as for my
place in the pecking order of this world—may I not be a "name dropper,"
seeking to upgrade myself with those who are famous and important;
may I be a "name lifter," seeking to honor the least of society. Amen.*

Jesus Saves

❖

An angel of the Lord appeared to him in a dream and said,
"Joseph son of David, do not be afraid to take Mary home as
your wife, because what is conceived in her is from the Holy
Spirit. She will give birth to a son, and you are to give him the
name Jesus, because he will save his people from their sins."

Matthew 1:20–21

The red neon sign JESUS SAVES isn't as common as it used to be, but you can still see it on a few buildings around the country. Those signs have sometimes embarrassed Christians who wonder if the average passerby has any idea what "Jesus saves" means.

Have you ever looked up your own name in a book of baby names to see what it means? I did it once and was sorry I did. My name, *Leith,* means "broad river," which didn't seem like a very good name to give someone. But look up the name *Jesus,* and you will see it means "Jehovah is salvation." In other words, Jesus *means* salvation. They are sort of one and the same thing. Not only does Jesus save people from their sins, but his very name announces he is salvation!

I guess that makes the sign JESUS SAVES a bit redundant, doesn't it?

❖

*Jesus, you are my Savior, and your name is a perfect
match to who you are. I want to say your name often and
tell others that Jesus really does save. Amen.*

Intended for Good

—⟨◈◈⟩—

"You intended to harm me, but God intended it for good to accomplish what is now being done, the saving of many lives."
Joseph, in Genesis 50:20

Young Joseph had a tough life. He was sold into slavery by his jealous brothers, then ended up in prison for a crime he did not commit. He had a lot to regret and plenty of cause for resentment. But God used the bad events in Joseph's life to bring him to a position of political prominence and power. And that position eventually enabled Joseph to save his own family—who had betrayed him—from starvation. The years in between had transformed Joseph's suffering to victory.

All of us go through pain in our own personal stories. The question is, what will you do with the rest of your life from now on? Will you do what God wants you to do? Will you let him renew you and heal your regrets? It may surprise you to find out what God has intended for good in your life.

—⟨◈⟩—

Others have intended to harm me. Lord, you know who they are and what they have done. Will you use their intentions for good? I pray that you will carry me past the hurt, change the bad to good, and use me to bless and benefit others. For this I must simply trust you, because I can't yet see the good coming from what has happened so far. Thank you, Jesus. Amen.

Wearing the Uniform of God

———❦———

Live such good lives among the pagans that, though they accuse you
of doing wrong, they may see your good deeds and glorify God.

1 Peter 2:12

When someone wears a company uniform, every word and action reflects
upon that company. If you have a really good or a really bad experience with
someone wearing a UPS uniform or a McDonald's uniform, you tend to
think of the company in terms of the way that person treated you.

Well, we Christians wear the uniform of God. Everything we say and do
either makes God look good—or bad. How can we make God look good? By
not doing bad things, and by doing good things, such as standing against
racism at work, helping someone looking for a job, offering free babysitting
for a friend who is broke, or sticking with a marriage that's bad and trying
to make it good.

Does that mean those around us will want to become Christians because they
are so impressed with how we act? Maybe yes, maybe no. But in everything,
we want to avoid evil and do good to reflect on God, regardless of how other
people respond.

———❧———

You are good. Others know I live and work for you. So that means
I wear your uniform, God. How I dress and behave always reflects
on you. Train me to represent you well. Give me the right words to
say in every situation. Allow me to make you look good. Amen.

You *Can* Make a Difference!

❧⌘❧

"If anyone gives even a cup of cold water to one of these little ones because he is my disciple, I tell you the truth, he will certainly not lose his reward."
Jesus, in Matthew 10:42

Seventeen-year-old Sonia Angeline lived at the garbage dump in Maputo, Mozambique. When she went into labor, her labor continued for four days with little progress. Sonia was dying, but her family couldn't come up with enough money for a taxi fare to get her to a hospital. The typical household savings in the country of Mozambique is ten cents.

Katrin Blackert, a twenty-three-year-old American volunteer, happened upon Sonia during her regular visits to the garage dump. Katrin quickly summoned a taxi, paid the fare with her own money, and took Sonia to the hospital, where her baby daughter was delivered by Caesarean section.

Do you know what the total cost—taxi fare and all medical charges including surgery—was? Two lives were saved for four dollars! Imagine how wonderful it would feel to make that kind of difference in somebody's life. Jesus said, "Love your neighbor as yourself." Look for opportunities to serve your neighbor, whether here or abroad. Ask God to show you how *you* can make a difference!

❧

Jesus, there are so many with needs that I wonder what difference I can make. May I see each one through your eyes—a God-given opportunity to help someone in need in your name. Lead me to that person today. Amen.

You Tell Me to Ask

—◆⬥◆—

You do not have because you do not ask God.

James 4:2

It's easy to misunderstand what James wrote—to think it means God will give us anything we ask for. But these words are not an open invitation to wealth, health, power, and success. God is not an Aladdin's lamp to be rubbed in order to make all our wishes come true.

It's what precedes this line that is extremely important: "Don't fights and quarrels come from your desires that battle within you?" The point is that anger, fights, and quarrels come naturally to us and fill our lives if we don't pray or "ask God." Sin grows like a virus, and we lack the strength to fight against it.

But if we regularly submit the control of our lives to God, his strength fills our souls on the inside. Suddenly, outside circumstances aren't so important. The battle is still there, but the need to fight and quarrel is gone when we can leave the outcome to God.

—◆⬥◆—

You tell me to ask, God. I'll start where James wrote about fights and quarrels. It is easy to argue with others at home, work, school, church, and just about anywhere. Quench the urge to fight that rises in my heart. Challenge me to see another's point of view. Answer these prayers, and then I will ask for more. Amen.

Privileges + Responsibilities

———◈———

"But you will receive power when the Holy Spirit comes on you;
and you will be my witnesses in Jerusalem, and in all Judea and
Samaria, and to the ends of the earth."

Acts 1:8

During one of Jesus' last meals with his disciples, he made a spectacular promise. He promised to send the Holy Spirit to give them supernatural power to live out the Christian life. The Spirit would reside inside them, guide them, encourage, instruct, and bless them. But they would also be given a job to do. They would become the messengers of God to tell about Jesus in Jerusalem, Judea, Samaria, and the rest of the world.

These words imply that Christians have responsibilities as well as privileges. Being a witness to what God has done may be difficult and come with a high price (the Greek word for "witness" is *martus,* from which we get our English word *martyr*). Jesus was giving the blueprint for Christians to change the world for God—from their hometown to province to neighbor nation to the whole globe.

That same Holy Spirit empowers every believer today. What are you doing to change the world for God?

———◈———

Welcome to my life, Holy Spirit. Fill and empower me just as Jesus promised. Lift me beyond the physical and natural to the spiritual and supernatural. I am so privileged to receive your blessings and so blessed to be given gospel responsibilities. Whatever the cost, I am Jesus' witness wherever you send me. Amen.

Praying to Our Father

Our Father, who art in heaven,
hallowed be thy name.
Thy Kingdom come,
thy will be done,
on earth as it is in heaven
Give us this day our daily bread.
And forgive us our trespasses,
as we forgive those who trespass against us.
And lead us not into temptation,
but deliver us from evil.

The Lord's Prayer

Before Jesus returned to heaven, he gave his followers a sample of how to pray. We call it "The Lord's Prayer." Actually, that's not a very good name, because Jesus didn't pray this prayer himself. It would be better to call it "The Disciples' Prayer," because it's a model of how they were to learn to pray. It was never intended to be memorized and prayed by rote. In fact, "The Lord's Prayer" appears in different words in the different biographies of Jesus in the New Testament. We are to think of it as a template, a form for us to fill in the blanks, an example for us to follow in our own words.

When you are praying, don't just repeat "The Lord's Prayer" verbatim out of the Bible. Instead, use it as a guide. Fill in the blanks with your own information, and make it your own!

For thine is the kingdom, the power and the glory, for ever and ever. Amen.

The Goodness of Work

Make it your ambition to lead a quiet life,
to mind your own business and to work with your hands…
so that your daily life may win the respect of outsiders
and so that you will not be dependent on anybody.

1 Thessalonians 4:11–12

The Bible establishes the goodness of work from page one, where it describes God's creation of the world. At each stage of creation the Bible says, "God saw that it was good." God takes great satisfaction in the work that he does, and he created humans to be like him.

Jesus even had a job waiting for him when he got back to heaven. Before his return, he told his followers that he was going there to prepare a place for them to live when they got to heaven.

The realization that we were created to work can revolutionize our lives. It can prevent us from viewing work as merely what we do in order to live—or as something we have to get done so we can get on with our real lives.

How would your perspective change if you saw work as something you were created to do? If you saw work itself as being "good"?

To you, the God Who Works, I dedicate my job and labors. Thank you for the work you have given to me. My desire is to perform so well that at the end of each day I can see that what I have accomplished is good. Amen.

A Heart for the Poor

There will always be poor people in the land. Therefore
I command you to be openhanded toward your brothers
and toward the poor and needy in your land.

Deuteronomy 15:11

Psychiatrist Karl Menninger was asked one time what people should do when they feel on the verge of a breakdown. Menninger answered, "Lock your house, go across the railroad tracks, find someone in need, and do something for him."

There is much that we can do for those who are in need. And, as Jesus' followers, we should have a heart for the poor. Why not mentor an immigrant who is trying to get established in this country and doesn't understand how the system works. Tutor a child who is struggling in school. Be an advocate for those who have less than you do, or for those who do not receive justice. If you have professional skills, offer them pro bono to someone who can't afford your services.

We all need to ask ourselves regularly, "When was the last time I spoke up for or did something to help someone in need?"

God bless the poor and needy. Give help and hope to the widow, orphan, alien, hungry, jobless, sick, disabled, and marginalized. Bless these through me, I pray. Get me beyond myself and the worries that monopolize my mind. I know that my own burdens may be lifted when I lift the burdens of others. Help me to get up and do it. For Jesus' sake, amen.

Take the Challenge!

———✦❦❧✦———

Suppose a brother or sister is without clothes and daily food. If one of you says to him, "Go, I wish you well; keep warm and well fed," but does nothing about his physical needs, what good is it? In the same way, faith by itself, if it is not accompanied by action, is dead.

James 2:15–17

A newspaper reporter once asked me why our church chose to get involved in helping people in Africa suffering from HIV/AIDS.

"We're just doing what Christians have always done," I told him. "Christians have responded with love and compassion during epidemics all the way back to the bubonic plague and smallpox epidemics of the Roman empire. That's what Christians do—they make a difference in the world."

No one wants to finish life poorly. I certainly don't want the measure of my life to be the money I earned, the education I received, or the possessions I accumulated. I want to make a real difference. Don't you?

One of the best ways to get started is to simply look for opportunities. Look for ways you can reach out and make a difference in the lives of others. I challenge you to try it for a week. You'll be amazed at the results!

———❧———

Open my eyes to the needs of others as you see them, Lord. May I see and then do something that truly helps. Forgive all my tired excuses. Stop me from blaming the needy. Push me to turn my faith into actual help. Amen.

Everything Changes

"Praise be to the name of God for ever and ever;
wisdom and power are his.
He changes times and seasons;
he sets up kings and deposes them."
Daniel 2:20–21

A generation ago there was a massive government effort to bring the United States into line with most of the rest of the world, switching from miles to kilometers and from Fahrenheit to Celsius. But millions of dollars in educational efforts didn't pay off. We stuck to our old ways and didn't budge a single centimeter! Canadians changed, but Americans didn't.

I guess the old adage is true that change comes more easily to some of us than it does to others of us. But whether we like it or not, change is inevitable. Every one of us experiences change every day—change in our family, job, finances, residence, church, friends, politics—you name it, everything changes!

Change may be hard, but change can also be very good. The healthiest attitude towards change is to trust in the God who is changing you step by step, all along the way.

You are the always-consistent God. We are your constantly changing
people. Please grant the special wisdom needed in fast-changing times.
Protect me from becoming bitter or angry because today is not the same
as yesterday. Multiply my trust so that you can use bad changes for good.
Keep me relevant for now rather than a relic from the past. Amen.

The Smartest Investment

"Where your treasure is, there your heart will be also."
Luke 12:34

I've always loved using my money to make a difference. I love to give to those in need, and I started giving money to spread the Good News of Jesus while I was in college. I didn't have much to give, but it felt great! Seeing the results of my continued giving was a great joy. When I saw lives changed, when I heard missionaries report about their work, when I knew that poor people were being helped, I was thrilled to know that I had a part.

To this day, I know that investing in people and the gospel are the best choices I could ever make. You see, I've regretted purchases I've made… money I've wasted. But I've never regretted giving generously to others. I'll admit there have been times when I thought I would, because I feared not having enough money for my expenses, but that's never happened. In fact, the more sacrificial the gift, the more I've grown in my faith. After all, everything we have is a gift from God anyway.

I want to be generous, my Savior, as you have been generous to me.
Open my wallet to donate more cash. Open my hand when it grasps
what is not mine to keep. Bestow wisdom to give to opportunity
and not only to need. Prevent me from pretending that giving is
the end of responsibility; may I also pray, go, and do. Amen.

Seventh Days Off

—❦—

Remember the Sabbath day by keeping it holy.
Exodus 20:8

The creation story tells us that God created the world in six days and took the seventh day off. It was his special day to stop and celebrate what he had done. In the Ten Commandments, God made it clear he wants us to have one day each week when we stop our usual work to celebrate God and his blessings. The word *Sabbath* actually means "stop"—to rest a day each week.

So work six days and take a day off. Enjoy your day of rest and focus on God. If Sunday is your Sabbath, great. If it can't be Sunday, pick a different day. But don't work seven days a week. This is a commandment of trust. It demonstrates that we trust God to help us accomplish our work in six days so we can celebrate this gift of a day from God. It demonstrates we are working for God, not ourselves.

∼❦∽

Lord of the Sabbath, I live in a world that never stops. My electronic connections are so many and frequent that I am always busy and never quiet. I don't really know how to take a day off. Show me the Sabbath way. Nurture my trust in you to make time to rest, renew, and be with you. Demonstrate that my work will go on, and life will be okay when I limit my labors to six days a week. Lead me to this discipline starting this week. Amen.

Tempted...

———◆❦◆———

"Worship the Lord your God and serve him only."
Jesus, in Matthew 4:10

When Jesus was alone in the wilderness, Satan took him up to a high place and showed him all the kingdoms of the world. By offering Jesus the rule of Earth, he was giving Jesus the opportunity to skip the cross and go directly to the throne of the world. Jesus could immediately stop all injustice, eliminate all poverty, and outlaw all sin, pain, and suffering. But it came with a high price. In order to become king of the world, Jesus was first required to worship Satan. It's a classic example of the end justifying the means. It was a powerful call for compromise, and it was tempting.

But Jesus insisted that there is only one God and only one right way. Jesus knew that giving allegiance to Satan is a guaranteed path to eventual destruction, even if it seems that some immediate good might come from it. God must be first. He alone deserves our worship.

———◆❦◆———

Temptation is dangerous stuff. You know better than anyone, Jesus. You've been tempted by Satan himself. When I face temptations that are obvious paths to sin, I pray for spiritual power to resist. When I face opportunities that seem good but could be disastrous, I ask for wisdom to discern, as well as courage to do what is right. Whatever the challenge, I repeatedly renew my worship of you and withhold worship from any other. Amen.

The Faithful Chauffeur

---❦---

> "His master replied, 'Well done, good and faithful servant!
> You have been faithful with a few things; I will put you in charge
> of many things. Come and share your master's happiness!'"
>
> *Jesus, in Matthew 25:23*

I grew up less than a mile from a very famous, wealthy man whose large garage was filled with very expensive limousines, sports cars, and various vintage automobiles. The family chauffeur lived on the property; his full-time job was to care for and drive all the vehicles. He worked for that family for decades and did an excellent job. I vividly remember how immaculate those vehicles were—they always looked brand new, as if someone waxed them every day.

That chauffeur treated the vehicles as if they were his own. They were his life's work. But they were not his. He was a servant, entrusted with a responsibility and accountable to his employer. He took his job very seriously. When the wealthy man died, he willed his vehicles to the faithful chauffeur, who received a fortune in valuable cars.

We too are called to be responsible and accountable for whatever resources Jesus puts under our care. If we are, we, like the faithful chauffeur, will be rewarded.

---❧---

*Master, everything belongs to you. There is nothing that is mine.
All that appear to be my possessions are entrusted by you. Tell
me how to manage what is yours. I promise to work hard and
do what you say. I very much want your approval. Amen.*

Jesus—Open 24/7

Jesus welcomed them and spoke to them about the kingdom
of God, and healed those who needed healing.
Luke 9:11

At first glance, the life of a celebrity might seem appealing. But when you look beyond the glamour to the lack of privacy, it loses some of its appeal.

Jesus was a celebrity. He attracted huge crowds. On one occasion Jesus took his twelve closest followers on a sort of debriefing retreat so they could all report on their travels to different villages to preach and heal. It was their special time to be alone with Jesus and was intended to be a well-deserved rest for Jesus as well.

But as often happens, someone leaked information. Word spread about Jesus' whereabouts, and crowds of people started showing up. They were attracted to Jesus like metal to a magnet. What did Jesus do? He welcomed the people!

Aren't you glad Jesus doesn't have a cut-off number? Think of what it would feel like to have the doors slam shut when you and your family are next in line.

With Jesus there is no limit. He always welcomes more!

Here I come again, Jesus. I have prayers to pray and problems for you to solve. Thank you for staying open 24 hours every day. You are always available, no matter how busy. You don't have limits like the rest of us. I love you for so many reasons, and your welcome is one of the best. Amen.

Ordinary Actions?

———◆◆◆◆———

"They do not need to go away. You give them something to eat."
Jesus, in Matthew 14:16

Jesus' twelve disciples were getting tired, hungry, and short-tempered with the late hour and the crowd. So they told Jesus, "This is a remote place, and it's already getting late. Send the crowds away, so they can go to the villages and buy themselves some food." It was a practical suggestion. After all, the disciples didn't have food or money to feed five thousand people.

But Jesus saw right through to his disciples' true motives. They really weren't thinking about the needs of the crowd; they wanted Jesus for themselves. So he directly challenged them, *"You* give them something to eat." He not only rejected their selfishness, he made them responsible for the solution.

Frankly, Jesus' answer makes me want to squirm. When I'm faced with needs, my first two responses are likely to be, "Let someone else do something" or, "Let God take care of this one." But I've learned that when I willingly step forward and offer what little I have for Jesus to use, anything becomes possible. Try it, and you'll see what I mean!

———◆◆◆———

Jesus, what do you want me to do? Tell me, and I'll try my best. I know that sometimes you let your followers start with ordinary actions that you later expand into miracles. My friends and I are reluctant to start because we don't see the miracle coming. Just help me get started. Amen.

Let Go and Fly

⎯⎯⎯⎯✦❧☙✦⎯⎯⎯⎯

When I am afraid,
I will trust in you.
In God, whose word I praise,
in God I trust; I will not be afraid.

Psalm 56:3-4

In Henri Nouwen's book *Sabbatical Journeys*, he describes the relationship between the "catcher" and the "flyer" in a circus trapeze performance. He says that the flyer swings on the trapeze and then, at precisely the right moment, lets go and flies through the air to be caught by the catcher, who is waiting a distance away. The hardest part of the whole dangerous journey is that the flyer has to hold his position as still as possible and just trust that the catcher will catch him.

It's like that with us and God. God has promised that he has a plan for each of our lives, but he doesn't want our hope centered on grabbing hold of his plan. He wants our hope centered on him. Just like the trapeze flyer in the circus, we must let go and fly through the dangerous journey of life—filled with trust and hope. It is our job to simply trust that God will catch us.

◆❧❧◆

Trustworthy God, I believe you will catch me. You'll never let me crash. Only because of you will I let go of the old and swing out to the new. It's scary. I feel vulnerable. Yet you have never let me down. My hands are outstretched. Catch me, Lord. Catch me! Amen.

NOVEMBER

The Slave Who Didn't Get Even

> Pharaoh said to Joseph, "I hereby put you in
> charge of the whole land of Egypt."
>
> *Genesis 41:41*

How would you treat those who had mistreated you if you were in the position of control?

Joseph, a young Hebrew, was sold into slavery in Egypt because his brothers hated him for being their father's favorite. Despite his hard life, Joseph remained faithful to God. After years of suffering, God rewarded that faithfulness by having the ruler of Egypt promote Joseph to the position of prime minister.

When drought spread throughout the region, only Egypt had food—all because of Joseph's wise management. Then one day his brothers, sent by their father in search of grain, stood before Joseph. When they discovered the powerful prime minister was actually the kid brother they'd sold into slavery, they were scared to death.

But Joseph's character shone brightly. He forgave his brothers, giving them food, protection, and land. He used his power for good, to accomplish the saving of many lives.

What a stunning perspective! People may intend to harm you, but God intends those very acts will be used for good.

*Joseph's God, you are my God too. May I forgive and
bless those who mistreat and curse me. Amen.*

Real Angels

—◦⟨⟨⟨⟩⟩⟩◦—

Praise the Lord, you his angels, you mighty ones
who do his bidding, who obey his word.
Psalm 103:20

Do you ever wonder what angels do? Do they sit around playing harps like you see in old paintings? The basic answer to that question is that angels do whatever God wants them to do. That's their job. The Greek word *angelos*, from which we get our word *angel*, was a common everyday term that means "messenger." So an angel, by definition, is a messenger of God—going where God wants and doing what God wants.

Angels do all kinds of good things to bless us, to help us, to strengthen and encourage us, but they don't take their assignments from us. They are not at our whim. They obey God, not us. Whenever you hear anyone say that an angel's job is to make us happy or to give us what we want, that is simply not true. Angels are not genies in bottles that we rub to make our wishes come true. Angels answer only to God's call—and do only his bidding.

—◦◦◦—

*King of the heavenly host, we join our voices with the angels in singing
your praises. Your angels are our celestial partners in serving you.
We, like they, await your orders. The difference is that they benefit
us, but we don't benefit them. Thank you, God, for every time you
have sent every angel to fulfill your wishes in our lives. Amen.*

Meaning—for Me

These are written that you may believe that Jesus is the Christ, the
Son of God, and that by believing you may have life in his name.

John 20:31

For the Bible to make a difference in your life, you need to ask yourself
three questions while reading it: What does the Bible say? What does it
mean? How does it apply to me?

For example, when John explained why Jesus came to earth, he said, "To all
who received him, to those who believed in his name, he gave the right to
become children of God" (John 1:12). The meaning of these words is that
anyone who personally believes in Jesus as Savior will be immediately and
forever adopted into the family of God.

But to make a difference in my life, I need to go beyond the meaning of
those words and ask, "What does that mean *to me*?" The personal application
of this Bible teaching is that if I receive Jesus as my Savior and believe in his
name, I will have the right to become a child of God. To personally apply
the Bible to yourself is to receive Jesus.

Have you done that?

*Open your truth and my mind, God my Teacher. Instruct me in the facts
of the Bible and sharpen my thoughts to understand. Guide me to the
meaning of the Bible and shape my thoughts to interpret. Show me the
application of the Bible and challenge me to do what you want. Amen.*

Honoring God's Name

---◈---

"This, then, is how you should pray:
'Our Father in heaven,
hallowed be your name.'"
Matthew 6:9

When a German manufacturer named Emil Jellinek decided to name a new car after his daughter, Mercedes, he made her name famous—a worldwide synonym for quality and excellence. In 1790 the Congress of the United States of America forever honored the name of the first President by naming the new capital "Washington." Perhaps you were named after a favorite relative or friend.

Names were even more important in ancient cultures than they are today. Back then it was typical to ask, "Who are you?" because it was assumed that the person and the name were the same. So, for example, the Old Testament woman named Naomi was "pleasant." After she faced famine, unemployment, a move to a foreign country, was widowed, and her two sons died, she changed her name to Mara, which means "bitter," to better reflect who she was.

When Jesus was teaching his followers how to pray, he taught them to value and honor God the Father by honoring his name. Do you honor God's name when you pray?

---◈---

God of Eternity, you are my heavenly Father whom I love. As often as my prayers call you "Father," it is an honor that I never fully grasp. My prayer is to you. My prayer is about you. My prayer honors you. You and your name are holy. Amen.

A God-Directed Life

The length of our days is seventy years—
or eighty, if we have the strength.
Psalm 90:10

In his heart a man plans his course,
but the Lord determines his steps.
Proverbs 16:9

One of my hobbies is collecting bits of wisdom and experiences from people in their seventies, eighties, and nineties whom I consider to have lived good, meaningful lives. I ask them to compare where they thought their lives were headed when they were younger, to where life ended up when they grew older.

They have repeatedly told how they had planned their lives, and then along came stunning opportunities and devastating disappointments that they never anticipated. No one has ever told me life has turned out exactly as planned. But the common thread I see running through their stories is that they did what God asked them to do, whether they liked it or understood it at the time.

I've learned from these senior Christians that I must do whatever God asks at the time and not worry too much about how it all hangs together. It is the mark of a God-directed life.

Lord of life, every day is a gift from you. I know when I was born, but you alone know how long I will live. Script my dreams and guide my plans. I know you bring surprises I never could have guessed. From opportunities to disappointments, I trust you to determine my steps and give me the strength to walk with you. Amen.

True Greatness

"Whoever wants to become great among you must be
your servant, and whoever wants to be first must be your
slave—just as the Son of Man did not come to be served,
but to serve, and to give his life as a ransom for many."
Matthew 20:26-28

Mrs. Zebedee, mother of the disciples James and John, came to Jesus to
ask for a favor. She wanted to know if her two sons could be seated—one at
Jesus' right hand and one at his left hand—in his kingdom. Jesus told her
that decision was not up to him. His Father would decide who would sit on
his right and on his left.

Centuries of Christians have passed judgment on Mrs. Zebedee for asking
that of Jesus and, frankly, I've never understood that criticism. What could
be better than a godly mother who wants her sons to be as close to Jesus as
they can possibly get?

You see, Jesus never condemns the desire for greatness or the quest for high
eternal rank. Rather, he explains how to be truly great. Referring to himself as
the "Son of Man," Jesus says that what is frequently mistaken for greatness in
our world is the opposite of the standards of heaven. Jesus, the most important
person in the universe, became a servant. Now that's true greatness!

*I'd like to sit next to you, Jesus. Not for the status
of your side but to be close to my Savior. Amen.*

The Main Truth

———◈———

"A man...fell into the hands of robbers. They...went away, leaving
him half dead. A priest...passed by on the other side. So too, a
Levite.... But a Samaritan...took care of him....
Which of these three do you think was a neighbor to the man who
fell into the hands of robbers?"
The expert in the law replied, "The one who had mercy on him."
Jesus told him, "Go and do likewise."
Luke 10:30-37

It's tempting to get carried away with our own cleverness when interpreting
the Bible. But it's a mistake to look for deep meaning in obscure details
while ignoring the main point being made.

For example, when a lawyer asked Jesus, "Who is my neighbor?" Jesus
responded with a story of a man who was robbed and left nearly dead as he
traveled from Jerusalem to Jericho. Both a priest and a Levite saw him and
passed by. But a Samaritan bandaged his wounds, loaded the injured man
on his own donkey, and took him to an inn to care for him.

So, what is the main truth? That we should watch out for robbers? That
priests don't care about victims of crime? That donkeys are good for
transporting injured people? No, the main point is that we're to love our
neighbors and that our neighbors are those with needs.

When reading the Bible, always look for the main truth.

———◈———

*Jesus, help me to read and understand what the Bible actually
says and not put my meanings in your mouth. Amen.*

Scrambling for the Bottom

———— ❧ ————

"If anyone wants to be first, he must be the very last,
and the servant of all."
He took a little child and had him stand among them. Taking
him in his arms, he said to them, "Whoever welcomes one of
these little children in my name welcomes me; and whoever
welcomes me does not welcome me but the one who sent me."
Jesus, in Mark 9:35–37

When I was a seminary student, each Sunday morning I'd try to teach the young children in our church what I had been studying that week. It was no small challenge! I'm not sure the children always understood what I was saying or that I made a lasting impact on their lives. Yet some of my best memories from those years are sitting on the floor with those children, and not the times when I was privileged as a student to preach in the "big church."

When Jesus took a little child in his arms as a lesson for his disciples, he was teaching about the hierarchy of heaven. He presented a principle so profound that we are still trying to figure it out two thousand years later.

True greatness is caring about those who are *not* famous, powerful, or important. As far as Jesus is concerned, the best way to the top is to scramble for the bottom.

———— ❧ ————

*Jesus, I am your child. Take me in your arms. There I do not
seek fame or importance. I just want to be like you. Amen.*

What If There Is a God?

---〰️---

The fool says in his heart,
"There is no God."
Psalm 53:1

I heard a conversation between a Christian and an atheist. They covered everything from the existence of God, heaven, and hell, to the authority of the Bible, until they were both exhausted from their debate.

Finally, the atheist said to the Christian, "So, what happens if you live your Christian life and at the end of it you discover that I was right and you were wrong?"

The Christian replied, "Then I will have lived a good life with great joy, and I will die and stay dead." Then he asked the atheist, "But what if I'm right and you are wrong?"

The atheist thought for a moment. "Then I will have made the worst possible mistake of all of eternity."

Our assumptions—whether they're right or wrong—shape our thinking on everything in life. But if our assumptions about God, the Bible, and life after death are wrong, the results are eternal.

---〰️---

God, I am completely counting on you to be real. My whole life is based on you and your teaching. My hope for life after death and eternity in heaven is because of faith in you. I believe in you and your salvation through Jesus, who came and died on the cross for me and rose again the third day. Amen.

A Seeker after God

On the way Jesus asked them, "Who do people say I am?"
They replied, "Some say John the Baptist; others say Elijah;
and still others, one of the prophets."
"But what about you?" he asked. "Who do you say I am?"
Peter answered, "You are the Christ."

Mark 8:27-29

St. Peter the apostle grew up by the shores of the Sea of Galilee and became a professional fisherman who was also a seeker after God. He was very attracted to the teachings of a charismatic young rabbi from Nazareth named Jesus. One day Jesus asked Peter to quit his fishing business to follow him. Peter instantly said, "Yes."

From that time on, no matter how much he got of Jesus, Peter always wanted more. When Jesus walked on water, Peter jumped out of the boat and went to him. When Jesus fed thousands with a boy's lunch, when he healed the sick and raised the dead, Peter was always close by. When Jesus asked his disciples who they thought he was, Peter was the only one with the courage to answer him, "You are the Christ, the Son of the living God."

Who do you believe Jesus is? How much do you seek after him? Why not be as eager as Peter?

Jesus, if you ask me who I think you are, I answer with Peter, "You are the Christ!" You are the One sent from God—the Son of God, my Savior, my Lord, my Friend, and even more. Amen.

Giving Thanks

❖

"Give thanks in all circumstances, for this
is God's will for you in Christ Jesus."
1 Thessalonians 5:18

If I send you a thank-you note for a present, I'm acknowledging that you are the one responsible for the gift to me. It would be nonsense for me to receive a gift from you and send a thank-you note to someone else, wouldn't it? The act of offering thanks acknowledges responsibility.

The Bible teaches that "Every good and perfect gift" (James 1:17) is from God. But some of us say, "Well, there's not much good in my life." My friend, even though your problems are real and many, don't let them blur your vision of God's goodness. Our lives are loaded with good. We have life. We have God. Through Jesus we have the offer of forgiveness of sin and the gift of eternal life in heaven to all who believe in him.

It is only when we acknowledge God's responsibility for the good in our lives that we are able to discover the true meaning of thanksgiving—that we experience God through giving thanks.

❧

*"Thanks be to God!" are the frequent words of St. Paul that I echo, Lord.
Forgive me for centering on what I lack. Push thoughts of what I do not
have to the edges of my mind and bring thoughts of your generosity to the
middle. I have so much to thank you for. Thanks be to God! Amen.*

Switching Allegiance

———◆◆———

"Great and marvelous are your deeds,
Lord God Almighty.
Just and true are your ways,
King of the ages.
All nations will come
and worship before you,
for your righteous acts have been revealed."
Revelation 15:3–4

After some years of living in England, a Frenchman decided to renounce his citizenship and become a British subject. Immediately after the legal ceremony, he was asked, "So, how does it feel? What's the difference?" His clever answer was especially meaningful to those interested in history: "Yesterday the Battle of Waterloo was a defeat. Today it is a victory."

By giving his allegiance to a different sovereign, he completely changed his perspective. You see, which king gets our allegiance determines how we interpret history and all of life. Christians are those who have renounced other allegiances in life and sworn loyalty to Jesus Christ as our King.

If you have never accepted Jesus Christ as your personal Savior, my prayer is that you would do it today. Tell God that you want to turn from your old life and switch your allegiance to Jesus Christ as your King. And then watch your perspective change.

———◆———

King Jesus, I renounce all other loyalty and swear my eternal allegiance to you. You are the Just Ruler, Sovereign Lord, and Eternal God. All of history and all of my life is defined and interpreted for you. Hail, King Jesus! Amen.

Stranded

❖❖❖

*Be imitators of God, therefore, as dearly loved children and live
a life of love, just as Christ loved us and gave himself up for us
as a fragrant offering and sacrifice to God.*

Ephesians 5:1–2

One year our family drove in our old station wagon from Minneapolis to
Phoenix. Just as we were nearing the summit of one of the highest, most
dangerous roads over the Continental Divide, the engine quit. Fortunately
there was a roadside pull-off close by, so we rolled the car there. A man
from the little town of Ouray stopped and transported all six of us into
town, where we got a motel. The next day, he graciously picked me up at the
motel and drove me back up the mountain to get the car.

"How can I thank you?" I asked him.

"Just treat somebody else well and remember me."

"That's all?" I asked.

"That's a lot," he replied.

And so, any time I ever help a stranded person, I remember that man and
experience his goodness all over again.

But how much more so with God! When we ask him, "How can I thank
you?" God says, "Love me, and love others the way I've loved you."

❧

*God, you have been good to me more times than I can remember.
You have often rescued me. Now I want to imitate you and be good
to others. Give me someone to rescue for Jesus' sake, amen.*

Sixpence None the Richer

———◆⟨⟨⟨◎⟩⟩⟩◆———

And now, brothers, we want you to know about the grace that God
has given the Macedonian churches. Out of the most severe trial,
their overflowing joy and their extreme poverty welled up in rich
generosity. For I testify that they gave as much as they were able, and
even beyond their ability.

2 Corinthians 8:1–3

After the musical group Sixpence None the Richer performed on *The Late
Show*, David Letterman asked Leigh Nash, the lead singer, where the group
got its name. Nash replied that the name came from C. S. Lewis's story of
a father giving his son sixpence (six pennies) to buy a gift for the father:
"When the father received the present, he was none the richer, because he
originally gave the sixpence to his son," Nash said. "The analogy is to God
who gives us gifts that we are to use to glorify him. He is not richer because
of our presentations, since he originally gave the gift."

David Letterman said, "That's a beautiful story. If people could actually hear
that and live by that sort of thing, then our world would be a better place."

Letterman was right. The world would be a better place if everyone realized
that all that we have comes from God. We will be blessed when we share our
blessings with others.

———◆⟨⟩◆———

*Everything comes from you, my Lord. I joyously give what you have
given to me. May I glorify you through giving in Jesus' name. Amen.*

Resolving Conflict

❦

"If your brother sins against you, go and show him
his fault, just between the two of you. If he listens to you,
you have won your brother over."

Jesus, in Matthew 18:15

Jesus taught that we are to love others—even our enemies. Nothing is more unnatural than loving your enemy! But loving an enemy doesn't mean giving in; it means helping out. If others' behavior is inappropriate or dysfunctional, it might be that no one else loved them enough earlier in their lives to deal with their unacceptable behavior. How we handle the conflict has the potential to bring about great good.

First of all, be a peacemaker, not a troublemaker. You need to think through your words, actions, and the consequences. Don't assume you know the motives of others. Avoid accusations and the use of words like *always* and *never*. Instead of spreading rumors and accusations, go directly to the person and try to be a reconciler, not an escalator.

Then trust God for a solution. Remain convinced that he can and will resolve conflict for the greatest good. Our role is not to fix everything, but to be faithful to God in everything.

❧

*Getting along with others can be painfully difficult. Sometimes they are mean
and deceptive—telling lies behind my back and tearing me down. Please,
God, give me patience and wisdom to know what to do. I'll try to love,
forgive, and even confront, but I'm going to need your help. Amen.*

Afloat with Hope

We wait in hope for the Lord;
he is our help and our shield.
In him our hearts rejoice,
for we trust in his holy name.
May your unfailing love rest upon us, O Lord,
even as we put our hope in you.

Psalm 33:20-22

We humans are amazingly resilient creatures. As long as we have hope, we can keep going through incredible setbacks and difficulties. Hope is like an inflatable raft with multiple chambers to blow up. Each chamber has to be inflated separately as a safety measure. If one chamber springs a leak and deflates, you're still okay because the other remaining chambers will keep you afloat.

And that's what God does in your life. He doesn't promise that every chamber of your life will always be full of hope, but when one chamber springs a slow leak or is ripped open, other parts have enough hope to keep you afloat and to get you into tomorrow. God is committed to your future. When things go terribly wrong, he gives new hope and new plans. So never give up hope! With God on your side, you can always expect a better tomorrow.

Keep me afloat, Jesus. I feel like my life raft is full of holes, and hope is rushing out. I'm sinking fast. Patch me up. Fill me full. Give me enough hope to make it through today and into tomorrow. You are my hope! Amen.

No Ordinary Teacher

———— ✦❦✦ ————

"Why are you thinking these things in your hearts? Which is easier:
to say, 'Your sins are forgiven,' or to say, 'Get up and walk'? But
that you may know that the Son of Man has authority on earth to
forgive sins...." He said to the paralyzed man, "I tell you, get up,
take your mat and go home."

Jesus, in Luke 5:22–24

Look at the tabloids at the checkout counter. It was no different in Jesus'
time. People are always attracted to the sensational, and the crowds were
drawn like a magnet to Jesus' miracles. Meanwhile, the religious leaders
were very upset when Jesus told people that their sins were forgiven. *That's
blasphemy,* the leaders insisted. *Only God can forgive sins! Who does this guy think he is?*

One day Jesus stopped his teaching when a paralyzed man was lowered from
the roof in front of him. Jesus told the man his sins were forgiven, chastised
the religious leaders for their thinking, then told the sick man to get up and
go home!

The crowd was awestruck, but the religious leaders were troubled. It was
becoming increasingly obvious that this was no ordinary teacher they were
dealing with. It was true then and it's true today: Jesus can both heal the sick
and forgive sins because he is truly God.

———— ❧ ————

*God of Miracles, we still need Jesus' forgiveness and healing.
I need Jesus' miraculous power in my life. May my traditions
never blind me to his presence and power. Amen.*

The Ticket

The first man was of the dust of the earth, the second man from
heaven. As was the earthly man, so are those who are of the earth;
and as is the man from heaven, so also are those who are of heaven.
And just as we have borne the likeness of the earthly man, so shall
we bear the likeness of the man from heaven.

1 Corinthians 15:47-49

The Bible compares Adam, the first man created, and Jesus. Adam was
from earth; he was weak, sinful, and he died. Jesus was from heaven; he
was powerful, sinless, and he came back to life after he died. The Bible goes
on to explain that anyone who has trusted in Jesus as Savior and Lord will
someday be resurrected as Jesus was. Right now we are more like Adam. But
our resurrection bodies will be like Jesus.

It's like trading in an old tent for a new mansion, a beat-up Taurus for a new
Lexus, or a maxed-out credit card for a billion-dollar checking account.
We're talking substantial improvement!

In heaven we need to be like Jesus, and that means a new resurrection body
like Jesus. When you put your faith in Jesus, death becomes more than the
end to this life. It's the ticket to a new body!

---

*I inherited weakness and sin. But now, because of you, Jesus,
I have spiritual strength and my sins are forgiven. Someday I will
have a resurrection body in heaven. Hallelujah! Amen.*

Avoiding Falling

You will never fall, and you will receive a rich welcome into
the eternal kingdom of our Lord and Savior Jesus Christ.
2 Peter 1:10–11

There are enormous benefits to being a Christian. St. Peter says that when
you put your faith and trust in Jesus, there is nothing that will take you down
or that God cannot overcome. At the time this verse was written, a unit of
one hundred soldiers in the Roman army was called a *century*. If the century
was marching along and one soldier tripped or fell, the century would never
leave that soldier behind. They would help the fallen soldier up.

The same promise is being made to Christians. Becoming a Christian
isn't just an insurance policy for heaven after we die; the benefits begin
immediately. And one of those benefits is that God will come alongside you
and help you not to fall or to be destroyed by the circumstances of life.

A second benefit is a rich welcome—a guaranteed place in the eternal
kingdom of God. When you think of it, this life is comparatively short,
while eternity lasts forever! Believing in Jesus fills our lives with joyful
anticipation of the destination that awaits us.

*Grab my hand, Lord. Some days I just lose my balance. Every
day I need you to keep me on my feet and going in the right
direction. Keep me going straight and strong until the day you
welcome me home in your eternal kingdom. Amen.*

No More Guessing

I write these things to you who believe in the name of the Son of
God so that you may know that you have eternal life.

1 John 5:13

In 2002 the *Philadelphia Enquirer* reported Alan Iverson, the superstar guard of
the Philadelphia 76ers, saying, in response to his friend Rah's murder: "I
want to go to heaven. When I die, I want to see Rah. I know he's in heaven,
and before I die, I want to know that's where I'm going. I don't want to have
to guess. "

Eternity is a very long time. In 1 John 5:13 St. John wanted us to know that,
through Jesus Christ, God has given us everything we need to succeed in this
life and to know for sure that we have eternal life. If you have doubts, I invite
you to tell God that you believe that Jesus died on the cross to pay the penalty
for your sins. Tell God that you trust Jesus for the forgiveness of your sin
and for eternal life. And then ask God to confirm your salvation, so you can
know where you are going. Why not make today the day you know for sure?

---

*There are days when I have doubts, God. I wonder if I am really
the Christian I say I am and if I truly have eternal life. Please
replace my doubt with confidence and my uncertainty with
assurance. Because of Jesus I can know for sure. Amen.*

A Simple Lunch

---

*They all ate and were satisfied, and the disciples picked up twelve
basketfuls of broken pieces that were left over.*
Matthew 14:20

I just love it that the story of Jesus' miracle of feeding the five thousand
ends with those words. The hungry crowd was satisfied because of Jesus,
not because they had a gourmet meal. Frankly, the food was very ordinary—
the simple lunch of a small boy. Only barley loaves and dried fish. No
other menu choices. It was "Take it, or leave it." I think it's significant that
Jesus met their needs, not their wants. Jesus not only was concerned and
compassionate for the hungry crowd, but he was generous. There was food
left over.

This is Thanksgiving week, and many of us are well fed to the point of
excess. To be absolutely candid, the garbage many have thrown away this
week would be considered meals for millions in some parts of the world.

I don't say that to make us feel guilty. But we should be grateful. May we
welcome others, feed others, and help others—trusting God to take what we
offer and use it to bless others in Jesus' name.

---

*Thank you, Father, for our daily bread. You are a generous provider
who faithfully feeds me. Often I take my food for granted and easily
forget the hunger of others. Thank you for what is on my plate.
Bless and feed those whose plates are empty this day. Amen.*

Doctor Jesus

———◦◦◦———

Jesus answered them, "It is not the healthy who need a doctor, but the sick. I have not come to call the righteous, but sinners to repentance."
Luke 5:31-32

One day Jesus approached a tax collection booth occupied by Matthew Levi Alphaeus. Because some tax collectors were dishonest, they were greatly disliked and unpopular as a group. As a result, having anything to do with tax collectors opened Jesus to criticism.

Matthew had no doubt seen and heard Jesus around town just like everyone else. When Jesus extended Matthew the simple invitation, "Follow me!" Matthew immediately left his franchise, followed Jesus, and never returned to his old business.

When Matthew later asked Jesus to come to his home for dinner and invited a broad cross section of his friends, Jesus' critics were enraged. "Why do you eat and drink with tax collectors and sinners?"

Jesus' answer was quick and to the point: "Healthy folk aren't the ones who need a doctor, but the sick." The implication of his answer stuns me. It doesn't matter what we've done, what sins we've committed, or what group we are part of. Jesus came to earth to save sinners—like you and me.

———◦◦◦———

Doctor Jesus, you are my skilled and loving Physician. I come to you for diagnosis—tell me what I need to know. I come to you for prescription—tell me what I need to do. Forgive my sins. Heal my diseases. Make me healthy and whole forever. Amen.

A Faith That's Alive

As the body without the spirit is dead,
so faith without deeds is dead.

James 2:26

Does St. James mean that faith is not enough? Do we have to *do* certain things? Imagine if God created Adam and Eve and never breathed life into them. They would be bodies without spirits, unable to do a thing. Obviously a dead body isn't much good. The same goes for a person who has faith and never does anything about it. Just as you want a body with a spirit that is alive and healthy, you want faith plus action. Faith that actively believes in God, has a heart for God, and demonstrates that faith by actions toward others is a faith that is alive—the best kind of faith.

Since you already believe in Jesus, take inventory of your actions to see if they match your beliefs. Ask God to help you live out your faith so that others can see it.

Have a faith that's alive!

Living Lord, you have breathed Christian faith into my soul. May the faith in my soul empower good deeds in my hands. Protect me from faith that is selfish and does not care about others. Show me those I may serve this day. Let my faith be confirmed in my behavior—may I respond graciously to criticism; kindly to harshness; lovingly to the undeserving. I want your righteousness to be seen in my life. Amen.

Superior Craftsmanship

Paul went to Corinth. There he met a Jew named Aquila,
a native of Pontus, who had recently come from Italy with
his wife Priscilla, because Claudius had ordered all the Jews
to leave Rome. Paul went to see them, and because he was a
tentmaker as they were, he stayed and worked with them.
Acts 18:1–3

"We work hard with our own hands."
Paul, in 1 Corinthians 4:12

A favorite sweater of mine says *Superior Norwegian Craftsmanship* on the label.
When I put it on, I'm always impressed by how good it looks on the inside,
where no one else sees it. Somewhere in Norway a worker executes superior
craftsmanship—even where it doesn't show.

As Christians, everything we do should wear the label, *Superior Christian
Craftsmanship*. We should delight in doing a good job whether our work is out
in the public or hidden on the inside.

Clearly what we do is important to God, because he identified people by their
occupation. Jesus was a carpenter. Peter, a fisherman. Lydia, a merchant of
purple cloth. Daniel and Nehemiah, politicians. Luke, a physician. Deborah,
a judge. Ezra, a scribe. Joshua, a general. And Mary, a homemaker.

Our attitude should always be, "Work is good to do. I work for God and
I do good work…even when no one else sees it."

*When you created our world, you said it was "very good." My Creator
and God, bless my work so that it too will be very good. Amen.*

Jesus in a Book

Jesus did many other things as well. If every one of them
were written down, I suppose that even the whole world would
not have room for the books that would be written.

John 21:25

A wonderful set of books was prominently displayed in my parents' home as I grew up. Beautiful red covers with gold leaf lettering, Carl Sandburg's multi-volume biography of Abraham Lincoln sat on a small table, held in place with impressive bookends, each with a brass head of Lincoln on a mahogany base. I was impressed with those books and have vivid memories of them, but I never opened one volume or read a single page. It's amazing how something can be so familiar, yet so unknown.

Most of us have Bibles in our homes. But how often do we crack them open? As you approach the month of December this year, instead of just reading the Christmas story, why not read the whole Gospel of Luke in the New Testament? Reading the biography of this most amazing and supernatural Jesus will not only educate you about his life, it can transform your life with the certainty of the knowledge and the experience of God himself.

As you read the story, you will never be the same!

---

*Dear Jesus, I want to learn as much as I can about you. From the
Christmas story of your birth to the Easter history of your death
and resurrection, let me experience you as if I was were there. Amen.*

Most Unusual Faith

My God will meet all your needs according
to his glorious riches in Christ Jesus.
To our God and Father be glory for ever and ever. Amen.
Philippians 4:19-20

George Mueller was a great man of faith whose compassion for the many orphans of his day led him to found and direct an orphanage in Bristol, England. Mueller based his life, and the running of the orphanage, on the premise of God's faithful provision for the needs of his children. Resources were meager, and Mueller would sometimes gather the children in the dining hall, have them bow their heads, and lead them in a prayer of thanksgiving for their food—even though there was no food.

Time after time, God provided food by the end of the prayer. Once a milk truck broke down in front of the orphanage. "The milk and other dairy products in my truck are going to spoil," the driver said. "Would you have any use for them?" Other times anonymous donors generously sent supplies without knowing what the needs were, and they would arrive just when they were needed.

George Mueller knew how to pray with thanksgiving in all circumstances, even when there was nothing apparent for which to give thanks. Do you?

God my Provider, my faith seems small compared to so many others. Grow my faith to trust you more. Remind me that you are the generous Lord who hears and answers the prayers of even the little-faith believer in Jesus. Amen.

Checkpoint Charlie

---•⟨⟨✦⟩⟩•---

Open for me the gates of righteousness;
I will enter and give thanks to the Lord.

Psalm 118:19

During the height of the Cold War, I spent a summer in Europe studying and traveling with a group of college students. One of the places we visited was the divided city of Berlin. We traveled by bus through the long corridor in Communist East Germany that connected West Berlin to the rest of West Germany. Later we crossed through the Berlin Wall into East Berlin. It felt so eerie and ominous that I was greatly relieved to be able to walk through Checkpoint Charlie—the gate into the American sector of Berlin—at the end of that brief visit. The soldiers were American, and the Stars and Stripes flew over the gatehouse. It was a feeling of "coming home."

Imagine how much better it will be someday to pass through the checkpoint of Christ. While we will not fully experience our ultimate "coming home" until we enter the gates of heaven itself, we can still experience the presence of God right now as we live lives of thanksgiving and praise.

∽⟨⟩∾

Someday I will walk through the gates of your heaven, God my King.
On that day I will step beyond the current limitations of this world
and this life with all of the woes of problems, pain, and death. Until
then, I live in anticipation. I'll see you at the gates! Amen.

An Attitude of the Heart

If you suffer as a Christian, do not be ashamed,
but praise God that you bear that name.
So then, those who suffer according to God's will should commit
themselves to their faithful Creator and continue to do good.

1 Peter 4:16, 19

Born in Wales in 1662, Matthew Henry devoted his life to preaching and writing and is best known for his popular devotional commentary on the Bible still in print today. We get insight into the kind of man he was from his diary. After he was beaten and robbed in London, Henry wrote: *Let me be thankful first because I was never robbed before; second, because although they took my purse they did not take my life; third, because although they took my all, it was not much; and fourth, because it was I who was robbed, not I who robbed.*

Matthew Henry had an amazing attitude of appreciation and gratefulness for God's goodness. When bad things happened to him, he focused on his gain, not his loss, and chose to be grateful instead of resentful. Gratefulness is an attitude of the heart. It is more a matter of choice than of circumstances.

Matthew Henry chose to have a grateful attitude. Do you?

*With gratitude I pray to see the best even in the worst. May Jesus
Christ mold my thoughts and behavior. Rather than bemoan
the bad things, may I celebrate your hidden grace. Amen.*

Dressed and Ready

—◆◈◆—

"Be dressed ready for service and keep your lamps burning,
like men waiting for their master to return from a wedding
banquet, so that when he comes and knocks they can
immediately open the door for him."

Jesus, in Luke 12:35–36

When I was a young pastor in a Colorado church, I was often on call during the night. Many times I spent hours at the bedside of someone desperately ill in the hospital and then slipped away to go home for a few hours' sleep. I would always lay out my clothes before going to bed so I could dress quickly if I got called back to the hospital. That way I was always ready to go.

And that's the way Jesus wants Christians to be. Jesus said to be dressed and ready for service. Don't get too comfortable. And when he said to keep the lamps burning, he was referring to oil lamps common in that day that needed to have their wicks regularly trimmed or they would go out. Jesus was saying, "Have your clothes ready and the lights on so you are ready when your master returns."

We need to ask ourselves, *If Jesus were to return to earth today, would I be ready?*

—◈◈◈—

*Jesus, I'm waiting for your call. Whether it is the ring of a phone
because of a hospital emergency or the song of a trumpet beckoning
me to heaven, I want to be prepared and ready to go. Amen.*

The Pull of the Star

———◦❦❦◦———

After Jesus was born in Bethlehem in Judea, during the time of
King Herod, Magi from the east came to Jerusalem and asked,
"Where is the one who has been born king of the Jews? We saw his
star in the east and have come to worship him."

Matthew 2:1-2

The Magi were an elite religious caste of ancient Persia—astrologers who
believed you could discern your destiny by studying the signs of the zodiac.
One historic night, as they studied the heavens, they saw a star unlike
anything they'd ever seen. A group of them risked everything to form a
caravan to follow the star. They had no idea they would journey two years
and a thousand miles—all the way from Persia to Palestine.

Why would they follow a maverick star? Curiosity? Superstition? Adventure?
It was almost as if that star had a magnetic pull on their hearts…the pull of
God's supernatural love bringing them to Jesus.

And it still happens today. The magnetic pull of God's love can move us
from where we are to destinations that we cannot foresee. Sometimes the
journey takes years and covers thousands of miles, but eventually it leads us,
like the Magi, to the Son of God.

～◦❧◦～

Lord God of the stars, I look to the heavens for your leading.
May I be a modern Magi looking for anything that points to Jesus
Christ. Show me your way. Draw me in your right direction.
Lead me to Jesus. I will follow—anywhere! Amen.

DECEMBER

Jesus' Baby Book

"Isn't this the carpenter's son? Isn't his mother's name
Mary, and aren't his brothers James, Joseph, Simon and Judas?
Aren't all his sisters with us?"

People in Jesus' hometown, in Matthew 13:55-56

Have you heard about the principle of diminishing baby books? It works like this: The first child has a well-documented book filled out in great detail with all kinds of pictures and mementos. The second child has a half-finished book with piles of snapshots stuffed into the back. The third child has a book—with the price tag still on it. It's never been opened.

Jesus was a first child, and Luke, chapter two, is his baby book. It tells the details of his life with precision. Information about Mary and Joseph's other sons—James, Joseph, Simon, and Judas—is sparse. We don't even know the names of his sisters.

When proud parents show me baby books, it's easy for me to become bored. But I'm never bored by the baby books that tell the stories of children to whom I'm related.

When you read Luke chapter two, do you find the story of Jesus boring or exciting? It all depends on whether you are related to him.

Father of Jesus, I love the Christmas story. You fulfilled prophecies about Jesus' birthplace and virgin mother. You chose Mary and Joseph to be his mom and dad. Every time I hear the details I want to listen again, because Jesus is my Savior and I'm related to you through him. Amen.

Old Prayer Answered

———•◦⟨✦⟩◦•———

Both of them were upright in the sight of God,
observing all the Lord's commandments and regulations
blamelessly. But they had no children, because Elizabeth
was barren; and they were both well along in years.

Luke 1:6–7

Over two thousand years ago in Judea a faithful priest named Zechariah
and his wife, Elizabeth, prayed for a baby. But Elizabeth never became
pregnant. They must have asked God, "Why are we being punished like
this?" But Zechariah and Elizabeth never stopped loving or serving God
even when their prayers were not answered.

One day, when it was Zechariah's turn to burn incense to God in the
Temple, the angel of God appeared to him and told him that the elderly
Elizabeth would bear a son who would be a prophet and bring people to
God. They were to name him John. And that's exactly what happened!

The next time you struggle with questions about unanswered prayer,
remember that God is the Master at taking seemingly unanswered prayers
and great disappointments and fitting them together into a perfect
masterpiece that could never have been imagined in advance. He did it for
Zechariah and Elizabeth, and he will do it for you!

∼⟨◦⟩∽

*You have heard my same prayers over and over, God. Should I give up and
be quiet? No answer seems to be a "no" answer. If you want me to keep
asking, please encourage me to keep praying. In Jesus' name, amen.*

The God of the Ordinary

"Do not be afraid, Mary, you have found favor with God.
You will be with child and give birth to a son, and you are
to give him the name Jesus."

Luke 1:30-31

The angel Gabriel appeared to Zechariah, the priest, to tell him that he and his wife would have a child in their old age. This was his first recorded appearance in more than six hundred years—when he had appeared to the prophet Daniel. After appearing to Zechariah, Gabriel received his next assignment. Imagine, he had been waiting six centuries between assignments, and now he had two in the same year!

Next, he was sent to a poor teenage virgin in the town of Nazareth, to announce the miraculous conception of the Messiah; Gabriel probably thought, *Isn't this just like God, to pick an unknown young girl in an unlikely place to do something supernaturally great?*

I find great comfort and hope in the fact that God is the God of the ordinary. He does his great things through ordinary people—like you and me—in ordinary places and sometimes even sends angel messengers.

Extraordinary God, I am so ordinary. Outside of family and friends there are few who know who I am. What matters is that you know me and that you delight to do supernatural things through everyday folk like me. Come to my place and do something special through ordinary me. Amen.

Whatever God Says

---❦---

> "I am the Lord's servant," Mary answered.
> "May it be to me as you have said."
> *Luke 1:38*

Imagine what it must have been like for Mary to suddenly have an angel appear to her. She was an unlikely recipient of an angelic visit—a very young, poor, unknown woman in a culture that respected age and often demeaned women.

The angel told Mary, "Don't be afraid." Then he explained what was going to happen to her—how she was going to become pregnant with the Son of God himself.

Now Mary was neither sophisticated nor educated, but she wasn't stupid. She knew pregnancy didn't just happen. She was a virgin; it simply didn't make sense! But Gabriel told her that the Holy Spirit would overshadow her and she would become pregnant but remain a virgin. "For," he said, "nothing is impossible with God."

Mary didn't understand virgin birth any more than we do, so her trusting response must have stunned the angel. When we hear from God, may our response be as Mary's: "I am the Lord's servant. May it be to me as you have said."

---❧---

Surprise me, Lord! Come and tell me things I never expected to hear. Use me in ways I would never guess. Bless me with the impossible. Whatever you ask, my answer in advance is "I am the Lord's servant. May it be to me as you have said." Let your supernatural adventure begin in me! Amen.

A Paradigm Shift

———— ✦❧✦ ————

Mary was pledged to be married to Joseph, but before they came together, she was found to be with child through the Holy Spirit.

Matthew 1:18

In *Seven Habits of Highly Effective People*, Stephen Covey tells about riding on a New York subway with a man and his rambunctious children. Everyone was irritated, so he finally confronted the man and asked him to control them a little better.

The man looked up in a daze and said softly, "Oh, you're right. I guess I should do something about it. We just came from the hospital, where their mother died about an hour ago. I don't know what to think, and I guess they don't know how to handle it, either."

Stephen Covey wrote, *Can you imagine how my paradigm shifted at that moment? My irritation vanished, and my heart was filled with this man's pain.*

An even greater paradigm shift occurred to Joseph, a carpenter who discovered his bride-to-be was pregnant. Joseph thought the baby was the result of sin. He saw her pregnancy as a source of pain and tragedy. It took an angel to tell him that the baby was coming to save people *from* sin and the pregnancy was a source of salvation and joy.

———— ❧ ————

My thinking is narrow, my perspective limited, and my assumptions quick, my Lord. Too often I imagine the worst when I should compassionately understand. Change my point-of-view to see what you see and transform my heart to feel what you feel. Amen.

Doing Right When Wounded

———— ❦ ————

This is how the birth of Jesus Christ came about:
His mother Mary was pledged to be married to Joseph,
but before they came together, she was found to be with
child through the Holy Spirit. Because Joseph her husband
was a righteous man and did not want to expose her to
public disgrace, he had in mind to divorce her quietly.

Matthew 1:18–19

Joseph was a good guy. He wanted to do everything the right way. He proposed to Mary, and there was no premarital sex. But then everything seemed to go wrong. The woman he loved was pregnant, and he felt betrayed.

Joseph did everything right but became the victim of someone else's choices. But even if Mary had done what was wrong, he wanted to do right by her before God. Heartbroken, he decided to end the engagement as quietly and respectfully as possible rather than publicly disgrace her. In the midst of his misery, an angel appeared to Joseph in a dream with a stunning message. And how did Joseph respond? He trusted God for what he could not fully understand. He sacrificed his reputation for a child with whom he shared no DNA and loved Jesus as his own son.

When dreams are shattered and hope is stolen, we too can choose not to be afraid and to trust in God's promises.

———— ❧ ————

*May I do what is right even when my heart is broken
and dreams are shattered. For Jesus' sake, amen.*

The Talk of the Village

In those days Caesar Augustus issued a decree that a census should
be taken of the entire Roman world. So Joseph also went up from
the town of Nazareth in Galilee to Judea, to Bethlehem the town
of David, because he belonged to the house and line of David.

Luke 2:1, 4

Have you ever thought how difficult it would have been for Mary and Joseph
to make the eighty-mile trip from Nazareth to Bethlehem? The census
couldn't have come at a worse time. Mary was due to have her child any day!

When they finally arrived, Bethlehem had no vacancy at the local inn, so they
ended up staying where the animals were kept. With the birth imminent,
it was too risky to start back to Nazareth after they finished their business.
So they stayed in the animal courtyard, awaiting the birth. Because it was
such a public place, others would have heard her cries when the contractions
started and as the labor intensified.

There was no keeping this birth a secret. It became the talk of the village.
But little did those gossiping villagers know the significance of what was
happening that night in Bethlehem. Two thousand years later we are still
talking about that extraordinary birth.

*God at Bethlehem, I've heard the story and seen the
Christmastime picture so often that it seems I am an eyewitness.
Although thousands of miles and years on this side of Jesus' birth,
I want to tell everyone exactly what happened. Amen.*

Good News!

———— ❦ ————

"Glory to God in the highest, and on earth peace
to men on whom his favor rests."
A great company of angels, in Luke 2:14

Imagine what it would have been like that first Christmas to have been the angel God sent to deliver this message: "Do not be afraid. I bring you good news of great joy that will be for all the people. Today in the town of David a Savior has been born to you; he is Christ the Lord. This will be a sign to you: You will find a baby wrapped in cloths and lying in a manger."

Suddenly the angel was joined by thousands of his buddies, and together they praised God. Then—*whoosh!*—the angels disappeared as quickly as they came. They just delivered their message and left, as if they disliked attracting attention to themselves. Their role, after all, is to praise and glorify God as his messengers.

I think the angels have something to teach us. Instead of drawing attention to ourselves, our worship should focus on bringing praise and glory to God.

———— ❧ ————

Christmas is not mostly about decorations, gifts, music, or me. It's all about you, Jesus Christ. I want to be your angel this Christmas season—telling others that you have come and pointing them to you without them much noticing me. My message is, "Joy to the world, the Lord is come!" Amen.

Love That Name

❧

When Joseph woke up, he…took Mary home as his wife.
But he had no union with her until she gave birth to a son.
And he gave him the name Jesus.
Matthew 1:24–25

When parents are expecting a new baby, choosing a name sometimes causes disagreement because, after all, it's an important decision. Mary and Joseph were spared the negotiations of choosing their baby's name when an angel appeared to Joseph and announced it.

Jesus is the Greek pronunciation of the very common Hebrew name *Joshua*. It was as common as "John" or "Jane" are in a modern list of names. Lots of Joshuas were running around the streets then. The name was not unique, but the meaning was special. *Jesus* or *Joshua* means "the Lord saves."

This promised child came with a powerful purpose. The angel told them that the baby to be born to Mary was all about salvation from sin and about eternal destiny. He was for all of humankind, not just for an obscure couple in an out-of-the-way little village. The purpose of his life was to save people from sin and the consequences of sin. And his name said it all.

❧

*Jesus, I love your name. When I speak it, my heart flows with joy.
When I hear it, my soul is full of salvation. When I pray it, my
words are heard in heaven. When I think it, my mind is purified.
When I sing it, my mouth is full of praise. Jesus! Amen.*

Child Born, Son Given

——⟨◈⟩——

For to us a child is born, to us a son is given, and the government
will be on his shoulders. And he will be called Wonderful
Counselor, Mighty God, Everlasting Father, Prince of Peace.
Isaiah 9:6

This beautiful poetry from the Old Testament is also profound theology.
The child was *born*—beginning in Bethlehem. The Son was *given* and is
eternal. He had no beginning, has always existed, and was *given* by God the
Father to earth as a gift. It is called the *incarnation*, which means "into flesh."
When he was born, the Son of God became human and was given a human
name—Jesus. Without the gift of Jesus, there would be no Christmas, no
salvation, no joy, and no reason to celebrate.

But here's the critical point: to experience the joy of Christmas first
requires receiving the gift of Jesus. Otherwise, Christmas is no more than a
commercial holiday one week before the end of the year.

If you have not yet received the gift of Jesus, there's no better time than the
present. Don't wait another moment. Wherever you are, just tell God in
prayer, "Yes, I accept your gift of Jesus. I accept him as my Savior and as
Leader of my life." Then thank him for sending Jesus—the best gift any of
us can ever receive.

——⟨◈⟩——

Thank you, Eternal Father, for your Son, Jesus. I believe. I accept.
Jesus is now my Savior and my Leader forever. Amen.

Supernaturally Interrupted

———————

"Do not be afraid. I bring you good news
of great joy that will be for all the people."
An angel, in Luke 2:10

I'd always pictured the Bethlehem shepherds as a group of about ten guys sitting around with a few sheep...until I observed working shepherds in New Zealand, a country with about four million people and around forty million sheep. Ten shepherds could have been in charge of hundreds of sheep—and the endless cycles of feeding, herding, shearing, birthing, and healing.

As the Bethlehem shepherds sat around their campfire late one night, exhausted from their long day, they were supernaturally interrupted by an angel telling them about a Savior who had been born nearby. Then the sky was filled with thousands of singing angels. It was quite a sight!

But there's a great point here. The birth of Jesus Christ has the power to break into every part of our lives—even the workplace. If God bursts into your routine at work, it may not be with angels, but with a sudden promotion or a termination, an unusual challenge, or a new coworker. When it comes, remember the shepherds, whose place of work became a place of worship.

———————

*Lord of Interruptions, break into my life with good news. Come
to where I work. Call me in the middle of the night. Wherever
I am and whatever I am doing, you are always welcome. Let me
see you in the surprises that interrupt my routines. Amen.*

The Biggest News of All History

———— ❧❦❧ ————

*"Today in the town of David a Savior has
been born to you; he is Christ the Lord."*
Luke 2:11

Did you know that most of the world—even the people who don't acknowledge Jesus Christ—date their calendars by his birth? AD is an abbreviation for the Latin words *Anno Domini,* which mean "the year of our Lord."

Why should this child's birth become the center point of history's calendar? The reason is explained in three key words spoken by the angel to the shepherds. *Savior* explains the whole purpose of Jesus' birth. He came to save us from sin. *Christ* is a title meaning "Messiah," the One chosen to represent God on earth and accomplish his great purposes in history. *Lord,* the word ancient Jews used to refer to God, is a most amazing word to be connected to Jesus, for it means Jesus is not just *from* God, but God himself.

The biggest news of all history is that God became human like us and came to earth to save us from sin so we can be forever with him in heaven. His birth is the most wonderful thing that has ever happened!

———— ❧❦ ————

*You are the center-point of history. You are the marker to date every
event. All our calendars point directly to you. Jesus, be the center-
point of my life. May the date of my personal faith be the marker for
all of my life. Absolutely everything is measured around you. Amen.*

Nothing Less Than Excellence

—⟨⟨❦⟩⟩—

> Since I myself have carefully investigated everything
> from the beginning, it seemed good also to me to write
> an orderly account for you...so that you may know the
> certainty of the things you have been taught.
>
> *Luke 1:3-4*

The writer of the Gospel of Luke, a physician named Luke, begins his account of Jesus' life by saying it is "carefully investigated" and "an orderly account." I suppose that says something about Dr. Luke himself—that he was a disciplined, well-organized researcher. That's the way he was wired; that's who he was. But I think there may be something more to why he investigated and wrote the way he did. Luke thought that Jesus deserved the very best! He believed that nothing less than excellence would do for anything that carried the name of Jesus Christ.

There is a powerful lesson here for us today, as well. Jesus still deserves the very best. Everything that we say about him and everything we do that carries the name of Jesus Christ should be done carefully and orderly, for only the best will do for Jesus.

—∞—

Jesus, you are the best. You deserve the best! I commit to serve you with excellence. Not that I think I am so great—you know my weaknesses and sins better than anyone. My desire is to take every skill you have given me, to work the way you have wired me, and to give you my very best. Amen.

Seekers of Truth

———◆◈◆———

On coming to the house they saw the child with his mother Mary,
and they bowed down and worshipped him.

Matthew 2:10

Christmas cards often show wise men on camels standing by the manger, but the Bible indicates the Magi didn't arrive until long after Christmas. They came to a *house,* not a stable, and saw *a child,* not a baby. By the time they arrived, Jesus may have been close to two years old, because when King Herod felt threatened by a coming king, he ordered the execution of all baby boys aged two and under. If the wise men started their journey when Jesus was born, it could have taken them up to twenty-four months to arrive.

These astrologers from Persia believed they could read a person's destiny in the stars. Today, they would author daily horoscopes. When they saw a previously unknown star they thought might lead them to a coming world leader, they decided to seek after it.

God's leading of the Magi reveals that a person doesn't need all the right knowledge and beliefs to come to him. Those who seek the truth and honestly desire God will be led to Jesus. Their route may be strange, but the destination is what counts.

———◈———

*Wise seekers still come to Jesus. I am a seeker. Guide me, God, to your beloved
Son. Through my ignorance and searching bring me to worship the child of
Christmas who became the Savior at Calvary and the Lord at Easter. Amen.*

The Three Gifts

Then they opened their treasures and presented him
with gifts of gold and of incense and of myrrh.

Matthew 2:11

The gifts the Magi brought on their long journey were not typical new-baby gifts but ones fit for a king: gold, incense, and myrrh.

Gold was the most royal gift of all. Since Joseph and Mary were of humble means, this was probably the only gold they ever touched in their whole lives.

Incense was a particularly religious gift, because the priest would burn incense every day in the Temple. As the fragrant smoke wafted heavenward, it symbolized the prayers of God's people. It was also fitting because Jesus is the only true mediator between us and God.

Myrrh, a valuable resin used for embalming a body prior to burial, was perhaps the strangest gift of the three. What an unusual item to bring to a baby—unless that baby was born to die. This Christmas gift was a portent of the child's future.

The Magi came looking for a king. Little did they know that the gifts they brought hinted at what was ahead for the child they came to worship.

Receive my gifts to you, Jesus of Bethlehem. My presents are not gold, incense, and myrrh. I bring to you my money, my prayers, and my life. I give to you my family, my home, my job, and any other relationship or possession I value. My gifts of worship come with my love and loyalty forever and ever. Amen.

Fully Committed

—⟨◈⟩—

The world and its desires pass away, but the man
who does the will of God lives forever.
1 John 2:17 (Verse on D. L. Moody's gravestone)

Dwight L. Moody, a great American evangelist in the 1800s, was once challenged by a friend who said, "The world has yet to see what God would do through a person fully committed to Jesus Christ." Moody responded by saying, "By God's grace, I'm going to be that person."

What if every one of us said that? What if we each decided we would be what God wants us to be? Say what God wants us to say? Give what God wants us to give? Go wherever God wants us to go?

The needs are all around us. People are hungry and hurting in our country and around the world. "How can one person, no matter how committed, make a difference?" you ask.

The answer is to join with others of like commitment. Imagine ten of us or one hundred or one million Christians saying "yes" to Jesus. Together, as the church of Jesus Christ, we can make a difference in our generation!

—⟨◈⟩—

God, I want to be that person who is fully committed to Jesus. Enroll me on the list of your most zealous disciples. Accomplish great things through me. And join me together with others who are passionate for our Savior. May we together be and do all you desire of the Church, the Body of Christ. Amen.

The Welfare Clause

*Though he was rich, yet for your sakes he became poor,
so that you through his poverty might become rich.*
2 Corinthians 8:9

According to Hebrew law, forty days after a baby boy was born, his parents were to bring him to the Temple to consecrate him to God. The law also required them to bring a lamb and a pigeon to be sacrificed. This was an event families eagerly anticipated. But Mary and Joseph could not afford a lamb, so they brought two pigeons instead. They were claiming the special exemption in the law—the "welfare clause"—for the very poorest in Israel.

Jesus was born into a poor family. His home was humble, and he must have gotten used to going without. I'm quite sure there isn't much correlation between the way most of us celebrate Christmas and the way that first Christmas was for Jesus. The poverty of Jesus is a powerful statement to us in our frenzied quest for prosperity. Jesus gave up heaven for a stable.

He was willing to give up his wealth for us! What are we willing to sacrifice for him?

Poor Jesus, you left heaven for earth and surrendered wealth for poverty. You are so amazing. Most of all, I am humbled and thrilled that you gave up so much for my sake. Thank you! I want to be just like you—willing to give up everything for you. Amen.

For—or Against?

❧

"This child is destined to cause the falling and rising of many
in Israel and to be a sign that will be spoken against, so that the
thoughts of many hearts will be revealed."
Simeon, in Luke 2:34–35

Simeon, a godly man who spent most of his time at the Temple in Jerusalem, had one last wish before he died: to meet the Messiah.

When Mary and Joseph brought the baby Jesus to the Temple to be blessed, the Holy Spirit enabled Simeon to recognize this baby as the Messiah. After he blessed Mary and Joseph and Jesus, he spoke some unusual prophetic words about the baby.

We don't usually think of Jesus as a stumbling block. But those who don't believe in him as Savior are uncomfortable with who Jesus is because Jesus reveals sin and judges us for falling short of God's expectations. To those who do not believe, Jesus is bad news, not good.

In contrast, Jesus causes those who believe in him to rise. Believing can bring stunning, positive changes for good. The point is, people are for Jesus or against him. They follow him or go their own way. As Simeon predicted, through Jesus, "The thoughts of our hearts are revealed."

❧

*My prayer is for those who stumble over Jesus. May my
unbelieving friends and family see Jesus in a new way this
Christmas so that they, too, will believe in him. Amen.*

An Unforgettable Christmas

---⟨❦⟩---

The Lord is my light and my salvation—
whom shall I fear?
The Lord is the stronghold of my life—
of whom shall I be afraid?

Psalm 27:1

All of us have fears. We fear sickness, financial hardship, failure, addictions. We fear infertility when others have babies, singleness when friends are getting married. After 9/11 we fear acts of terrorism. Our fears are as individual as we are.

On the first Christmas the angel told the terrified shepherds not to fear. Today, we still need the angel's answers to our fears: *Do not be afraid. Jesus will be your Savior if you will invite him in.* That's what being a Christian is: someone who invites Jesus inside to live and take charge.

A man once came to a Christmas Eve candlelight service at a time when his life was steeped in sin and fear. During the beauty and quiet of that service, God spoke to him, and he said a simple prayer of faith—confessing his sins and fears and inviting Jesus inside as his Savior and Lord. It was the Christmas he'll never forget...when his fears were chased away.

May his Christmas story become your own Christmas story.

---⟨❧⟩---

Take my fears away. Replace them with the peace of Jesus. Make this a memorable Christmas when my heartaches are healed, my worries are forgotten, and my hope is renewed. Settle my soul with the presence of Jesus in my life. Amen.

Just Like Anna

❧

Anna gave thanks to God and spoke about the child to all
who were looking forward to the redemption of Jerusalem.

Luke 2:38

Anna, the prophetess, had been married for only seven years when her
husband died. She spent a large part of her life alone (when we meet her
in the New Testament, she had been a widow for eighty-four years). Most
widows were very poor at that time, so she knew firsthand about life's
difficulties. Yet Anna was not bitter. She was a gracious and godly old lady.
There was no spiritual retirement for this wonderful woman. Much of her
time was spent at the Temple centered on the worship of God. She lived and
breathed God; he was central to everything she did.

Her reward was to see the baby Jesus face to face when Mary and Joseph
brought him to the Temple to be blessed. Her response? She thanked God
and then did what a prophetess is supposed to do: she told others.

As you experience the Christ of Christmas, why not be like Anna? Share the
good news with others!

❧

*How long will I live, Lord? Will I become old like Anna? If I do,
I want to grow old worshipping you. May I experience Jesus
every day from this day to my last day. Along the way I will thank
you for my Messiah and will tell others about him. At every
age of my life I want to tell others who Jesus is. Amen.*

Thumbs-Up!

"My soul glorifies the Lord and my spirit
rejoices in God my Savior."
Luke 1:46-47

After Bobbi McCaughey gave birth to septuplets, her husband, Kenny,
stepped out of the delivery room and gave a thumbs-up sign to his waiting
family and friends. Later, he praised God over and over in front of the TV
cameras as he described the miraculous sevenfold birth.

The mood was similar when Mary, a pregnant teenager from Nazareth,
went to visit her cousin Elizabeth, who was also pregnant. The Bible
describes, "When Elizabeth heard Mary's greeting, the baby leaped in her
womb, and Elizabeth was filled with the Holy Spirit. In a loud voice she
exclaimed: 'Blessed are you among women, and blessed is the child you
will bear!'" It was Elizabeth's equivalent to a modern thumbs-up!

Mary could have complained. After all, she was poor, unmarried, and
pregnant. Instead, she glorified God. Why are some people with the worst
circumstances the most joyful while others with the best circumstances are the
most miserable? Some interpret everything that happens in terms of *me* while
others interpret everything in terms of *God*. Which perspective is yours?

*God of heaven, you do so many wonderful acts on earth. Some people seem
to miss all the good you do. Not me! I see you all over the place—when babies
are born, when flowers bloom, when children pray, when bodies are healed,
and when lives are changed. Thumbs-up to you, God! Amen.*

What Do You Want for Christmas?

———⁓⧉⁓———

If anyone acknowledges that Jesus is the Son of God, God lives in him and he in God.... God is love. Whoever lives in love lives in God, and God in him. In this way, love is made complete among us.

1 John 4:15–17

When a woman decided to trust in Jesus as her Savior, her life was completely transformed. Shortly before Christmas the year she became a believer, she was talking to her mother on the phone. When her mother asked her, "What do you want for Christmas this year, dear?" the daughter blurted, "Mom, what I want more than anything else this year is for you to accept Jesus Christ as your Savior."

The mother caught her newly Christian daughter by surprise when she answered, "I already did that. I already accepted Jesus as my Savior."

The stunned daughter asked, "But Mom, why don't you live like you believe in Jesus?"

God used that conversation to draw them together in a closer bond than ever before.

What do I want more than anything else for Christmas this year? Everyone reading these words to accept Jesus as Savior. Tell God today that you believe in Jesus Christ. And then live the way you believe!

⁓⧉⁓

Giver of Christmas, thank you for the fabulous gift of Jesus! I accept your gift as my Savior and want to live like I believe. And, I pray for those I love to accept Jesus and live for him too. Amen.

Living in the Meantime

"Be careful, or your hearts will be weighed down with dissipation, drunkenness and the anxieties of life, and that day will close on you unexpectedly like a trap. For it will come upon all those who live on the face of the whole earth. Be always on the watch...."

Jesus, in Luke 21:34-36

In earthquake zones many houses are built over faults. If you live with danger every day, you might just start ignoring it. Jesus told his followers that someday he would return to earth as the powerful and triumphant conqueror. But he also told them how to live "in the meantime." Think about his advice as specific for us today: "Don't let your heart get weighed down so you are distracted. Don't get lazy or lose your focus. Don't use alcohol or drugs to deal with life's disappointments. And don't spend your time worrying about the stuff that fills up your life. Always be on the watch for when I might return."

How can we prepare for the future? Just as regular tune-ups keep a car running and a piano on key, prayer keeps us in tune with God so we can be prepared to stand before Jesus Christ on that glorious day when he returns.

God of the Meantime, my yesterdays are past and my tomorrows are yet to come. Today is my in-between; today is my meantime. Keep me centered, focused, sober, diligent, joyful, and watchful. I pray to make this day count for Christ. Amen.

From Getter to Giver

"It is more blessed to give than to receive."
Jesus, in Acts 20:35

Every December 25 of my life has begun, due to my mother's English tradition, with gifts exchanged on Christmas morning. Funny thing is, all I remember from my childhood are the gifts I received. I cannot recall a single gift I gave anyone. Now, as an adult, I can barely remember any of the gifts I've received. Instead, I remember the gifts I have given.

The change happened gradually. But there was one Christmas when the transformation seemed to permanently take hold. It was my first Christmas as a father. I no longer cared what I got because all I could think about was our four-month-old daughter. I wanted to give her everything in the world!

Changing from a "getter" to a "giver" is one of the most wonderful changes that can happen to a person. Only when that change takes place do you begin to understand that the most intense joy of gifts comes from giving, more than receiving.

*It's Christmastime, Lord. Days have been busy with decorating, shopping,
parties, cards, food, and festivities. And stress, worry, and weariness.
Now it's almost time to give away my Christmas gifts. With every present
I give, I pray your blessing on the one who receives. With every
present I give, I think of Jesus, who is the best Christmas gift of all.
I rejoice in the delight of giving. In Jesus' Christmas name, amen.*

El Niño

————◦≪∘≫◦————

> While they were there, the time came for El Niño to be born, and
> she gave birth to her firstborn, a son. She wrapped him in cloths
> and placed him in a manger.
>
> *Luke 2:6–7*

The weather phenomenon El Niño is a climatic change that raises the temperature of the Pacific Ocean just a few degrees but has consequences around the globe. In some places it brings warm weather during winter. In others it brings flooding or drought.

In Spanish, *El Niño* means "the child." It's named after Jesus because the warm waters of El Niño always come around Christmastime. It's a fitting title because the El Niño weather phenomenon has far-reaching results—some of them good and others difficult and devastating. So it is with the coming of the child Jesus; it has far-reaching results. For some, his coming is wonderfully good and pleasant; for others, it is dangerous and devastating. Depending on how we respond, the Christ child may bring us peace and salvation and eternal life or judgment and eternity without God.

At Christmastime the most important El Niño is not the climate, but the Christ. May we welcome his warm coming and all the wondrous changes he can and will bring into our lives.

————◦≫∘◦————

*El Niño! Happy birthday, Jesus! Your warm love has reached
all the way to me, and I am blessed. Thank you ten thousand
times. I love you and celebrate you today. Amen.*

No Limits!

"With man this is impossible, but with God all things are possible."
Jesus, in Matthew 19:26

What do you picture when you imagine a throne room? A majestic space with marvelous tapestries, precious jewels embedded in the furniture, and a solid gold throne? An awesome monarch who has the power of life and death over his subjects?

God is the King of kings and Lord of heaven and earth. His throne room is far greater than anything we could imagine. He is richer, more magnificent, and stronger than any earthly ruler, and what he says goes.

That means God can do anything. If he wants a new universe, he snaps his fingers and it's done. If he wants to form the dust of the earth into a man, *poof*, he does it. He speaks a word, and the Red Sea has a dry path through it. He makes a virgin conceive, a lame man walk, a dead man live. Whatever he says, happens. Knowing there are no limits with God makes my confidence soar to the limit!

Almighty, All-Powerful, All-Wise, Magnificent God...you are God, and there is none other like you. You never began and you will never end. Your presence and power are infinite. Nothing is impossible for you. You can and do perform any miracle you choose. When I acknowledge who you are my heart beats faster, my faith grows stronger, and my confidence in you soars. You are the Unlimited God—Father, Son, and Holy Spirit. Amen.

The Best Days of All

—◆─◈─◆—

"How can I be sure of this? I am an old man
and my wife is well along in years."
Zechariah, in Luke 1:18

Zechariah, a godly man who lived two thousand years ago, grew up, married, worked, and hoped for children who did not come. Finally, when he was finishing out his career as a priest, a series of unusual events occurred.

He was awarded the once-in-a-lifetime opportunity to offer incense in the Temple. The angel Gabriel appeared to him. His elderly wife, Elizabeth, became pregnant, and their son, John, was born. Zechariah had more excitement in one year than in the rest of his life combined. Interesting, isn't it, that it wasn't until Zechariah was an old man that he made his greatest contribution?

Most of us assume the best days of life are the earlier days. We rarely imagine that a person's greatest work will be done after age sixty-five. But what if we lived as if *every* day is not only the most significant and important but is also preparation for our greatest days of all? With God the best days are often ahead!

—◈—

God of every age, make my best days begin today. Looking forward and not backward, surprise me with your grace and grant me new opportunities that only you can give. I ask you not for Zechariah's blessing, but for my own. Bless me this day and prepare me for tomorrow. In Jesus' name, amen.

A Twist on Giving

An angel of the Lord appeared to Joseph in a dream.
"Get up," he said, "take the child and his mother and escape
to Egypt. Stay there until I tell you, for Herod is going to
search for the child to kill him."

Matthew 2:13

After the Magi visited Mary, Joseph, and Jesus in Bethlehem, Joseph had a troubling dream. In that dream an angel warned him to flee with his family to Egypt because King Herod wanted to kill Jesus.

So Joseph took his wife and child to Africa, where they went into hiding as refugees in Egypt. How did they live? Where did they stay? How did they support themselves for the next couple of years until it was safe to return home to Nazareth? A good possibility is that they financed the trip and supported themselves with the proceeds from selling the gifts the Magi had presented to Jesus. Gifts given as an act of worship became the means by which Jesus was kept alive and safe.

So what can we learn from this after-Christmas story of the Magi? First the Magi met Jesus; *then* they gave him gifts. It is only as we meet Jesus and receive him as God's gift to us that we are motivated to give to others.

*As this year nears its end, I pray to finish it well with Jesus.
As you have given to me, may I give to others—especially
those who, like Jesus' family, face great need. Amen.*

How to Be Remembered

───◆❦❦◆───

"Praise be to the Lord, the God of Israel."
Zechariah, in Luke 1:68

The prolific American author James Michener wrote very long novels with
very short titles, like *Hawaii*, *Texas*, and *Centennial*. They all begin with more
background information about the setting and history than most of us want
to know. Maybe that's how you feel when you read the first chapter of Luke.
You may be thinking, *Let's get on with the story of Jesus.* After all, the first chapter is
about Jesus' cousin John and barely mentions Jesus.

But Luke was anxious for us to know the story behind the story—about an old
man named Zechariah and his newborn son who would grow up to prepare
the way for Jesus. Zechariah's last words are a song of praise to God. Then
Zechariah is never mentioned again.

What would you like your last remembered words to be? "I made a lot
of money" or, "I had a nice car"? Probably not. How much better to be
remembered, like Zechariah, for praising God.

───❧───

*As this year ends, I thank you, God, for getting me through to today.
Yet, with each additional year, I wonder when my life will end and
how I will be remembered. May I not be so occupied with this life
that I neglect the life to come. Help me to live today for you and
so be ready for the future. May I be remembered not for the things
I leave behind, but for the God I loved and served. Amen.*

Singled Out

❦

I urge you to live a life worthy of the calling you have received.
Ephesians 4:1

Everyone appreciates being singled out as special. When the angel told Mary she was chosen to be the mother of God's Son, she realized she was special to God and part of his plan for history. You might think, *Well, I'd feel special too if God sent an angel to me and did a miracle in my body.* But God's call is different for everyone. God has not called you to be the mother of Jesus, living in poverty in first-century Palestine. He has called you to be you.

Each of us is special to God. He cares about every detail of our lives. He has called us to be what he wants us to be in our time, in our bodies, and with our problems and our opportunities.

Some of us face lifelong misunderstanding, as Mary did. Others of us live with limitations and challenges. Still others are called to live with the awesome responsibility of enormous gifts or significant influence. We all need to focus on living out God's unique call for us.

❧

You designed me just the way you want me to be, didn't you, God? No one else is wired as I am or has my personal combination of strengths and weakness, joys and sorrows, opportunities and limitations. My prayer to you and resolution to me is that I will be exactly who you want me to be. Amen.

The Best Is Yet to Come!

When the Chief Shepherd appears, you will receive
the crown of glory that will never fade away.
1 Peter 5:4

Every night and every morning I read the words embroidered on a small pillow on my wife's and my bed: *The Best Is Yet to Come*. At the end of really tough days when I'm tired, discouraged, and ready to quit, I'm reminded that God promises to bring good out of suffering. On satisfying days, when life is sweet, I'm reminded that something even better is ahead.

The apostle Peter describes a crowning ceremony for faithful Christians when Jesus returns. Today we might think of it as receiving a Congressional Medal of Honor, a Nobel Prize, or an honorary doctorate. At that awesome moment, the experiences of this life will be seen from a different perspective. Our worst days will be distant memories, and what we thought was the best of the best will be nothing compared to what we will experience in the presence of God. If you trust in Jesus as Savior, the best is truly yet to come!

*My hope is in you, God of All Tomorrows. Because of you, the failures
and sorrows of the past can be left behind, and I can step into the future
with hope and promise. My future is bright. Your promises are good.
My best days are ahead. The best is yet to come, with Jesus. Amen.*

About the Author

The heart of a pastor
The mind of a scholar
The influence of a leader

Leith Anderson is senior pastor of Wooddale Church in Eden Prairie, Minnesota, which not only ministers to thousands in metropolitan Minneapolis but also serves as a teaching laboratory across denominational lines to churches throughout the nation. He also serves as president of the National Association of Evangelicals headquartered in Washington, D.C., which represents about 45,000 American churches. He is frequently interviewed and quoted by publications and broadcasts including *The New York Times*, *The Washington Post*, *TIME*, *Newsweek*, PBS, CNN, the BBC, NBC *Nightly News*, and National Public Radio.

Educated in sociology, Bible, and theology, Leith holds university and seminary degrees from schools in Illinois, Colorado, and California. He grew up in the parsonage of a New Jersey church, where his father ministered for thirty-three years. Of his three older brothers, one became a missionary, another a pastor, and the third a fundraiser for Christian colleges and mission organizations. In his travels to seven continents, Leith's care for others and for ministry has built valued and meaningful relationships with a broad array of people—pastors of mini-churches and mega-churches, religious leaders, denominational executives, and government officials from local communities to the highest levels of Washington. He has been invited to speak at international conferences of leaders from non-Christian world religions to present and explain evangelical Christian faith. His friends are young and old, racially diverse, famous and not famous, women and men. But his number-one passion is Jesus Christ—Jesus as the Lord and Center of everything.

Leith is the author of more than a dozen books, including *Dying for Change*; *A Church for the Twenty-First Century*; *Winning the Values War*; *Praying to the God You Can Trust*; *Leadership That Works*; *Becoming Friends with God*; *JESUS: An Intimate Portrait of the Man, His Land, and His People*; *How to Act Like a Christian*; and *The Jesus Revolution*.

His radio programs sponsored by Woodvale Church—*Faith Matters*, a daily two-minute radio program, and *Faith Minute*, a daily one-minute radio program—provide brief and targeted messages of practical wisdom, personal challenge, and unshakeable hope. They are heard on stations across America and overseas.

Leith and his wife, Charleen, have known each other all their lives and have been married for most of their lives. They have four children and make their home in Minnesota.

Website visits are welcome for:
Wooddale Church at **wooddale.org**
National Association of Evangelicals at **nae.net**
Faith Matters radio programs at **faithmatters.fm**